LET THERE BE LIGHT

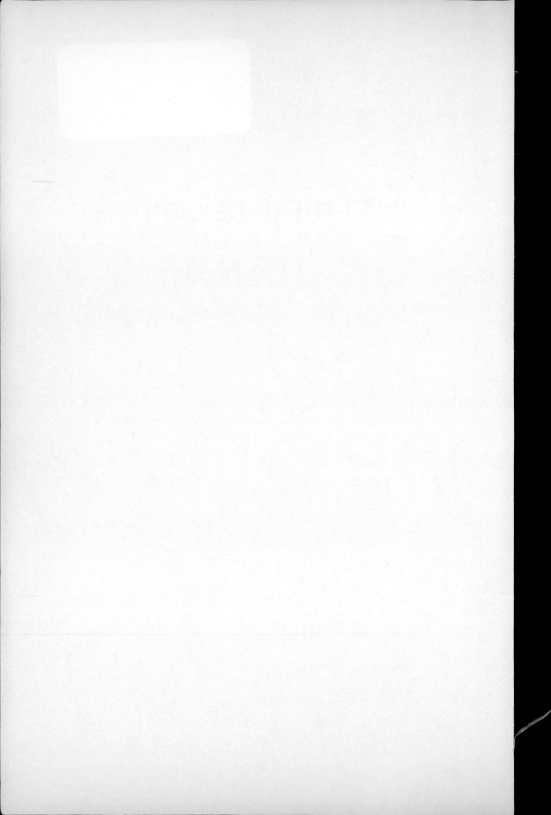

LET THERE BE LIGHT

MODERN COSMOLOGY AND KABBALAH
A NEW CONVERSATION BETWEEN SCIENCE AND RELIGION

HOWARD SMITH

New World Library
Novato, California

New World Library
14 Pamaron Way
Novato, California 94949

Text design by Tona Pearce Myers

Library of Congress Cataloging-in-Publication Data
Smith, Howard A., 1944–
Let there be light : modern cosmology and Kabbalah — a new conversation between science and religion / Howard A. Smith.
p. cm.
Includes bibliographical references and index.
ISBN-13: 978-1-57731-548-3 (pbk. : alk. paper)
1. Judaism and science. 2. Cosmology. 3. Cabala—History. 4. Sefirot (Cabala) 5. Creation. I. Title.
BM538.S3S65 2006
296.3'75—dc22 2006020910

First printing, November 2006
ISBN-10: 1-57731-548-0
ISBN-13: 978-1-57731-548-3
Printed in Canada on acid-free, partially recycled paper

New World Library is a proud member of the Green Press Initiative.

Distributed by Publishers Group West

10 9 8 7 6 5 4 3 2 1

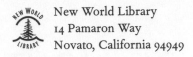

To My Family

אבי, שרה, מירה,
ובילה- "לבבתני אחתי כלה"

And God said: Let there be Light. And there was light.

— Genesis 1:3

From this verse [Genesis 1:3] we can begin to uncover the hidden mysteries: how the world was created in detail from the mystery of Thought.... This Light expanded and extended itself, having burst through from the mysterious primal vacuum.

— Zohar

It was the discovery of the microwave background in 1965 that showed that the universe really did have its origin in a Big Bang, and that the early phases of the universe were dominated by radiation. The universe was, in fact, born in a blaze of light.

— Michael Rowan-Robinson, *Ripples in the Cosmos*

One of the great afflictions of man's spiritual world is that every discipline of knowledge, every feeling, impedes the emergence of the other. The result is that most people remain limited and one-sided.... This defect cannot continue permanently. Man's nobler future is destined to come when he will develop to a sound spiritual state so that instead of each discipline negating the other, all knowledge, all feeling will be envisioned from any branch of it. This is precisely the true nature of reality.

— Rabbi Abraham Isaac Kook, *The Lights of Holiness*

CONTENTS

PREFACE

This is a book for people wondering about modern science and religion, and what each has to say to the other, if anything. It is also for people curious about the discoveries of modern cosmology and physics, or about the insights of Kabbalah and Jewish mysticism, but who know little about them. Those who may never before have picked up a book on popular science, or who think of themselves as indifferent to or inept at science, should find the material here both fascinating and understandable. On the other hand, scientifically literate readers who may never have heard of the Kabbalah or who have decided they are uninterested in religion, will, I hope, take away a new appreciation of religion, as well as learn something more about our current understanding of the world. I have written this book for all of you, and I have tried to make it completely and easily accessible.

Let There Be Light is deliberately not a scholarly work. I have gone out of my way to avoid jargon, footnoted attributions, and even the expansive and detailed thoroughness of most popular science books. I am not trying to explain these subjects comprehensively. Actually, quite the opposite: I worked hard to keep each theme short and completely approachable, and I restricted my discussions to what I thought was the minimum necessary to interest, inform, and intrigue you. I certainly steered clear of the academic diligence of my technical articles. This book is, however, meant to educate and perhaps enlighten you. Brian Greene remarks that his book *The Elegant Universe*, an excellent and readable volume, was sufficiently complicated to give his mother a headache. I wrote this book to give your mind, and your spirit, a tingle.

The creation of the universe, quantum physics, and Jewish mysticism are profound and intricate subjects. My strategy is to hold your interest as we navigate among them. I have learned from years of lecturing on this subject that I stand a good chance of losing your attention if I introduce unnecessary, albeit interesting, tangents. Mathematical equations, historical background, and even important physical stipulations can be distractions, and I avoid them whenever they are parenthetical to my main message. While I will not be able to teach you the subtleties of these topics in this small volume, I do hope to explain their essential ideas clearly and painlessly, and I even hope to persuade you that such exploration can intensify your appreciation of this world — God's world.

As a result of brevity and simplification, the book will no doubt leave some readers wanting more, while others who are familiar with the scientific or mystical ideas may criticize me for oversimplifying the explanations and perhaps allowing for some misconceptions. I ask your indulgence if you think my balancing act sometimes teeters. Occasionally I do plunge into the nitty-gritty, as I will when discussing the first moments of the Creation, because then my overarching theme — the compatible discourse between science and religion — requires such specific arguments. I want to reassure nonscientifically inclined readers that they do not have to remember all the definitions and relationships in those sections; I will recapitulate the essential points when needed. What is important to remember from these passages are the take-away messages and the realization that a body of knowledge exists with a carefully constructed justification behind it. As for those interesting tangents, in the Notes and Comments I provide extensive recommendations to many excellent books that describe in more detail the circumstances, the intricacies, the uncertainties, the personalities, and the fascinating historical contexts of our venerable search into the nature of our universe.

Books on modern science these days tend to be filled with personal anecdotes and recollections. I include none because I don't want to be distracting, and I want to keep things focused and moving along. Moreover, this is not a story about me. I do appreciate, though, that I am the person writing this book, because I am probably one of the very few people in the world capable of writing it: an observant Jew, a practicing research astrophysicist, and an educator. So here, in the preface, let me provide a few words for those interested in who I am and why I wrote *Let There Be Light*.

I love science, and as far as I can remember, I always have. The universe is an amazing place, and I remember as a child being curious about what was out there, and why things were the way they were. No wonder I always wanted to be a physicist — this kind of knowledge brings me great pleasure. In the words of Psalm 92:5–7: "He makes me happy with His works... [in a way that] an unlearned person just doesn't get." My teachers in high school and during my undergraduate years at MIT nurtured these interests. After graduation I enrolled at UC Berkeley for a Ph.D. in physics and quantum optics — the field that includes lasers and all the fascinating phenomena that laser light can induce in matter. My thesis advisor at Berkeley had been a mentor of mine at MIT: the inventor of masers and lasers, the Nobel laureate Charles H. Townes. When he left MIT for UC Berkeley, I accompanied him. He became increasingly involved in astronomy research there, and so did I.

I love being Jewish too, and as far as I can remember, I always have. To me, being Jewish means being aware: cognizant of the holiness in all things. Awareness in the context of relationships, whether with people or with God's Creation, embraces a sensitivity to their circumstances and needs. Awareness is cultivated with ceremony; the Sabbath discipline, for example, nurtures appreciation of the holiness in the Creation that saw its completion with the Sabbath day. Being Jewish calls for refining this consciousness with caring and the fulfillment of divinely obligated responsibilities. As the sage Hillel put it, "If I am not for myself, who will be for me? But if I am for myself only, what am I? And if not now, when?" And not least, being Jewish to me means applying intellect as well as soul toward these holy ends by embracing thinking and questioning, two concentrated states of mind that sharpen awareness and can educe a meditative consciousness.

I suppose it makes perfect sense that a scientist would find such an intellectual approach to religion appealing, but that is not why I love being Jewish, or why I love science, either. Love is an emotional, irrational, blessed feeling. All those other things — awareness, responsibility, intellectual struggle — help to ground life in meaning and purpose, but alone they are emotionally vacuous. In my case, love came first from being raised in a caring, traditional Jewish family which kept kosher, observed the Sabbath, and celebrated the holidays in ways that brought joy, affection, emotional intensity, personal expression, beauty, and much color to ancient and potent rituals. Later in life I also came to appreciate "the abundant love with which God loves us."

During my years as a graduate student in California I developed new instruments for studying the stars. I traveled to large telescopes on high mountaintops around the world, experienced incredibly lucid night skies, and mixed with professional astronomers around the midnight lunch tables. I had many influential Jewish teachers during my student days as well, and studying ancient and modern rabbinical texts took on a whole new perspective as an adult. In

Berkeley, with its richness of passionate and alternative spirituality, there was much to reconsider, but as I suggested earlier, to me being Jewish means embracing challenge and paradox. When it comes to living life, God demands that we "inquire diligently" and "choose life" (Deuteronomy 13:15, 30:19); authentic choosing requires a diligent inquiry into what those choices are. It was a transformative time during which I learned with and benefited from many skilled teachers and guides from diverse traditions, non-Jewish and Jewish. I am not a Judaic scholar, however, nor did I ever study for the rabbinate. I am just an educated layperson when it comes to religious texts, and readers should feel free to disagree with my interpretations of the Jewish sources or, for that matter, my nonliteral — but, I think, still faithful — translations of the material.

After graduating from UC Berkeley I accepted a postdoctoral position in astronomy at the University of Arizona in Tucson and subsequently took my first astrophysics job at the E. O. Hulbert Center for Space Research at the Naval Research Laboratory in Washington, D.C. My research used data from NASA's Infrared Astronomy Satellite, a mission that surveyed the whole sky at infrared wavelengths and provided humanity its first sensitive look at the heavens in this normally invisible kind of light. I became a co-investigator on the next-generation infrared space mission, and I continue to be active in space-based astronomy.

I have been lecturing on cosmology and the Kabbalah since my Berkeley days and have always enjoyed teaching in public. I therefore joined the Smithsonian's National Air and Space Museum, in Washington, D.C., where I led the Laboratory for Astrophysics, one of the Smithsonian's museum-based departments conducting science research and developing exhibitions and educational programs. During my years there I learned much more about the extraordinarily complex task of communicating technical material to the general public, and I helped to develop numerous educational programs, exhibitions, videos, IMAX movies, shows, and lectures. Later I accepted the position of senior astrophysicist at the Smithsonian's primary astronomy center, the Smithsonian Astrophysical Observatory, in Cambridge, Massachusetts, as part of the joint Harvard-Smithsonian Center for Astrophysics. Before moving north to Cambridge I spent two and a half years at NASA headquarters in Washington.

Today my research uses the infrared light coming from cosmic sources — stars, interstellar gas and dust, and galaxies — to investigate the intimacies of stellar birth and how those processes help to power the fantastically luminous, distant galaxies we see glowing in the early epochs of the universe. ("Early" here means only a billion years or so after the big bang.) I regularly teach students and the public and often try to weave together the astonishing story of modern astronomy with the personal meaning people associate with religion. I have come to realize that listeners who are not all that interested in science or astronomy will sit up and take notice when I make a connection to something they do care about, such as biblical texts. Many of my best students have been the ones who were in some way spiritually engaged. In response to frequent requests for copies of my lecture notes, I decided to write down my thoughts in a coherent way. This book is the result.

"רבון העולמים...אל יהיו עונותינו מבדילים בינינו לבינך...
ותפתח לבינו בסודות תורתיך ויהיה לימודינו זה נחת רוח...
יהיו לרצון אמרי פי והגיון ליבי לפניך ה' צורי וגואלי."

"May my many errors be forgiven, may my heart and mind stay open, and 'May the words that I speak and the heartfelt thoughts I express be acceptable before You' (Psalm 19:15)."

— From the prayer of Isaac Luria

A NOTE ABOUT LANGUAGE: GENDER AND SCIENTIFIC NOTATION

The Bible explains that God created "Man in His image, male and female" (Genesis 1:27). God, to the extent we can use language and anthropomorphic imagery, is both male and female. I could have used the word *she*, or *he/she*, everywhere in the book to refer to God, but since each of these alternatives is also imprecise I decided just to stick with the conventional masculine form when that form was a more accurate translation of the original.

The cosmos is a very big place, and it is also manifold. Although language runs out of descriptive words soon after *million*, *billion*, and *trillion*, we will definitely not run out of things to talk about. To comprehend and track all the meaningful distinctions we will encounter, we must be quantitative. The solution to the paucity of language is scientific notation, which tracks the number of zeros after (or before) the decimal place and uses that number as a positive (or negative) exponent of ten. Ten (10) is 10^1, one (1) is 10^0, and one-tenth (0.1, or $^1/_{10}$) is 10^{-1}. One million is 1,000,000 (a one with six zeros), or 10^6; one trillion is 1,000,000,000,000 (a one with twelve zeros) or 10^{12}; and one-trillionth is 0.000000000001 (a one following eleven zeros, with the twelfth "zero" being the place-holding decimal point), or 10^{-12}. The biggest number we will encounter in this book is 10^{500}, and the smallest one is 10^{-43}. Both are pretty dramatic, with just enough space on a page to write them out the ordinary, longhand way, but scientific notation allows us to see at a glance exactly how large or small a value really is, and to compare it to other very big or small values.

ACKNOWLEDGMENTS

People are just as amazing as the rest of the created universe, and one of the rewards of writing *Let There Be Light* has been a chance to interact with my teachers, students, colleagues, friends, and strangers in entirely new ways. I have certainly learned much about myself in the course of writing this book; indeed, I hope the ideas in this book lead everyone to new personal insights. I am particularly thankful to those people who have heard me lecture over the years about cosmology and the Kabbalah and asked me to please write down my notes. This book is the direct result of your nonstop prodding. I received hundreds of helpful comments from colleagues and readers during its preparation, but I particularly want to acknowledge the warm and enthusiastic encouragement I got early on from Len Lyons, Rabbi Lawrence Kushner, Phil Clayton, and Charlie Townes; I am also indebted to them for their many thoughtful suggestions. Versions of the semifinal drafts (there were many drafts) were meticulously read by Irwin Shapiro, Daniel Matt, Jonathan Rhodes, Larry Smith, and Rabbi Benjamin Samuels; their criticisms, suggestions, corrections, and questions have gone a long way toward improving this book.

In my search for a publisher I discovered that writing a book combining serious science and mainstream religion is asking for trouble — the subject simply does not fit neatly into any of the pre-assigned categories. I want to thank Arthur Kurzweil, who has been a continuing source of thoughtful advice and support throughout the publishing process. My editor at New World Library, Jason Gardner, has been consistently supportive, cooperative, and helpful, and I am very appreciative of him and his staff.

Most of all, I want to thank my wonderful family — my wife, Nancy, and my children, Avi, Sarah, and Mira — for their love and encouragement, and for nourishing a husband and father who spent so much of his free time (think of those beautiful weekends) staring at a monitor instead of exploring the world with them.

1 RELIGION AND SCIENCE IN HARMONY

This is a book about modern scientific cosmology and the Jewish mystical tradition of the Kabbalah. Cosmology is the study of the universe as a whole, its creation, and its future evolution. The Kabbalah, "the Received," is a Jewish mystical tradition that originated more than two thousand years ago and remains vigorous today; its earliest text, the *Sefer Yetzirah*, is an explicitly cosmological inquiry probing the inner workings of the Divine in the world. Modern cosmology and Kabbalah are complementary in essential ways, and I hope to persuade you that they serve to illustrate a much broader principle, the underlying harmony of science and religion.

There is a perceived division between our routine lives and our spiritual selves, one that has been accentuated by the pervasive, intrusive success of modern technology. To the extent that people don't particularly understand either technology or science, this gap widens. Two approaches have predominated in recent struggles to harmonize these two facets of our existence. The first one, simply stated, argues that science and religion are separate but equal. The Bible is a source of ethical and religious inspiration, and science deals with an objective, quantitative modeling of physical phenomena. In the words of Galileo (originally expressed by Cesare Cardinal

Baronio), the Bible tells us how to go to heaven, but not how the heavens go. George Lemaître, a Catholic priest and a pioneer of modern cosmology, put it more bluntly: "The idea that because they [the writers of the Bible] were right in their doctrine of immortality and salvation they must also be right on all other subjects is simply the fallacy of people who have an incomplete understanding of why the Bible was given to us at all." Scientists commonly articulate this attitude, but to me it is disconcerting, because it formally segregates two elemental areas of our lives and imposes a dissonance that is awkward, uncomfortable, and, when you think about it, a priori peculiar. I also believe it is unnecessary.

The second approach, likewise stated simply, holds that the Bible and science are in agreement when one or the other is nudged, or interpreted, into conformity. Those who treat the scriptures literally argue that today's scientific theories are conjectures: incorrect or incomplete theoretical models that are doomed to be forever "only models," even if they improve. Literalists often take specific issue with models of the Creation, many of which we will be discussing later. Other proponents of conformance admit that science is probably correct, but they interpret the Bible broadly to find consistency, suggesting, for example, that people naturally lived longer before the time of Noah than they do now because the conditions on Earth were different, changing for the worse after the Flood. Both of these alternatives are, at least to me, ad hoc at best and apologetic at worst.

Over the past twenty years or so, an active group of Christian theologians with strong backgrounds in science have attempted to classify and analyze the various ways in which people can integrate science and religion. Ian Barbour, Arthur Peacocke, and Sir John Polkinghorne, for example, look beyond what Barbour terms the "independent" or the "conflicting" attitudes I just mentioned to interactions characterized by respectful dialogue and a sharing of ideas. It is relatively easy, according to Polkinghorne, for people to develop what he calls a "Deistic" view of the universe, in which an appreciation of its scientific wonders and mysteries inspires a spiritual awareness, with or without a sense of some larger purpose. But they feel, as I do, that this is insufficient, and one of their aims has been to find ways to integrate the role of a personal God into a scientific worldview.

Efforts to harmonize religion and science are typically undertaken by people who are religious, while nonreligious scientists rarely even wonder about the matter; it is simply not that important to them. This book, for example, is my attempt to work through issues that many religious people find profoundly significant. One important motivation for the religious, it seems to me, is a nagging concern that if scripture is true about some things, then it ought to be "true" about all things, including its descriptions of the natural world. There is, of course, a different worry, too: if scripture is wrong about some things, perhaps it is also wrong about others. How can it be Divine? Some religious-minded people seek reconciliation with science not necessarily to gain new insights into the real workings of God's world, but rather to reinforce or even justify a belief in other matters, such as a promise of redemption, the moral commandments, or an assurance that our lives have meaning. As the modern Christian astronomer and fundamentalist Hugh Ross puts it, "Many [believers] fear that believing in a billions-of-years-old Earth and universe means they must accept a multimillion-year history for the human species" or, even worse, a universe without any need for God. People feel threatened. It perhaps goes without saying that underlying these struggles for reconciliation, and exacerbating some of their current political controversy, is people's presumptive faith in the accuracy of science.

A search for spiritual harmony should be motivated by nobler feelings than those of being threatened, sentiments that can lead to spiritually debilitating, parochial, or needlessly defensive views. A search for truth and meaning should not presuppose its answers, either scientific or scriptural, and humility, at least to me, dictates an awareness that one does not yet fully understand the natural world or the biblical texts. We should seek in order to find and inquire in order to learn and grow. I write about the harmony of religion and science not because I feel under siege, but because I want to understand — and there *is* more, much more, to understand. Consider the invigorating words of Rabbi Abraham Isaac Kook (1865–1935), the chief rabbi in Israel prior to the establishment of the Israeli state: "We should not immediately refute any [scientific] idea [such as evolution, anthropology, cosmology, or biology]... but rather we should build the palace of Torah [the first five books of the Bible] above it. In so doing we are exalted by the Torah, and through this exaltation the ideas are revealed... to raise the banner in the name of God above the blowing of the winds for the benefit of all."

Do I hope to convince atheists to become believers, or textual literalists to become scientists? Not at all. Not only is it not my intention to try, it actually would be contrary to my intention to try. To the atheists among my readers, I say in all honesty that I respect your considered principles. Nevertheless, I do hope that you live your lives in what I would describe as a "God-fearing" way: one that is caring and respectful of humanity, life, and the Creation. I also want you to know that you are missing something — a rich perspective of thought about complex issues, and a community of love and ritual. As for the religious among my readers who are skeptical (or dismissive) of science, let me be equally clear: I respect your beliefs as well. At the same time, I hope you live your lives realizing that, as God's stewards of the Earth, we must all apply our most rigorous intellectual efforts in science and technology to the task of caring for our world. Regardless of what you believe, it is vital to have a basic understanding of modern science. And I want you to know that you are missing something as well — a sense of wonder about and appreciation of God's majestic creation that can come only from a better understanding of it, just as every musician's appreciation of music has a depth that eludes those who only listen. God has clearly made the world in an ordered way, and given us analytic minds and free choice. These are precious gifts. Surely we are expected to use them; perhaps they have a purpose.

The most frequent question I am asked about this material is, If science and religion can have a dialogue, can religion answer any of the questions raised by science? There was certainly a time when the answer to this question would have been yes. The very questions we are considering in this book, on the origins of the universe, of the Earth, and of life, were posed by philosophers and scientists and answered by theologians for hundreds of years. Today, I think the answer would have to be no. In fact, the various disciplines of science have discovered so much, so quickly, that all of these traditionally religious themes are now firmly in the domain of the natural sciences. It is a curious outcome that science's ability to address with seriousness, and even answer, many great spiritual mysteries has not in general resulted in its becoming more religiously acceptable. On the contrary, science stands accused of *impoverishing* the spiritual dimension by providing convincing answers! To me, the spiritual value of a wonder lies not in the ignorance of its particulars, but in the fact that it exists. Will this standoff continue? I don't know. We will look at a few intransigent mysteries later in this book — consciousness, quantum mechanics, and some aspects of the Creation — and I will leave it to you to arrive at your own conclusions.

I am also asked the opposite question: Can science answer any of the questions posed by religion? Here I am unequivocal: at least in the domain of Jewish mysticism, science is essential to a sophisticated understanding of the nature of the world, the essence of the Creation, the possible meaning of unity, and many other topics, some of which we will address later.

I suggest asking two different questions, namely, Can religion answer any of the questions raised by scientists? and correspondingly, Can science answer any of the questions raised by spiritual seekers? The answer to both of these is surely yes. In the following pages I will present a harmonized account in which religion and science form an alliance that looks beyond literal interpretations to conceptual intent in a mutually enriching synthesis intended to further our understanding of the creation of the universe.

COSMOLOGY AND KABBALAH

Why have I chosen cosmology, from all possible scientific disciplines, to present these ideas? For one thing, the idea that the universe began somehow with a "big bang" is widely familiar. Perhaps in part this is because the eminent British astrophysicist Fred Hoyle popularized the concept over four decades ago by giving it such a descriptive and memorable name (although, ironically, he meant the term to be derogatory). Hundreds of excellent and up-to-date science books on the market have popularized the success of this revolution in cosmology. The basic theory and its derivatives have enabled scientists to explain with remarkable accuracy the intricate birth and early evolution of the universe and to understand its salient attributes, such as the rapid expansion that we see. Many subtle predictions have been verified, and meanwhile, as increasingly ethereal features of the observed universe are being uncovered, the model continues to provide either credible explanations or a solid framework for variant ideas. So far, the essential picture remains robust.

There is another, more important consideration. Cosmology is not just familiar to people, it is also *important* to them. Popular books on astronomy and cosmology fill shelf upon shelf in bookstores because people buy them. Newspapers frequently and prominently feature new discoveries about the age of the cosmos because their readers want to hear about them. People care. Despite its subtleties, complexities, or even perceived heresies, theories about the creation of the universe directly affect our sense of ourselves. No other branch of astronomy — all of which is immensely fascinating to people — appeals as directly to our spiritual needs as the study of the Creation. Even the search for planets around other stars is less compelling, perhaps because so many people have adopted the opinion that life is common in space and is just waiting to be discovered.

Astronomers share this sense of the importance of cosmology. In the Bahcall Report, the scientific community's report to NASA and the U.S. Congress on the priorities for astronomy in the decade of the 1990s, the section on cosmology is titled, "Our Place in the Universe." The double entendre is intended. Astronomy can tell us firmly where we are situated in the cosmos with respect to the nearby stars, and by its study of the origin and evolution of the universe it also fixes the framework within which we must find our purpose. Finally, I have chosen cosmology as the lens through which to examine these questions because I am a research astrophysicist. Cosmology is a discipline I understand and teach.

The biblical version of the Creation is, of course, even better known than the scientific one. An essential component of our Judeo-Christian and Western worldviews, biblical cosmology provides a concrete example we can use to compare with the scientific account. Like scientific cosmology, the biblical creation story is important to people, I think for the same reason: it constitutes a broad framework within which we find meaning in our lives. Yet these two popular narratives about our origins and our place are rarely woven together. On the contrary, as I mentioned before, there tends to be an uneasy sense that either the two are in conflict, in which case adherents of one often decide not to bother investigating the other, or there is a sense that they are in vague congruence, in which case people might conclude there isn't all that much to learn from the other. Religious believers may be wary of big bang cosmology because it appears threatening, while believers in science may be unfamiliar with, skeptical of, or even hostile to religious ideas about cosmology that appear to them as superstitious. These attitudes extend to views on religion and science overall. Both attitudes are, in my opinion, sadly mistaken. In this book I hope to illustrate how closely twined the physical and spiritual worlds really are and offer my personal view that they are complementary in ways that can provide insight and perspective to seekers trying to understand a little bit more about the world's mysteries, and what they might mean.

Why compare scientific cosmology to the Kabbalah, a branch of Jewish mysticism? After all, the biblical creation narrative has inspired a diverse and sophisticated literature, with many traditions to draw upon as resources for exploring the compatibility of science and religion. Furthermore, mysticism is notorious for being personal, even "irrational"; how can it be associated with science?

The term *mysticism* is even difficult to define. The pioneer of modern Jewish mystical scholarship, Gershom Scholem, refused to be pinned down to a narrow definition because, as he put it, "There is no such thing as mysticism in the abstract.... There is only the mysticism of a particular religious system." Nevertheless, it is generally fair to say that religious mysticism, Jewish mysticism included, incorporates a personal experience of the Divine of the kind the psalmist describes (Psalm 34:9): "Taste, and see that God is good" (using the literal meaning of the Hebrew *ta'amu*, taste).

The Kabbalah emerged as a distinct movement of Jewish mysticism in twelfth- and thirteenth-century Spain, where it first became public, but it traces its roots all the way back to the patriarchs Abraham, Isaac, and Jacob. The oldest work of Kabbalah is the *Sefer Yetzirah* (The Book of Formation), a book that is cited in texts dating from the first century of the Common Era and which by the tenth century had its own set of commentaries. Another very early mystical work is *The Bahir* (The Illumination), a book referenced in the kabbalistic literature as early as the twelfth century, whose authorship is attributed to a first-century sage in Israel, Rabbi Nehuniah ben HaKana. The essential text of the Kabbalah, however, is the *Zohar*, which appeared around the year 1300 in Spain. The *Zohar* claims the inspired authorship of the great personality Rabbi Shimon ben Yohai, who lived and taught with a group of his companions in Galilee during the second century CE. Like other works of Jewish mysticism, the *Zohar* makes use of earlier esoteric material, as well as mystical passages in the Bible, the Song of Songs and the books of Ezekiel and Daniel being prime examples. The majority of the *Zohar* is structured as a mystical commentary on the Torah, but a very unusual commentary, one framed in a landscape of personal exploration. Daniel Matt, the translator and explicator of the new Pritzker English edition of the *Zohar*, describes it as "a mystical novel. . . . The text of the Torah is simply the starting point, a springboard for the imagination. At times the commentators become the main characters, and we read about dramatic mystical sessions with Rabbi Shimon or about the companions' encounters with strange characters on the road, such as an old donkey driver who turns out to be a master of wisdom in disguise." I will rely on the *Zohar* and its commentators for most of the cosmological concepts I compare.

Following the expulsion of the Jews from Spain in 1492, some Kabbalists settled in the Galilean community of Tzefat (Safed), Israel, in part to be close to the tomb of Rabbi Shimon ben Yohai. There, during the sixteenth century, the Kabbalah matured and flourished, especially in the school of Isaac Luria (1534–1572). Luria's systematic analysis and innovative teachings were written down as the *Etz Hayyim* (The Tree of Life) by his follower, Hayyim Vital, and circulated in handwritten copies for more than a century before they were published. Lurianic Kabbalah is what Gershom Scholem has called "Jewish theosophy: a doctrine that attempts to perceive and describe the workings of the Divine, in particular as manifested in the acts of Creation, Revelation, and Redemption." The Kabbalists strove to understand God the Creator. The Kabbalah explores the spiritual world and our connections to the Divine by offering a paradoxical understanding of God as concurrently manifest but hidden, omnipresent in the gross world yet holy.

The Judaic scholar Rabbi Louis Jacobs cautions, however, against inferring too much about the Kabbalah and mysticism. He observes that the term *mysticism* has many meanings, and that there is an inaccurate tendency to equate the Kabbalah with all forms of Jewish mysticism: "The Kabbalah was indeed produced by mystics, and it contains both the fruit of profound religious meditation and instruments used by later mystics to attain the aim of encountering God. However there were many mystics who flourished before the kabbalistic era and the Kabbalah deals with many matters that are not mystical."

If the explication of these apparent paradoxes did not make the Kabbalah confusing enough, its texts are written in Hebrew or in a difficult Aramaic (the latter being particularly the case for the *Zohar*). The books of the Kabbalah are also poetically constructed, replete with wordplay and ellipses, and they weave their own ideas together with subtle allusions to biblical texts and early rabbinic concepts such as are found, for example, in the Talmud and associated literature. In short, all these features of the Kabbalah make it difficult for the uninitiated to understand. On the other hand, the spiritual world is also the world of the human soul. The Kabbalah offers psychological insights that can lead to personal growth, and spiritual guidelines that have helped it acquire a measure of popular appeal today. One graphic image commonly associated with this form of Jewish mysticism, and which many may find familiar, is the "Tree of Life," or "ladder of sefirot," a diagram of ten labeled circles, arranged into three columns and further grouped into sets, shown with lines interconnecting the ten (see p. 220). This visual image was developed in particular by the Tzefat Kabbalists to express many of the sophisticated relationships between these mystical entities. We will explore the sefirot in considerable detail in chapter 4. For now, it is enough to recognize them as a key concept of the Kabbalah, representing ten aspects of the Divine that act as a conduit to the world of our reality.

The books of the Kabbalah explore the workings of Creation in an attempt to comprehend how a purely spiritual being could create a physical world, with the aim of helping seekers perhaps retrace some of the steps of the Creation to return, in a fashion, closer to the spiritual One. As a result, the Kabbalah concerns itself with how — *exactly how* — God created the world. As the *Etz Hayyim* puts it, "How? And how many? And when?" It is this aspect of the Kabbalah that invites a comparison with scientific cosmology and provides a powerful framework connecting the two worlds of science and religion. This is the first reason I draw on the Kabbalah. The other is that I am not only a practicing scientist, I am also a conscious and traditional Jew and am familiar with some of the traditions of the Kabbalah. My examples in this book, therefore, often derive from Jewish theology, the body of understanding that I am most conversant with, and which I can best describe to you. I believe this wisdom will give us a foundation from which to explore the essential unity of the world, a unity that underlies what Rabbi Abraham Isaac Kook called "the true nature of reality." I will restate my conclusions at the end of this journey, when of course it will be up to you to consider your own.

PRECONCEPTIONS AND PREJUDICES

Mysticism is commonly but unfairly disparaged because of its emphasis on personal, versus objective, experience, but mysticism is rooted in rational insights and the logical development of ideas, not just personal revelations. Plato, a founder of Western philosophy and logic, was of course also the exponent of the view that the reality we perceive is like a shadow on a cave wall, cast by an unseen, fundamental reality that we aspire to comprehend. Inspired religious and spiritual leaders were also great rational thinkers.

The opposite perception of science — that it is purely rational and objective — is equally misleading. While science as a discipline is rooted in objective measurements — that is, a reality independent of the observer — individual scientists are motivated by many personal concerns. These include the search for beauty, as well as the same issues of purpose and caring that attract people to the subject of Creation. In the words of Albert Einstein, "Cosmic religious experience is the strongest and noblest driving force behind scientific research." Scientists also generally acknowledge that intuition, accident, or even personality play a dynamic role in the development of scientific theories and in the occurrence of "revolutions" in scientific thought. So do the limitations of language and culture. Furthermore, as we shall see in chapter 7, modern science is no longer quite so sure what an "objective" measurement is, or even if such a measurement is possible. As a result, there is an unexpected and deep ontological link between modern physics and mysticism, which numerous authors have emphasized, especially those who approach mysticism from the perspective of Eastern religions. These all become relevant when we consider the issue of truth, which we will do in chapter 10.

The "god of the gaps" is a popular expression currently used by some scientists to refer to God. With this phrase, they assert that God is invoked only to explain those things that science cannot, such as Creation, death, or the human sense of ethics or beauty. Where science leaves a gap in understanding, according to this view, is just where theologians posit God's central manifestation. As science confronts incredible new realms, such as the human genome and even the Creation itself, the gaps available for God to fill are getting narrower.

Religious people can be equally deprecatory toward science. They argue that science is naively pursuing a reductionist approach that leaves it intrinsically blind to deeper truths and oblivious to how human language and societal concerns shape it — influences, they feel, that ensure science's failure to meet its own ideal of "objective truth."

I hope to illustrate that these attitudes are not only mistaken, they are naive in their own right, and corrosive. Each approach, whether grounded in science or in religion, offers a vital and insightful perspective that is complemented — not threatened — by the other.

Many scientists, philosophers, and mystics would agree that knowledge of both worlds, natural and spiritual, leads a person to greater fulfillment. Illustrious founders of modern science such as Isaac Newton were particularly impressed by the apparent "perfection" of the natural world they studied, and they maintained that such order was a clear sign of God's hand in the world. Newton and his contemporaries did not know what we know today: that the Earth is very old, and evolution, with billions of years to operate, provides a conclusive architecture for the natural order we see on Earth. Nevertheless, the same sense of perfection that motivated these thinkers has a contemporary counterpart in the anthropic principle, which we will discuss at length in chapter 6.

By way of illustration, let me share with you one of my favorite quotations about religion and science, from Maimonides' (Rabbi Moses ben Maimon, 1135–1204) *Guide for the Perplexed*:

> Those who desire to arrive at the palace [of God — that is, an understanding of the Divine] and to enter it, but have never yet seen it, are the masses of religious people, the multitude that are righteous but ignorant... [while even] those who investigate the principles of religion have [only] come into the ante-chamber .... My son, when you understand Physics, you have entered the hall, and when, after completing the study of Natural Philosophy, you master Metaphysics, you have entered the innermost court, and are with the King.... For it is said (Deuteronomy xi:13), [that you are] "to love the Lord your God, and to serve Him with all your heart and all your soul," and as we have shown several times, man's love of God is identical with his knowledge of Him.

MOTIVATIONS AND QUESTIONS

We find ourselves in a bewildering world.
We want to make sense of what we see around us and to ask:
What is the nature of the universe? What is our place in it and
where did it and we come from? Why is it the way it is?

— Stephen Hawking, *A Brief History of Time*

Where were you when I secreted matter?
Speak up if you really understand... how the flow was
contained, or how it burst forth!

— Job 38:4

Many questions come immediately to mind as we begin to ponder the origin of the universe, but before starting we ought to consider for a moment how best to ask them. A poorly posed question will, more often than not, lead to an unsatisfying answer. If we are interested in the reason why the universe was created, for example, we should not expect an answer to come from science, nor should we be disappointed if scientific opinion on the matter seems beside the point. Similarly, we should not expect a theological answer to why the cosmic microwave background radiation — the remnant of the big bang — has a temperature of 2.725 degrees kelvin or, for that matter, why our body temperature is about 98.6 degrees Fahrenheit. No, the wonderful thing to appreciate is that science and religion are at least talking about and struggling with the same mysteries of origin, of destiny, and of the human condition.

There are four broad sets of questions that I think are helpful to set down at the outset, and which any theory of creation, religious or scientific, ought to address. Answering them will help us sort through the details of what follows.

The first set of questions asks whether or not the Creation took place at some specific time, and if so, when this was. Alternatively, perhaps there was no Creation, and the universe has existed eternally, either without essential changes or perhaps with evolutionary or periodic changes.

The second set of questions, one of the most nonintuitive, addresses what might be considered the geometrical questions about space: If the universe has not existed eternally, where did the Creation take place — in some empty location? Further, if the universe is the totality of what exists, what does it mean to say that it was not in existence and then it was created in some spot? What place could this be? For a religious thinker, these questions are folded into at least two separate mysteries of the Divine. First, a creation that occurs in time obviously entails some change in time, but what does it mean for an omnipresent, perfect God to change? Second, how can God, who must be considered complete, whole, and eternal, create a universe that is or is not a part of Himself, and in any case that is manifestly imperfect? Auxiliary questions can be asked about the size and shape of the universe and our own location within it.

The third set of questions asks, How did the Creation happen? Was Creation ex nihilo — from nothing — or from some preexisting matter? Was it a miraculous event, in the sense of being beyond the laws of physics, and if not, then how was Creation physically possible? Were the processes involved unique to that event?

Finally, an inclusive theory of Creation must address the role, if any, of life in the universe and, more fundamentally, the role of intelligent or human life. After all, we are the creatures asking the questions. Is it not an amazing, direct, and perhaps purposeful consequence of the Creation that beings evolved who would ask about that same Creation?

The Kabbalah and scientific cosmology each think about these four sets of questions and provide answers that, in my opinion, can be considered jointly. Can they be compared? It does not necessarily follow that because they address the same questions, they can share their ideas. Literature, music, and art also express ideas about the Creation. Science is the objective observation and the systematic distillation of facts into natural laws; mysticism is typically concerned with a personal awareness of the Divine and the world of the spirit. Science is quantitative; mysticism, qualitative. Science is grounded in this world; mysticism is otherworldly. It is not obvious that there is much of substance to discuss between these two.

I think that the disciplines of cosmology and the Kabbalah actually do provide an opportunity to go beyond a vague reconciliation of sensibilities and to initiate a meaningful dialogue. Their subject matter and their approaches overlap in numerous details. Kabbalah poses questions normally thought of as belonging to physics, and it provides answers that can be roughly compared to those of science. Admittedly, drawing comparisons is problematic, if only because the language of each discipline is so vastly different, complex, technical, and obscure. My goal is to capture the essential ideas of each and to show how complementary they are to each other in their descriptions of the Creation. The result will be much richer than when each is isolated in its separate context.

Like the story we are about to begin, our lives are mixed metaphors of spirit and substance: "You have made humans only slightly less than Divine, adorned with glory and majesty, and [yet] given them responsibility for the material world created beneath their feet" (Psalm 8:6–7). Surely this is a mandate to contemplate science and religion as partners cooperating in the human quest.

THE PATH AHEAD

The imageries of cosmology and Kabbalah are conspicuously dissimilar and are attended by many mixed metaphors. Nonetheless, I will weave these disparate descriptions together in this book because I think they provide a useful rhetorical device for thinking about things in new ways. I caution you, however, to approach this material with your eyes open.

A few words of encouragement are likewise in order before we go on. The ensuing chapters present a story that is exciting, but it can frequently become complex. Scientific discussions normally carry with them a lot of jargon and mathematics, almost all of which I will try to avoid. The broad principles of the big bang are generally grasped by the public, but the subtleties that form the great framework of observation and explanation related to this theory, and that mark the connections to our more everyday existence, are not widely understood. Let me reassure you that your efforts at deeper understanding will be amply rewarded. Nevertheless, I intend to provide only the fundamentals. Over many years of teaching this material to students of widely varying backgrounds, I have concluded that it is more effective to keep the story line flowing with broad concepts and plausible ideas than to dwell on detailed technical descriptions. Often this complex material, although it provides context and proof, can leave people more confused than they were when they started, especially if it is presented too succinctly. I have found that at first, people usually prefer to take the scientist at his or her word and get on with it. My experience also suggests that people more readily absorb the material and digest new ideas if I change course at the right junctures, retrace my steps, and reconsider the same topics with a different, more informed vocabulary. I hope those readers familiar with the more comprehensive scientific explanations will not be troubled when my presentations skip over pertinent details, and I apologize for the ambiguities that brevity has introduced. I suspect, though, that most readers will be more spiritually connected than scientifically literate. I hope that those who may be encountering the incredible power and personal relevance of modern cosmology for the first time will not simply accept my word, but will be tempted to explore further for more complete explanations. Certainly in a few years' time there will be new discoveries to marvel at and to assimilate.

The Kabbalah, like science, is complex, and like science it carries its own jargon, although instead of mathematics it uses Hebrew and Aramaic texts to develop its intricate concepts. It is also currently popular, and like the literature on cosmology, paperbacks on the Kabbalah fill considerable shelf space in bookstores. Some of these works are excellent and sensitively explain an esoteric subject to interested laypeople. I recommend some in the Notes and Comments. But, as with the scientific ideas in this book, I will not try to offer detailed explanations or attempt to repeat all of the spiritual or mystical ideas contained in Kabbalah. The Kabbalah is sophisticated, complex, and multitiered. It is esoteric on purpose. I hope our deliberations will be fascinating and convincing, but they will expose virtually none of the deeper riches. Readers should appreciate that our brief, almost superficial, encounter with the Kabbalah is meant to hint at the wealth of imagination and insight that lies beyond these just-barely-opened doors. My aim is to explain two arcane subjects simply but fairly, offer enough detail to show how they are richly complementary, and whet your appetite for further study, which is its own reward, and which, in the words of Psalm 19:8, "refreshes the soul."

Chapter 2 summarizes the conventional debate between science and religion and presents the current scientific picture. In chapters 3, 4, and 5, I present science's answers, profound and increasingly detailed, to the questions about the creation of the universe and the possible role of humanity, while weaving in kabbalistic imagery. Chapter 6 steps back for some perspective and introduces anthropic ideas. The key insights of quantum mechanics are discussed in chapter 7, and the final three chapters explore related mysteries — free will, miracles, life elsewhere in the universe — some of which are not part of science's usual cosmological discourse, but which are featured in kabbalistic literature.

2 TWO VIEWS OF COSMOLOGY

The Torah, the five books of Moses, is my spiritual starting point. Its unembroidered opening verses provide a straightforward account of the creation of the world. Just as science explains that the world is structured in layers, from atoms to galaxies, concisely described with mathematical symbols, so too the Hebrew text is layered and contains within its sentences, words, letters, and even punctuation clues not only to basic meaning but also to more subtle teachings implied by analogy. These lessons and ideas are developed and expressed through human interpretation and imagination, often in storylike extrapolations called "midrash" by the ancient rabbis. (Classical midrashic literature was written down beginning in about the fourth century CE.) Derived from the Hebrew word meaning "to seek" or "to examine," midrash is the creative explication and amplification of scriptural texts by means of legends, parables, and homilies that build on word or name associations and on ellipses in the narrative. The Kabbalists were masters of midrash. In addition to excelling in common homiletic techniques, they used numerology (in Hebrew, *gematria*, the correlation of letters with numbers, e.g., A=1, B=2) to explore quasi-mathematical linkages between words, created new words by transposing the letters of existing ones, and invoked Hebrew punctuation marks to draw analogies, among other creative associations.

The first word of the Torah is בראשית *B'Resheit*. "In the beginning" is its usual translation, although perhaps just "B'ginning" would be better, since this translation and spelling have the same sharp exhalation of breath as the Hebrew word: "B'ginning: God created the heavens and the Earth — the Earth was chaos and void and the spirit of God hovered over the surface of the water" (Genesis 1:1).

The first-century Rabbi Yonah reveals the significance of the Hebrew letters quoted above. In the classic midrash to the Torah, the *B'Resheit Rabbah*, he states that his teacher, Rabbi Levi, would ask, "Why does the Torah start with the letter *bet* בּ? [Hebrew is read from right to left.] Because its shape is like that of a bracket" — that is, the punctuation mark] — "which is closed behind and open in front: so we have no permission to discuss what is above or below, in front or in back, only onwards from the moment of creation."

This rabbinic dictum might appear to be antiscientific, presuming to rule some area of inquiry off-limits. I take it otherwise, as a statement that the biblical Creation engendered *time* as well as *space*, and that we cannot sensibly ask about "before" with reference to the period before time began. We can formulate questions that are not meaningful, and we are advised to beware. Elsewhere in the midrash itself, the rabbis speculate at length on what may have preceded the creation of our world.

Take a closer look at the Hebrew text above. What does come first in the Hebrew, immediately after that "bracket" (the letter *bet*), where we are granted permission to consider such matters? A small diacritical point called a *dagesh* comes first. When it appears within the letter *bet*, it hardens the sound of the spoken letter, which without it would be pronounced as a *v* rather than a *b*. This particular dot, inside the bracket that forms the letter *bet* of the first word describing the Creation, has a special name in the Kabbalah: it is called the *Resheit*. The word *resheit* itself means "beginning." In Hebrew the letter *bet* is used as a prefix to words, adding, among other possibilities, the meaning "in the" or "with the." The first word of the Bible, then, can mean either "In the beginning" or, if *resheit* is taken to be a proper noun, "With the *Resheit*"; thus the whole sentence reads: "With [a point, named] the *Resheit*, God created the heavens and the Earth."

As is typical of midrashic exegesis, the wordplay reflects and inspires a much deeper philosophical inquiry about the Creation. This is as it should be: the poetry of words is part of their effect. After all, if God creates with language, then words themselves have significance beyond their plain meanings. Even the order of the letters in words may be transposed in an effort to decipher hidden or multiple implications. In the kabbalistic literature, and especially in the imagery of Isaac Luria, the first word of the Torah is unpacked to mean many things at once:

B'Resheit: In the beginning (that is, of time itself).

B'Resheit: With the dot named Resheit.

B'reit Esh (rearranging the Hebrew letters): literally, "In a covenant of fire."

Shir Ta'eb (again rearranging the letters): literally, "A song of desire."

Bre Sheit (and again rearranging the letters): literally, "He created from nothing, Six" (referring to the days or stages of creation, excluding the Sabbath).

So: At the beginning of time, the universe was created from *nothing* in a series of stages initiated by an intentional act of desire or will, with a burst of covenantal fire expanding dramatically outward from a microscopic point called the *Resheit*.

DISPARATE VIEWS OF CREATION

As science matured over the centuries, and as the great natural philosophers such as Bacon, Galileo, and Newton refined its methodologies, it endorsed and elaborated on the cosmological position first asserted by the Greek philosophers, Aristotle in particular: the universe is eternal and unchanging. That it had to be so followed from Aristotle's principles of perfection. However, the static universe puzzled Newton. He wondered why the universe did not collapse, being, as it is, filled with matter, with the force of gravity tending to draw everything together. He concluded (arguing incorrectly, we now realize) that the universe must be infinite, because then the inward pull of gravity from matter on the inside would be balanced by the outward pull of gravity from matter on the outside. Einstein puzzled over the same thing and was prompted to introduce an otherwise unnecessary mathematical variable into his equations for general relativity for the sake of balance, as a way to express the inhibition of a cosmic gravitational collapse. This term was his famous "cosmological constant"; I will return to it shortly.

The Greek (that is, Aristotelian) model of a static universe conflicted with the opening words of the Bible, which certainly suggest that there was a "beginning," but in general the biblical verses were taken by most philosophers to be in conformity with the Greek view. Many (though not all) Jewish theologians objected. Philo of Alexandria (circa 20 BCE) and Maimonides strongly defended the literal biblical picture of creation in time. In his *Guide for the Perplexed*, Maimonides criticized the Aristotelian claim that "the Universe in its totality has never been different, nor will it ever change" and the Platonic view, which claims "the heavens did come into existence, but were created from pre-existent, eternal matter." Instead, said Maimonides, "Those who follow the Law of Moses our teacher hold that the whole Universe, i.e., everything except God, has been brought by Him into existence out of nonexistence."

The Kabbalists, including Isaac Luria, elaborated on the circumstances of the beginning as described by the Bible and introduced a dynamic expansion and subsequent evolution to the new cosmos. They imagined that the center of activity was not the Earth, but rather the tiny point called the *Resheit*. They developed their picture in great detail, because they saw in the secrets of God's creation some hints at human purpose and an explanation for the course of history. Thus the Jewish mainline and the mystical biblical pictures stood for more than two thousand years in contradiction to nearly every fashionable scientific model, all of which presented the universe as eternal and unchanging.

It is curious that these two contradictory views of creation in time, so glaring to modern eyes, did not spur nearly the controversy as did an ancillary theological point not particularly significant to the biblical creation story: the geocentric nature of the universe. In the Aristotelian universe, the Earth lay at the center in part because the geocentric perspective seemed obvious, but also because this picture conformed in beauty and simplicity to a cosmology of nested concentric crystalline spheres whose models did a respectable job of predicting observed eclipses and planetary motions. Copernican theory shifted the center from the Earth to the Sun. Galileo's discovery, using his newly perfected telescope, that the planet Jupiter had four circling moons confirmed that other celestial bodies besides the Earth could have subordinate worlds orbiting them. Galileo called this proof from "the open book of Heaven." He wrote:

> I believe that the intention of Holy Writ was to persuade men of the truths necessary for salvation such as neither science nor any other means could render credible, but only the voice of the Holy Spirit. But I do not think it necessary to believe that the same God who gave us our senses, our speech, our intellect, would have put aside the use of these to teach us instead such things as with their help we could find out for ourselves.... To prohibit the whole science [of astronomy] would be but to censure a hundred passages of Holy Scripture which teach us that the glory and greatness of almighty God are marvelously discerned in all his works and divinely read in the open book of Heaven. For let no one believe that reading the lofty concepts written in that book leads to nothing further than the mere seeing of the splendor of the Sun and the stars and their rising and setting, which is as far as the eyes of brutes and of the vulgar can penetrate. Within its pages are couched mysteries profound and concepts so sublime that the vigils, labors and studies of hundreds upon hundreds of the most acute minds have still not pierced them, even after continual investigations for thousands of years.

Indeed, Galileo was the first modern scientist to formulate one of the arguments I adopt: God's book of Heaven is equal to a book of the Bible as a source of truth and can be studied as such. In time, of course, the theological opposition to a nongeocentric worldview dissipated. Today, the sophisticated public is more likely to criticize biblical metaphors for the opposite reasons, namely, that they are not scientific enough: the biblical Earth is not the insignificant speck in a vast cosmos we know it to be — and of course the biblical Creation is apparently missing the rapid expansion of the universe that, as we are about to see, is one of its most distinguishing characteristics. In fact the Kabbalah, well before science, developed a model that is impressively close to the modern image.

THE MODERN SCIENTIFIC PICTURE

The Expanding Universe

The early scientific picture of a static, finite, and Sun-centric (if not geocentric) universe persisted into the nineteenth century. By the twentieth, it was generally recognized that the Sun was not precisely at the center of the universe, although it was thought to be nearby it. Puzzling questions had been raised over the years, including one put forward by Edmund Halley (of comet fame) and Jean-Philippe Loys de Cheseaux in the seventeenth century, and by Heinrich Olbers in the eighteenth century, that is notable for its simplicity and profundity: Why is it dark at night? If the universe were truly infinite, eternal, and homogeneous (that is, the same everywhere), with stars scattered uniformly throughout space, then upon looking out at the night sky the blackness between stars should be filled in by more and more distant stars, to infinity, with the result that the whole sky ought to appear as bright as a star's surface. Since it is dark, one or more of these assumptions must be wrong. This puzzle is known as "Olbers's Paradox."

The starting point for our exploration of modern cosmology is Edwin Hubble's detection of other galaxies and a cosmic expansion, findings that came as something of a shock. In the 1920s, Hubble realized that many of the nebulous objects he saw in the sky are not fuzzy patches of hot gas, glowing brightly like the great nebula in Orion. No: they are tremendous ensembles of stars — now called galaxies — that appear fuzzy because their multitudinous stars are not separately distinguishable to the eye at such a great distance.

A galaxy is a massive collection of stars, gas, dust, and other things (including planets) held together by gravity to form a distinct object in space. Our own galaxy is called the Milky Way, and on a dark, clear night we can see it stretching across the sky from the northern constellations of Cassiopeia through Cygnus and Sagittarius (the center of our galaxy is in the direction of Sagittarius) and on past Scorpius and Crux in the southern sky. Our Milky Way has about a hundred billion stars. Today, using large modern telescopes, astronomers can see other galaxies — hundreds of billions of them — of various shapes and sizes. Perhaps the most striking feature of these other galaxies is Hubble's second discovery: they are all moving *away from us*.

Hubble's discovery demonstrated that the universe is in fact not static, but is expanding, a finding that reputedly prompted Einstein to refer to his cosmological constant — the one he had introduced into his equations to keep the universe in static equilibrium — as his greatest blunder. (Recently, however, this cosmological constant has again become indispensable, in the formulation of the so-called inflationary theory of the universe and the discovery of apparent cosmic gravitational repulsion at the farthest reaches of the universe — two ideas that I will develop in chapter 4.) Hubble discovered something else about this motion: the galaxies are not receding randomly — they all follow a regular pattern such that the galaxies farther away from us move systematically faster than those that are closer to us. Knowing the distances to galaxies and their speeds makes it easy to approximate how long they have been moving. Simple division gives an answer: about 13.7 billion years. If galaxies have all been traveling away from us for this amount of time, then in the distant past, before they moved so far apart, these galaxies must have been much closer together. In fact, scientists think they must have been extremely close together, as close together as is imaginable, because there is no known force — nor any logical reason we can think of — to keep them suspended in a volume even as big as the size of our solar system, or of the Earth, or for that matter, as big as the period at the end of this sentence. All galaxies, and hence all matter — all stars, planets, everything, even space itself — were concentrated in a tiny, pointlike dot, which exploded 13.7 billion years ago in the event that the astrophysicist Fred Hoyle dubbed "the big bang." Hubble's measurements and the ensuing big bang explanation of the universe's creation identified the assumption that lay behind Olbers's Paradox, and did so in the spirit of the sixteenth-century Kabbalist Isaac Luria: the universe is neither eternal nor static — it is finite in age and rapidly expanding.

Corroborating Evidence

In the last century three quite independent scientific methods estimated roughly comparable ages for the cosmos. The first method calculated the geologic age of the Earth by dating its rocks, using as a chronometer the radioactive decay of the isotopes of elements within them. The nuclei of atoms contain particles called protons and neutrons, and individual chemical elements are specified by the number of protons in their nuclei, since chemical behavior is related to protons. The neutrons — that is, the neutral particles — add stability to the nuclei; isotopes of an element differ from one another in the number of neutrons present in that element's nucleus. The isotopes of some elements, for example uranium, have nuclei with more than the optimum number of neutrons for stability; they are unstable and eject protons, thereby transmuting into other elements in a precise, timed fashion. One particular isotope of uranium, for example, decays steadily into lead with a timescale of 4.5 billion years. The oldest rocks on Earth contain radioactive rubidium, whose decay into strontium provides a clock by which we can fix the time when rocks on Earth hardened from a molten stage: about 4 billion years ago. The Earth is at least as old as this, and the universe must be too.

The second method determined the age of the universe from the age of the oldest cosmic objects known, namely, the oldest stars. These are located in the Milky Way's "globular clusters," magnificent, roughly spherical collections of tens of thousands (or sometimes millions) of stars on the outskirts of the Milky Way. Our Sun, a middle-aged star in our galaxy, is older than the Earth; it's about 5.5 billion years old. According to our best current understanding of stellar evolution, stars in the globular clusters are considerably older than the Sun — they are 12 to 14 billion years old; like the Earth and Sun, these stars could in principle be much younger than the universe itself, but our current understanding of the nuclear power in stars, and how stars form and age, suggests that they cannot be even as much as ten times younger.

The third and last method — the "cosmological method" of Hubble — measured the rate at which the universe is expanding and extrapolated backward to the time when it was very small. Using current data this technique gives an age of 13.7 billion years. When these three timescales were first estimated, the data used to derive them were less reliable than the data we have today, and yielded values appreciably different from one another, prompting intense efforts to resolve the apparent discrepancies, especially between the latter two. (Such efforts continue even today, as astronomers work to refine a slight disparity between the apparent ages of the oldest stars and of the universe.) Nevertheless, before long these three methods gave remarkably consistent results, lending tremendous support to Hubble's picture of an expanding cosmos.

The picture developed from the cosmological method quickly garnered support from other disciplines. In 1915 Albert Einstein had published his theory of gravitation, general relativity. Several detailed mathematical models were developed using Einstein's theory, especially one by Alexander Friedmann, who in the 1920s developed a consistent framework, grounded in the nonintuitive ideas of general relativity, by which the universe could expand from a primordial point of ultradense matter. Other implications of such an explosive expansion were soon proposed and were confirmed to in fact be the case. Most notable of these were two quantitative predictions: most of the matter in the universe should exist as hydrogen and helium (the two lightest elements), and remnant light from this creative event should still be permeating space.

The relative abundance of hydrogen and helium (and a few other, much rarer, elements, such as deuterium and lithium) is indeed within a few percent of what is calculated by the big bang model, and the remnant light, the "cosmic microwave background radiation," was detected in the 1960s with all its predicted characteristics. More recently, two NASA satellites, the Cosmic Background Explorer (COBE) and Wilkinson Microwave Anisotropy Probe (WMAP), have measured this cosmic background radiation precisely, as have several sophisticated balloon- and ground-based facilities. These experiments are no longer trying to confirm the big bang model; they are now determining its particulars to greater precision, and more measurements of the remnant background light are planned to improve our understanding of the physical state of the primitive universe.

In chapter 5, I will discuss the origin of this cosmic background radiation in some detail. This light is a wonderful exemplar of the manifest presence of ancient cosmic milestones. Although primordial, this light bathes us today in its faint glow — like sunlight, except much fainter and present always, even at night. This light, the light of the Creation, appeared well before the formation of the Sun or any other stars.

Ideas about the big bang continue to undergo vigorous refinement. Astronomers are constantly modeling substantive new details

— after all, the whole universe is under consideration — and measuring their consequences. Paradoxically, the most important other discipline contributing to our understanding of the cosmos is one that examines the opposite extreme: the field studying submicroscopic elementary particles. At the close of the twentieth century, physicists probing the tiniest scales of matter with giant particle accelerators developed a self-consistent description of matter. The primary constituents of atoms — protons and neutrons — were discovered to be composed of even more elementary particles, all of which are intimately related to one another and, gratifyingly, to three of the four basic forces of nature: electromagnetism, the strong force, and the weak force. (I introduce the four forces in detail in chapter 4.) The "standard model" is the name given to this current theory of particle physics; it has components to describe these three forces, although it does so somewhat imperfectly. The "grand unified theory" (GUT), still being fashioned, would encompass these ideas in a more unified and successful way. Although still manifestly incomplete, because it does not yet include a quantum mechanical description of the fourth force (gravity), GUT can explain what happened in the earliest microscopic split-second of the universe: how nothing — or more precisely, how the vacuum — was able to bring forth our universe of matter and do so in a way that naturally resulted in rapid expansion, just as Hubble's observations implied.

Despite creative and considered attempts to present alternative scientific scenarios to the big bang, none have succeeded in explaining all of the many and varied observations in a consistent way. The most notable effort was the "steady-state" picture proposed by Fred Hoyle, Herman Bondi, and Tommy Gold in 1948, which posited that new matter is continually being created to fill the volumes of expanding space in a way that leaves an eternal universe unchanging in its local appearance. However, evidence from the cosmic background radiation, and from progress in particle physics like cosmic nucleosynthesis that Hoyle himself helped to pioneer, makes the steady-state alternative seem implausible today. In contrast, one of the most impressive achievements of the big bang models is their ability not only to explain all the results that scientists have obtained through their observations (at least so far), but also to anticipate many of them.

The Isotropic, Expanding, Homogeneous Universe

The oldest light that we can see has been journeying toward us from remote parts of the universe for about 13.7 billion years, the age of the cosmos. In order to talk about distances, especially the large astronomical distances we will encounter in this book, I need to introduce the *light-year*, one of the astronomer's preferred measures of distance. Light is unique. Its speed, about three hundred thousand kilometers per second, is the fastest possible; nothing can travel faster than this speed. A light-year is the distance that light travels in one year — about ten trillion kilometers, a range well beyond our solar system and its farthest planets, but only about one-quarter of the way to the *closest* star to Earth not counting the Sun. If the universe were static, its radius as measured by light 13.7 billion years old would be 13.7 billion light-years. But it is expanding. During the time that the light from the far reaches of space was making its way toward us, the cosmos increased in size, and its current corresponding dimension is therefore more like about 46 billion light-years. Unlike the value for the age of the universe, which is quite firm, the estimated current size of the universe depends on the details of how it expanded once the light departed. Furthermore, some variants on the standard model of cosmology (we will encounter one of these in chapter 9) suggest that the universe might actually be vastly larger than either of these preceding two values; it's just that we cannot in principle see anything that distant.

The modern depiction of the cosmos directly confronts three of the most general properties of the universe. First, the universe is *isotropic*: regardless of the direction in which one looks, the universe appears more or less the same. Now obviously this is not true in detail. The Sun and the Moon, for example, and the constellations we see at night, are proof that unique structures are everywhere. But cosmology deals with a bigger picture, hundreds of millions of times larger and more encompassing than the distance to the nearby stars, or even to nearby galaxies. Just as we might study demographics of the population but know full well that our immediate neighborhoods differ from one another, so too cosmology examines the universe on a scale at which local irregularities smooth out.

Second, the universe appears to be *expanding*. Edwin Hubble's observation means that the universe is filled with organized motion: it is changing with time. During the past few years, a new revolution in observational cosmology has raised an even more incredible possibility. The universe is expanding outward, but apparently not at a steady pace. Astronomers had long theorized that the expansion might not be constant. It should be slowing as the attractive force of gravity from cosmic matter in the universe retards the velocities of outbound galaxies. What they actually found amazed everyone: the outward speeds of remote galaxies seem to be *increasing*, not decreasing. The distant universe is *accelerating* away. This conclusion was originally advanced by teams of astronomers studying the light from distant supernovas, dying massive stars each of whose brilliant, explosive demise can shine as brightly as an entire galaxy, at least for a few days. The phenomenal intrinsic brightness of supernovas means that we can see ones that are very, very distant. If astronomers know a supernova's true light output — and most supernovas can be classified according to their characteristics and associated with well-understood prototypes or models — then measuring the amount of light that arrives here at Earth provides a direct measure of the object's distance from Earth, since, like the emission from a candle or any other uniformly shining light, its light propagates in all directions, spreads and dims, and the amount actually collected by a telescope depends on its distance. Supernovas in very remote galaxies have enabled astronomers to estimate distances to these galaxies accurately, and by comparing each galaxy's distance to its velocity, astronomers have been able to measure the Hubble expansion (the velocity of a galaxy as a function of its distance) out to the distant reaches of space. The measured velocities of distant galaxies are larger than expected from Hubble's relation, implying that they are accelerating away.

The presence of acceleration at the largest scales suggests some kind of cosmic repulsion. Einstein's theory of general relativity allows for the possibility that gravity has a repulsive aspect in addition to its familiar attractive component; this is his cosmological constant. If this repulsion indeed exists — the research is still new — it becomes apparent on cosmological scales only because its strength is directly proportional to the separation between masses, instead of inversely proportional to the square of their separation (the behavior of the normal gravitational force). Only objects very far apart would feel a noticeable effective repulsive gravitational force.

The last of the three general properties of the universe is its apparent *homogeneity*. This is a more dramatic feature than isotropy because it implies that every large volume of the universe is the same as every other, regardless of where in the universe that volume is situated. There may be local variations, but again, on a large scale — dimensions of the size of clusters of galaxies, for example — such fluctuations become relatively insignificant. A homogeneous universe is automatically an isotropic universe for viewers at its center. Early philosophy imagined the Earth to be surrounded by crystalline spheres, an isotropic but thoroughly nonhomogeneous picture. In the modern description, the universe is homogeneous. On its face, Hubble's observation of an expanding universe appears inconsistent with the principles of isotropy and homogeneity unless we are somehow specially situated — for example, at the center of the expansion. As we are about to learn, we are so situated — albeit in a very particular sense.

Two other lines of recent evidence have corroborated the astounding implications of these supernova studies. The WMAP satellite images of the cosmic microwave background radiation, and the other probes of this light, do more than confirm a big bang birth — they have spotted a complex patchwork of faint but distinct bright and dim speckles superposed on an almost perfectly uniform (or, isotropic) background. Cosmologists who model the early universe understand that the sizes and separations of these speckles depend on the interplay between the gravity holding matter together and the effects of the expansion pushing masses apart during the primal epochs. Detailed calculations based on these cosmic structures lend powerful support to the idea of an accelerating expansion.

The faint structures, by the way, turn out to be the seeds of future clusters of galaxies. A few hundred million years from the date of this primordial radiation, the first galaxies would materialize from these beginnings, and later other generations of galaxies would develop as well. Astronomers mapping the patterns of these galaxies on the sky have been able to analyze how matter in the universe is distributed on a scale vast enough to incorporate millions of galaxies out to distances of hundreds of millions of light-years. Their cartography reveals that galaxies in the universe are not randomly scattered, like poppy seeds in a cake. They are organized into stupendous crisscrossing strands and filaments that are interspersed with enormous voids. This topography is consistent with the clusters' origins from those early seeds of matter, and also with the existence of a cosmic acceleration balancing, in part, the inward pull of gravity. This portrait also highlights the unfolding of the universe we know today from an epoch characterized by almost uniform radiation into one with galaxies and stars.

All of these modern ideas — an expanding, even accelerating, universe that was born from a tiny point in a burst of energy in the remote past and then evolved into galaxies — would have seemed ludicrous to scientists a hundred years ago. But they leave us with a cosmology that is in remarkable conformity with the biblical one:

At the beginning of time, 13.7 billion years ago, the universe was created from nothing (more precisely, from the vacuum) in a burst of radiation that expanded dramatically outward from an infinitesimal point, in a process that has been termed the big bang; then, in stages, the universe evolved into its present form. This infinitesimal point, or at least its metaphysical equivalent, may be considered analogous to what the sages of the Kabbalah called the *Resheit*.

3 THE PARADOX OF "WITHOUT-LIMIT"

THE AGE AND SHAPE OF THE UNIVERSE

The *Zohar* expounds on the first word of the Torah:

> In the beginning [*B'Resheit*]: At the very beginning of the King's authority, He made engravings in the supernal purity. A spark of blackness emerged in the sealed within the sealed from the mystery of *Ein-Sof* ["Without-Limit/End"], a mist within matter, implanted within a ring, not white, not black, not red, not yellow — no color at all. Within the spark, in the innermost part, emerged a source.... It was not known at all until, from the pressure of its penetration, a single point shone. Beyond this point nothing is known, and so it is called "*Resheit*," the first word of all.

In this passage expanding on the first word of the Bible, the *Zohar* uses ambiguous terminology and indeterminate mystical metaphors to introduce several cosmological principles. Most apparent of these is the assertion that there was in fact a beginning, in agreement with a simple reading of the biblical account. The passage invokes the Divine using the consequential kabbalistic term for God, *Ein-Sof* ("Without-Limit") and elaborates on the brief biblical description by positing that the universe began as (or from) a "single point," one so minuscule that the eminent medieval Spanish commentator and mystic Nachmanides (Rabbi Moshe ben

Nachman, 1194–1270) describes it in size as being "like a very tiny point, having no substance." Finally, the *Zohar* notes a further feature: the *Resheit* was all-inclusive ("Beyond this point nothing is known"). Such a concept is impossible to visualize because we naturally imagine a point as being located somewhere *in* space — and wouldn't that space be "beyond" the *Resheit*? For comparison, a good nutshell description of the "beginning," as presented by Joseph Silk, a modern astrophysicist, reads as follows: "The universe began at time zero in a state of infinite density. . . . At [such] a singularity [i.e., point], matter and energy can be created, and come spewing forth, unheralded and intertwined, into the universe. . . . The big bang was an act of creation."

Hubble's discovery of a universe expanding in all directions raises many evident questions and challenges common sense. Does it imply we are at the center of the expansion, and perhaps therefore at the center of the universe? If so, why don't we see an "edge" beyond the farthest galaxies? Why don't we appear to be the oldest region of space, if the rest is more newly occupied? If there were some special reason, a Divine purpose perhaps, for us to be at the center of things, why could it not be achieved in some less unique place in space? Is there any purpose to the rest of the vast, expanding universe? Perhaps the most difficult question of all is, If we modern, post-Copernican people are averse to perceiving ourselves as living in a privileged location, then how can any sense be made of the observation of a universe expanding away from us?

The well-known answer raises fewer questions — indeed, it may really pose no serious problems: our conventional conception of expansion in a volume is faulty. A more useful way to visualize the universe was suggested by George Gamow in his popular book *One, Two, Three — Infinity* and is based on general relativity. The universe in a way resembles the surface of a cosmic inflating balloon.

We and all other galaxies reside, antlike, on the surface, watching one another move apart as the balloon inflates. This model has two immediate and useful consequences. Every ant, or galaxy, sees all the others moving away from it as the balloon gets larger and larger, illustrating the concept that in some geometries there is no privileged position: all galaxies are equivalent, and all see the same receding motions. Second, as a natural consequence, although the closest neighboring galaxies are not moving apart particularly fast, the ones farthest apart are separating very rapidly indeed, just as observed. This description can be made both mathematically precise and more nuanced, and it implies that all matter was once together in one place. Human observers, by determining how far apart galaxies are now and how fast they are moving, can tell how long the universe has been expanding: 13.7 billion years since it was small and pointlike in the *Resheit*.

The expanding-balloon model resolves the dilemmas about living in an Earth-centered universe but raises more of its own. The space we live in is clearly not a two-dimensional surface like the skin of a balloon. We live in a three-dimensional world. Furthermore, an expanding balloon does have a center, albeit one that is not on the surface, the "space" of the ants, and we can legitimately ask where in the cosmos this "center" is. For that matter, we might ask the same questions we could ask about the simpler view, namely, what is the balloon expanding into, and how big is that space? The scientific model, like the description in the *Zohar*, poses an apparently absurd paradox. Into what kind of space did the early universe, or *Resheit*, expand? Where in our current universe is that supernal location where it all started? Did this empty space exist before creation? It is no coincidence that the questions that cascade into our minds from these two portrayals are so similar, because indeed, the emerging pictures are strikingly similar.

GENERAL RELATIVITY: A SCIENTIFIC PERSPECTIVE ON UNITY

From the *Zohar*:

> When the Holy One, Blessed Be He, wished to create the world He brought forth a single hidden light so that from this light all the revealed lights would emerge and shine. . . . This light extended itself. . . .
>
> . . . The primal point [is] the beginning of the extension of another thing: light. . . . This light is a sealed mystery: the expansion that extended itself and burst through from the secret mystery of the hidden primal vacuum. First of all the expansion burst through and produced a single hidden point from its own mystery. . . . Once [it] extended itself, whatever remained of the mystery of the hidden primal vacuum was light.

A prominent but counterintuitive feature of the universe we live in is that it is *curved*. Space has properties that in essential, geometrical ways resemble the properties of either the round surface of a ball or, in the opposite sense, the open curves of a saddle. A flat surface provides a contrasting example. On a flat sheet of paper the three angles of a triangle sum exactly to 180 degrees. A flat surface is therefore said to have Euclidean geometry (named for Euclid, the author of the most prominent book on geometry in antiquity). However, the sum of the three angles of a triangle drawn on the surface of a balloon, to use the earlier example from a description of the expanding universe, is not 180 degrees; it is more than that, because of how the surface is curved. Triangles drawn on a saddle-shaped surface have a sum that is less than 180 degrees. Were we to measure carefully the angles of a triangle drawn on the surface of the Earth, we would immediately realize that the Earth is round, not flat. Non-Euclidean geometry describes such curved surfaces. Space in our universe is non-Euclidean, as determined by what are in effect the measurements of cosmos-size triangles. There is one important proviso. On a local scale, smaller than clusters of galaxies, the curvature of space is quite distinct, but on the cosmological scale the curvature of the universe is very small and, given the current uncertainties, the universe might even be flat. Whatever its value, the curvature of space is described by general relativity.

It is natural to want to visualize space, but how can we visualize curved space? What does it even mean for space to be curved? The surface of a balloon, after all, is two-dimensional and rests on a three-dimensional object; how can three-dimension space be curved like the surface of a ball or a saddle? Is there some fourth dimension? Furthermore, what does it mean for the universe at the Creation to have once been a point, as implied by the big bang scenario? Where in our universe was the *Resheit*? And what is outside our balloon, beyond the "edge" of our universe? In order to speak about space and its shape we must somehow be able to measure it. A ruler, a marked device to measure distances, is impractical because (as we will see more clearly in the next section) any such device will appear deformed to experimenters in motion, and our universe is filled with motion. Light and its measurement, however, play a pivotal role both in the mystical explanations of the Creation and in Einstein's description of space and time. We know that light has a unique property: its speed is constant, regardless of the frame of reference or the motion of the measurer. Furthermore, light always travels along the shortest possible path, just as a straight line is the shortest distance between two points. Light rays, therefore, are the optimum "rulers" to measure and demarcate space. A crisscrossing network of intense laser beams, for example, may be visualized as forming a web, or grid, that traces space as the rays propagate in different directions.

Light obeys physical laws, and one particular property of light is crucial to realize: light rays *bend* in a gravitational field. At first this may seem strange or unbelievable, but it is not too difficult to see why it's true. Consider the following argument: Matter has two independent but often confused fundamental properties. The first, a quantity that determines how a body moves, is called its *inertial mass*. Objects at rest or moving with a constant speed will continue to do so indefinitely unless a force is applied — they have inertia, and the amount of inertia is proportional to their inertial mass. A skidding truck is much harder to bring to a halt than a skidding bicycle, because the truck has much more inertial mass. For the same reason a truck at rest is much harder to push up to speed. The second, quite different, quantity determines the strength of a body's gravitational attraction to another body and is called its *gravitational mass*. The truck is much harder to lift off the ground than the bike, because its gravitational mass is larger. We should remember that *weight* is not a useful term when talking precisely about the amount of a substance, because it refers not to the quantity itself, but to the way the substance responds to gravity from another body. That truck, for example, will weigh approximately six times less on the Moon, whose gravity is weaker, but there is just as much truck, and it will be just as hard to stop when it skids. I will always use the term *mass* in this book, rather than *weight*.

To better understand the significance of gravitational mass, consider a related example, oppositely charged objects, and think about the electrical force between them. Electrically charged bodies attract each other, but the attraction between them has nothing whatsoever to do with their inertial masses; it depends only on their electric charges and separation. Their inertial masses enter the picture only if the charges begin to move in response to the electrical force. The gravitational force behaves the same way, only depending on the "gravitational charges" of, and the separation between, the bodies. The name for this "gravitational charge" is gravitational mass.

The inertial mass of a substance, in contrast, is the property that determines how it moves and, in particular, how rapidly a body changes speed when it is accelerated or decelerated by a force. Inertial mass has nothing to do with how bodies attract or repel one another, only with how they move. (So a truck on the Moon is easier to lift than one on Earth, but just as hard to bring to a halt.) Einstein postulated that these two nominally independent characteristics of matter, inertial and gravitational mass, were identical. This postulate about the nature of mass is called the "principle of equivalence," meaning that inertial mass is equivalent to gravitational mass. Therefore, we usually dispense with the preliminary descriptive adjectives *inertial* or *gravitational* and simply say "mass." Many observations have confirmed the accuracy of this equivalence, but scientists continue to probe its applicability at ever finer levels of precision. Current measurements find that the two kinds of masses are identical with an uncertainty of less than one part in a trillion, and ongoing experiments on Earth and in space satellites are attempting to reduce this uncertainty to even tinier values.

A direct consequence of this principle is that the effects of gravity (that is, force) are indistinguishable from the effects of acceleration (that is, motion). Consider travelers in a spaceship. The equivalence principle implies that astronauts will never be able to tell from a downward force on their bodies whether they are enclosed in a rocket ship accelerating (that is, moving) upward, or sitting at rest on a planet, held there by the planet's gravitational field (that is, its attraction). The two cases feel the same to our astronauts, and any possible experiments they could perform would yield the same results, because the two kinds of masses are the same. Now imagine that their rocket ship has a laser mounted on one wall, with its bright beam illuminating a crosshair on the opposite wall. One day, the astronauts awaken to realize that the engine must have started up, because the rocket seems to be accelerating upward; at least, they certainly feel a downward force. They check their laser. The whole room does seem to have moved upward in response to the engine's acceleration, because by the time the laser beam reaches the opposite wall, it strikes just below the crosshair, as expected. But wait — the travelers look out a window and discover that their ship is actually resting on a large planet with a strong gravitational field, and the force they felt was due to gravity, not acceleration. The principle of equivalence explains that both situations are the same. Everything that happened onboard — including the laser beam's illuminating the wall below the crosshair — will be the same whether the ship accelerates upward or gravity pulls downward. Gravity must have pulled the laser beam down.

This implication of the equivalence principle is enormous: gravity bends the path of light. In this example, the planet's mass bends the path of the laser beam, which started out pointed directly toward the crosshair, into a curve, such that the beam strikes the rocket's wall below the crosshair. Precisely the same thing happens to light from a star when it passes by the Sun on its way to Earth. The Sun's mass manifestly bends the path of the light, and the star's position with respect to other stars appears to shift when the star is seen close to the solar disk, as though a distorting lens were disfiguring the pattern of stars around the Sun. This subtle effect was first definitively observed during the solar eclipse of 1919, when background stars that were seen close to the limb of the darkened Sun appeared to shift their positions with respect to stars farther away from the Sun's disk. The result provided a dramatic confirmation of Einstein's theory of general relativity.

Since light marks out the web of space, the remarkable and inescapable physical conclusion is that gravity "bends this web" — and thus curves space itself. Gravity results from the attractive force between matter, that is to say, mass, and so the presence of matter causes space to curve. Space is often depicted in science graphics as having the properties of a rubber sheet, crisscrossed with a grid of lines. In this metaphor, mass is what pulls and stretches the sheet into valleys, basins, or, if a black hole is present, even sinkholes. The universe is filled with matter, and matter defines the space in which it resides. As beams of light pass by clumps of matter, they bend in toward the matter, curving around stars and sweeping in great arcs around galaxies or clusters of galaxies as they trace the fabric of space like the lines on that stretched rubber sheet, whose dips and deep depressions signal the presence of mass.

The *Zohar* exclaims "Come see!" when it wants to call a reader's attention to dramatic new ideas. Come see! At the time of the Creation, as the matter created from the *Resheit* began its expansion outward after the big bang, there was no "space" outside of it. Light beams emanating outward from the newly created volume of matter were bent back, pulled inward by the attraction of gravity from that same matter. There was no outside to the volume of space that the matter occupied. The separation between clumps of matter was increasing with time, however, in response to the expansion, and the volume of space that matter occupied was therefore increasing as well: new space was "created." Like ants on the surface of an expanding balloon who can always walk around their complete world even while it increases in size, so too we residents of the cosmos can see that our universe is complete and inclusive, even though its size has stretched immensely, and despite the very nonintuitive conclusion that there is no "outside." The location of the *Resheit* is here, as everywhere.

The equivalence principle conveys two profound, coupled ideas: that the ostensibly different qualities of matter — how it moves and how it attracts — are quantitatively the same, and that matter curves space by virtue of its bending the path of light. In the words of the *Zohar*:

> Come see the secret of the affair!... Each level is independent even though they are all one, and all are bound together as one, and not separated from each other.... Behold, everything is bound together in one thing. It includes everything because, since the paths are hidden and are not separable, and are gathered together in one place, it is called *Ehyeh* [the first name used for God in Exodus 3:14].... Now, let everything emerge and be perfectly arranged.

For the Jewish mystics, a transcendent philosophical issue is the meaning of unity. As they struggled to conceptualize the universe and its creation, they encountered questions such as, How can there be something outside of God? Or similarly, If God is everywhere, how can He find space in which to create something? Maimonides put it succinctly in *Guide for the Perplexed*: "God's unity is not an element superadded, but He is One without possessing the attribute of unity." Every human being is unique, but only in comparison to other humans, and things we create, such as this book, are unique only in comparison to others of its kind. The inclusive Oneness of God implies no "other." The general relativistic description of the universe, self-referential and complete, captures a sense of the oneness of space in a way that helps us grasp what such inclusive oneness means. Of course, general relativity is much more than a description: it is a mathematical tool that allows us to describe and predict our world in great detail, and with great precision.

I do not suggest that it is easy to visualize a universe with no "outside." The analogy of a balloon's surface is a flimsy one because, as noted earlier, a balloon sits in a three-dimensional space and, moreover, has both a center and an outside, although they do not reside on the surface itself. The self-referential relationship between matter and space, wedded through gravity, is one of the most difficult, counterintuitive, and yet indispensable concepts in modern cosmology and mystical imagery. I will return over and over again to the idea of a system that itself determines its own boundaries — including those in space and time. All of the deepest concepts of our inquiry are intimately linked to this notion. Self-reference is the nature of oneness.

We always must be open to the notion that our ability to conceptualize things may be so biased by our everyday experience that intuition is not a reliable guide either to truth or to reality. It is a disconcerting realization, and there are many ways to deal with the discomfort it causes. For the scientist, training and experience have taught that logic, powered by mathematics and rooted in experimentation, is by far more reliable than gut instinct, although an equally important part of the scientist's task is to judge and refine models in order to understand them more clearly, draw new conclusions, make new predictions, or even disprove the original ideas. For the spiritual seeker, such paradoxes themselves may reinforce a faith in the mysterious; an acceptance of the actuality of a phenomenon that is incompletely understood is a valuable lesson in humility. Each person must find his or her own unique balance between these approaches.

SPECIAL RELATIVITY: THE COUPLING OF SPACE AND TIME

General relativity describes space and addresses the nature of gravity. It also enables us to understand how objects "accelerate"; that is, how they change their speed or direction of motion when influenced by a force like gravity. Special relativity, on the other hand, explains how to view the world under the more quiescent conditions of motionlessness or its effective equivalent, uniform motion. Just as the equivalence of inertial and gravitational mass is an unexpected but observed fact, so too is another remarkable finding, one that is almost harder to comprehend: the speed of light is a constant. Unlike everything else with which we are familiar — atoms, baseballs, planets — light is always and only found moving at a speed of about 300,000 kilometers per second (or about 186,000 miles per second) in a vacuum. For simplicity, I will always cite the approximate value of 300,000 kilometers per second. Light effectively slows down, however, in a material like glass or water as it interacts with that material's atoms.

The constancy of the speed of light in a vacuum has bizarre implications. Should a train traveling east at 100 kilometers per hour (kph) pass alongside a train going west at 100 kph, they would pass each other at a relative speed of 200 kph. If someone onboard that west-moving train were to pitch balls westward at 100 kph, the balls would zip past the east-moving train at 300 kph. The velocities all add together, so that in this example the velocity of the ball relative to the east-moving train, 300 kph, is much faster than the pitched-ball velocity of 100 kph. But here is the completely unexpected phenomenon: should the pitcher shine a beam of light westward, its photons (that is, its particles of light) would zip past the other train at exactly the speed of light — not a fraction faster. Furthermore, the photons would zip past at exactly this same speed,

300,000 kilometers per second, even if either or both trains were themselves moving at nearly the speed of light.

Does nature use different rules of motion when light is involved? Not at all. Special relativity does not make an exception for light. In truth, everything obeys the same rule for summing velocities for the net relative velocity. But in our world the accurate expression for adding speeds is more complicated than the ordinary, intuitive one. Special relativity formalizes what scientists see subtly happening into a rule containing a nonintuitive provision that is negligible until speeds approach the speed of light. Once objects move that fast, their relative values of speed no longer add directly, but rather in a way that gives a much smaller net value, consistent with the observed behavior that no relative speed can be faster than that of light itself.

Einstein and others built a mathematical framework and consistent worldview in which the apparent absurdity of this observation not only makes sense, it is quite a rational — and even the most plausible — arrangement for the universe to have adopted. It ensures that everyone, regardless of his or her movements, can use the same set of equations and physical laws. Scientists on a rapidly moving planet do not need to adjust their physical equations to take into account their particular motion, whatever it may be. Neither do they need to ask in what way (that is, with respect to what frame of reference) their speed qualifies as being "rapid." Special relativity explains that all uniformly moving frames of reference are equivalent.

Einstein also found that in order to achieve such universal consistency, other physical properties besides velocity must become "relative." The principle that velocities do not combine in a simple additive way may seem strange, but the implications for other physical behaviors are, on their face, downright weird. In the following paragraphs I offer a brief explanation of some of these bizarre realities. It is not meant as proof, and it might not be for everyone, but I hope it will give you a feeling for why these effects, although not intuitive, do make sense.

Consider our earlier train example and imagine a clock on the train moving west. Since time ought to pass at the same rate independent of how a clock's mechanism works, suppose our train uses a clock that works like this: it counts one "second" each time a beam of light bounces back and forth vertically once between two parallel mirrors. To passengers on the train, that time interval is exactly equivalent to the distance between the mirrors divided by the speed of light. But if we are on the platform watching the train zoom past at nearly the speed of light, we clearly see that during the brief, "one-half second" time interval that the light beam in the clock travels from one mirror to the next, the second mirror has moved — and quite a long way too, since it is on a fast-moving train. (The same thing happens on the light's return path to the first mirror.) The mostly horizontal path in space that we see the light traverse as the train zooms past horizontally, taking its light with it, is, in fact, much longer than the plain vertical mirror separation the train's passengers witness in their reference frame. Since relativity asserts that the speed of light is the same even though it is on a rapidly moving train, the time the light beam takes to cover that longer distance must also be longer. We find that the time is longer: we observe that the clock on the train is running slow compared to our clock on the platform. Meanwhile, the passengers on the train see nothing at all odd in the behavior of their clock, but they notice that *our* clock (the one on — to them — the rapidly moving platform going east) appears to be running slow.

Not only are velocity and time "relative" in relativity, so is space. Speed, after all, is a combined measure of distance and time;

if both speed and time are relative, and if at least one thing — light — has an absolute value of speed, then distance should also be relative. Indeed, if we were to do an experiment to measure the length of a stick on the train (with the stick lying in the same direction as the train's motion, not perpendicular to it), we on the platform would measure a length that is shorter than the length that the train passengers themselves would determine. Both space and time appear distorted; they are coupled together because the speed of light is constant.

The relative nature of time results in other curious, *Alice in Wonderland* phenomena. Events that occur simultaneously in their own reference frames do not appear to be simultaneous to observers in other, moving frames of reference. Let's try one last thought experiment. We will measure the entire length of the moving train by placing remotely activated electronic sensors all along its track; each sensor is designed to turn red if (and only if) one end of the train is passing immediately over it when they are switched on. We power the experiment on and off quickly and then measure the distance between the two red sensors — the places where the two ends of the train were at the moment the experiment was activated. We already know that the measured length of something that moves very fast appears shortened when it lies along the direction of motion, so we are amazed, but not wholly surprised, to see that the separation of the red markers is considerably shorter than the actual length of the train as measured by the travelers on board. Later we ask the passengers on the train what *they* saw as they passed by the sensors, since their measurement of their own train's length is inflexible. They respond that, yes, they saw two of the sensors turn red, but, they report, *not* at the same time! They saw the sensor under the front of the train switch on a little bit earlier than the one at the rear, and meanwhile the train moved forward a little bit before the rear sensor flashed on. What we saw as happening at the same time, they saw as occurring at different times. We measured a shorter train, and they measured a normal one. We each have our own perfectly self-consistent explanations for length and time, and we each understand exactly why the other's measurements differ.

Special relativity theory has the great power of ensuring that all observers, no matter how fast they may be moving, arrive at exactly the same understanding of all physical laws: relativity describes universal laws of physics for any and all observers moving at any constant speed. General relativity extends this framework to observers experiencing acceleration or gravity. Space and time depend on the relative motion of observers and are intertwined with each other. The consequence of this intimate interconnection is that our universe is not a three-dimensional space in which objects move in time, but rather a coupled, four-dimensional "space-time."

We saw in the previous section that general relativity can describe space as complete, without an "outside." With this very brief introduction to special relativity, perhaps we also can imagine that a similar kind of wholeness applies to space-time. It can also be complete but finite, with no "outside," or, in the case of time, no "before." Indeed, Stephen Hawking and James Hartle have argued, using some of the principles of quantum mechanics, that at the creation event, not only was space created, but time also began. It makes no sense to ask about a "before" — there can be no "before." The universe is eternal (that is, there was no time when it did not exist), yet it had a beginning.

Come see! An equally fantastic implication of special relativity is that energy and mass are similarly intertwined. Energy is a well-defined physical quantity, a measure of the capacity to do work.

Energy is conserved, which is to say that it is neither created nor destroyed, but rather undergoes changes in form between chemical energy, nuclear energy, kinetic energy, and other types of energy, but none of it is lost. The energy of a body in motion had to come from energy somewhere else — chemical fuel, for example. A body in motion has *kinetic energy* equal to one-half its mass times its speed squared. Speeds are relative, as we have just seen, and do not add up simply as the plain sum but are always smaller in value. Conservation of energy therefore implies that the mass must somehow increase correspondingly... and so it does. The mass of an object increases rapidly as its speed approaches the limit of the speed of light. For example, when you kick (that is, add energy to) a soccer ball, it will speed up, but if it's already moving at close to the speed of light when you kick it, it can't speed up much more — so the energy in your kick goes instead into increasing the ball's mass. This phenomenon is the source of Einstein's famous conclusion about the equivalence of energy and mass, $E=mc^2$ (c is the common abbreviation for the value of the speed of light). As the mass of an object increases, proportionately more energy is needed to accelerate it further, such that an object's speed can only approach — but never reach — that of light.

Once we grasp the equivalence between mass and energy, we also can appreciate that the creation of matter is not fundamentally different from the creation of energy. Furthermore, we can fathom why light, a form of energy (called electromagnetic energy), has a mass equivalent to this energy, and it may not be surprising that light is attracted by a gravitational field. Before this book is finished, we will contemplate the first quantum micromoments of the big bang and reflect on the vast energy emerging from it, energy that would soon turn into matter.

We now have access to the central tools needed to grasp the

two crucial features of biblical mystical creation: it occurred with a beginning (our universe is not eternally old), and, although the universe was created to be in some way separate from God, still God and the universe are one: complete, whole, and eternal. In the words of the *Zohar*: "Each level is independent even though they are all one, and all are bound together as one, and not separated from each other.... Behold, everything is bound together in one thing."

4 THE COSMIC CAST

THE FOUR FORCES

The universe, although it is an infinitely rich and complex place, is also surprisingly regular, harmonious, and predictable. It runs with just a few basic laws, which can be expressed using only several dozen mathematical symbols, and which, thanks to the principles of relativity, are applicable everywhere. The values for only thirty-one physical quantities (at least according to one recent analysis) specify everything fundamental about our universe, from its age and dimension to the strengths of its forces and the masses of its atomic particles. As for the constituents of the universe, they are likewise composed of relatively few fundamental kinds of matter, and they interact according to these same rules. In this chapter I will summarize the current scientific understanding of the fundamental forces and particles of the universe, and in the next I will use this background to describe the Creation as formulated by modern physics and as pictured in the Kabbalah. As we wade into these deeper waters, you will be invited to do a bit of swimming. Let me take a moment to reiterate my earlier reassurances and persuade nonscientifically inclined readers not to feel discouraged by the details. Some people will enjoy following the arguments closely, and others won't. Just remember that it is not necessary to remember all the definitions and relationships discussed in these chapters. I do want to emphasize, however, that the conclusions we reach in the end rest on carefully constructed logical arguments and precise measurements.

Forces enable objects to influence one another: the strength of a force is measured by the acceleration it imparts to an object, although for convenience we often use a calibrated counterbalanced force, such as a scale, to measure strength. In all the universe we know of only four forces. The first, the *electromagnetic force*, enables magnets to push or pull and causes objects with electrical charges to attract or repel one another, depending on whether the charges — positive and negative — are opposite or the same. The electromagnetic force is called a "long-range" force, because the strength of the attraction or repulsion between charges decreases only gradually with their separation. The force varies inversely with the square of the distance between charges: doubling the distance between particles reduces the strength of the force to one quarter of its original value. The force has a range that spans very large distances, and even though its effect decreases with distance, it never reaches zero. The electromagnetic force binds electrons to orbit the nuclei of atoms and governs their collective behavior, and so it is responsible for all of chemistry and biology. Electromagnetism keeps the surface of a water drop round, prevents books from falling through desktops, powers combustion, and enables computers to process information and display it on well-lit screens. It can be described fairly well by classical physics in a theory that was perfected in 1864 by the Scottish physicist James Clerk Maxwell, but in many cases, and certainly in extreme environments like the early universe, its behavior can be described only by comprehensive quantum mechanical theory.

An altogether different force is *gravity*. Like electromagnetism, gravity is a long-range force. Unlike electromagnetism, however, gravity comes with only one kind of "charge" — gravitational mass — and has no opposing force of repulsion. (As mentioned, Einstein's cosmological constant describes a possible exception, the hypothetical presence of a cosmic repulsion.) Gravity is the force that caused Newton's mythical apple to fall on his head. As Newton discovered, gravity is also the force that causes the Moon to "fall" toward Earth as it circles, except that its falling motion and its forward motion are perfectly balanced, so that it forever misses the Earth; that is, it orbits. As the Moon orbits the Earth, its gravitational pull causes the ocean's tides. Gravity likewise keeps the Earth in orbit around the Sun, constrains the Sun in its path through the Milky Way, and binds together the galaxies of the universe in a vast network of clumps and filaments.

Although gravity dominates the dynamics of the universe, it is easy to see that compared to electromagnetism, its strength is puny. A tiny magnet can suspend a nail, even though the entire Earth, with a mass of about six trillion trillion kilograms (6×10^{24} kg), is pulling down on that nail. This example is accessible but illustrative only, since the magnet is held quite close to the nail, while most of the Earth's mass is thousands of miles away. Here is a more precise one: when two protons (elementary atomic particles we will meet shortly) are side by side, the gravitational force between them is a fantastically inconsequential 10^{38} times weaker than the electromagnetic force between them. Compared to the electromagnetic force — and to the other two forces as well — gravity is inconsequential. It may make Newton's apple drop, but electromagnetism, in concert with the rules of quantum mechanics, makes it stop falling when it hits the ground. Why, then, is gravity important at all? Because the electromagnetic force involves both positive and negative charges, and there are nearly always equal numbers of each kind, so that matter is usually neutral, with no net charge. In our everyday world, we never worry that an electrically charged pencil, for example, will be sucked from our hand by an oppositely charged desk. The gravitational force, by contrast, involves particles that only attract each other. It gets cumulatively stronger as larger volumes of space that include larger quantities of matter participate. This unique ability ensures that gravity dominates the dynamic processes of cosmology.

As mentioned in chapter 2, the nucleus of an atom contains two kinds of particles: protons (positively charged particles) and neutrons (particles that have no charge). A neutron is about the same mass as a proton. Each chemical element is identified by the number of protons in its atomic nuclei. The dimensions of a nucleus are microscopic, typically about 10^{-15} meters across. How can an atomic nucleus exist and remain in a stable configuration when it is full of positively charged protons that repel one another with tremendous electromagnetic force? The answer lies in the existence of the third great force of nature, the *strong force*. Two adjacent protons are attracted by the strong force with a strength that is approximately a hundred times greater than that of the repulsive electromagnetic force. The strong force is the strongest of all forces and the one that binds together the nuclei of atoms. Unlike electromagnetism and gravity, however, the strong force is not in practice long-range. It does not operate over distances much larger than an atomic nucleus, so it is not normally apparent to us in our macroscopic world. The nuclei of the atoms of the heaviest elements, such as uranium, with 92 protons and as many as 146 neutrons, can become relatively large as all of these particles cluster together, large enough to weaken the binding power of the strong force and make these nuclei unstable and prone to spontaneous fragmentation, or fission. That is why there are not many more than about a hundred elements in nature: heavier elements would need even more protons and neutrons in their nuclei. Physicists have artificially produced some additional elements using particle accelerators, but these elements are unstable.

The fourth and last of the forces is also confined to the strange world of subatomic particle physics. It is called the *weak force*, because the distance over which it can exert influence is only about a hundredth that of the strong force. In the case of two adjacent protons, the effect of the weak force is about one ten-millionth that of the strong force. The weak force controls how particles decay into other particles, particularly in processes during which ghost-like particles called *neutrinos* are produced. The weak force may be unfamiliar to most people, but it is far from unimportant. The fusion of hydrogen into helium, for example, involves the conversion of hydrogen nuclei (single protons) into helium nuclei (two protons and two neutrons), with the resulting release of neutrinos. This is the process that powers our Sun. The weak force thus helps enable the Sun and other normal stars to shine. As we explore the earliest moments of the Creation we will find that the weak force, and neutrinos, played a crucial role there as well.

There are no other forces, nor are there any known phenomena that these four forces might not in principle explain. This is by no means to claim that our current theories are perfect, or that we understand everything we see. Far from it: one of the greatest unsolved mysteries of science is why there *are* only four forces, and why each has its own particular attributes. In our everyday world, the forces appear to be distinct and independent. But many physicists suspect that in environments where the energies are tremendous and temperatures fantastically hot — above 10^{32} degrees kelvin — these four will behave with comparable strengths. Temperature, of course, quantifies how hot or cold something is. For matter, temperature is a measure of the energy in the random motion of its constituent particles; more motion implies a higher temperature. (For normal situations the astrophysical convention for temperature is to use degrees on the Kelvin scale, in which water freezes at 273.15 kelvin and boils at 373.15 kelvin. All atomic and molecular thermal motions stop at 0 kelvin. Temperatures discussed in the rest of the book are expressed using the Kelvin scale unless otherwise noted.) At phenomenally high temperatures, the four forces can be described as behaving like four different aspects of a single force.

Key to our investigation of the Creation will be the "theory of everything," optimistically predicted by physicists who suspect that each of the four forces really is one facet of some meta-force. Physicists have achieved remarkable successes in their efforts to formulate a grand unified theory (or, GUT) that can explain the relationship between three of the four forces (all except gravity). It is fervently anticipated that GUT, intrinsically a quantum mechanical theory, will eventually be extended to include gravity. The theoretical physicist, Nobel laureate, and prolific author Steven Weinberg calls it the particle physicist's "dream," and I too presume that this kind of unity infuses the world, and that physics will uncover it. Once that is accomplished, there will be a single explanation for all four forces, as well as a formulation that includes both general relativity and quantum mechanics: a theory of everything.

If the four forces ever had been united as one force in the past, it could only have been in a place with extraordinarily high temperatures, far hotter than the centers of the hottest stars, whose cores burn at tens of millions of degrees. There is only one place we know of in the universe with the incredible energy and temperature necessary to allow the four forces to have been unified. That place was the *Resheit* of the big bang.

THE PARTICLES AND THEIR FORMS

We are not accustomed to thinking of our world as being particularly narrow in its variety. Whether a gas, liquid, or solid, a planet or a paramecium, objects come with an apparently limitless diversity of qualities and behaviors. Yet the truth is that all material things are built from only a few kinds of matter — using fewer than a hundred types of atoms — with a relatively narrow set of physical attributes. It is a remarkable fact that our astonishingly diverse world is built from these few constituents combining in myriad subtle forms. Physicists have discovered that atoms themselves are composed of a relatively small set of even more basic "elementary" particles that have tightly constrained properties. Only twenty-nine of these fundamental particles have been discovered. Two more have not yet been discovered, but all the evidence points to their existence. Together with their variants, these thirty-one particles form an interrelated, recognizable class of particles that appears to constitute a mathematically symmetric system of properties in much the same way that the properties of the atomic elements fill out the periodic table of elements.

The elementary particles are not a collection of disparate entities. Apples and oranges may appear to be very different, but both are fruits. In a roughly similar way, the elementary particles seem at first to be unrelated: some are hundreds of billions of times more massive than others; some carry a positive or negative charge, while others have no charge; some can exist on their own (electrons, for example), while others can survive only when combined in tight sets. Despite these considerable differences, and not to mention the manifest difference between, say, air and rocks, all matter and particles fall into just two groups, or classes. Particles in one class tend to aggregate together and are statistically indistinguishable from one another; these are called *bosons* (pronounced

"BO-zahns"). Exactly the converse applies to the other class, in which particles segregate themselves in the sense that no two identical particles of this class can be in the same physical state at one time; these particles are called *fermions*, and they are distinguishable from one another. These two classes are named, respectively, after Satyendra Bose and Enrico Fermi, the two physicists who, with their respective colleagues, Albert Einstein and Paul A. M. Dirac, described how particles behave collectively; that is, they calculated the particles' statistical behavior. The "physical state" of a particle is the set of all physical parameters that completely describe it, including, for example, its position and its motion in space. When physicists say that electrons, being fermions, are distinguishable, they do not mean that each electron is different. They mean that, like two peas in a pod, electrons may look the same, but they cannot have exactly the same position, velocity, and other properties — they cannot be in the same physical state.

The Bosons

Light is the most familiar kind of boson. Light is an electromagnetic phenomenon — a propagating wave of joint electric and magnetic fields that is characterized by the distance from wave crest to wave crest: the wavelength. Light has a common visible manifestation, optical light, but it also comes in myriad invisible forms, from the so-called gamma rays and X-rays at the shortest wavelengths to radio radiation at long wavelengths. James Clerk Maxwell discovered the basic equations that governed electric and magnetic fields and showed that these fields are not fundamentally different kinds of phenomena, but are closely related to one another. Light has both electric and magnetic components, whose joint natures determine the speed at which it travels. Light, also called electromagnetic radiation, is therefore associated with the electromagnetic force.

"Particles" and "waves" are two different but useful metaphors for describing the behavior of elementary matter. Although electromagnetic radiation (light) is usually thought of as a wave, it can also behave like a stream of particles. These particles of light are called *photons*, and photons are therefore the most familiar kind of boson. Light is produced (or, "radiated") by the movement of electrically charged particles: hot, rapidly moving electrons in a lightbulb filament, for example, or in a fire, or on the surface of the Sun. Since light is associated with the electromagnetic force, photons are also associated with that force.

There are bosons affiliated with the other three forces as well: the bosons in the family of particles associated with the strong force are called the *gluons*; those associated with the weak force (there are three of them) are called *intermediate vector bosons*; and those associated with gravity are called *gravitons*. Altogether there are five kinds of bosons that have been directly discovered which are associated with forces, with the *graviton* (not yet actually discovered) being a probable sixth. There also are bosons that are not directly associated with any force.

I explained earlier that all particles are either bosons or fermions. Particles can be characterized another way as well, by their masses, and this seems like the right place to mention it. Some particles have the familiar kind of mass; these include atoms and molecules, or their constituents the electrons, protons, and neutrons. Of the bosons, those with mass include the mesons (strong-force related) and the intermediate vector bosons (weak-force related). A second group of bosons exists as packets of energy that are always moving at the speed of light; they don't exist at rest. These packets of energy can't have mass in the conventional sense, since, as explained by special relativity, the mass of any body increases toward an infinite quantity when its speed approaches that universal speed limit, the speed of light. The mass of these particles derives only by association with their energy (from Einstein's mass-energy equivalence relation, $E=mc^2$). These particles are sometimes said to be "massless," but to be more precise, they have no "rest mass." The photon is the principal member of the group of particles with no rest mass, but the group may include other bosons, for example, perhaps the gravitons, the particles associated with the gravitational force. (Gluons may or may not be massless — we don't yet know, but if they have any mass, it is modest.)

The features to keep in mind from all of this are the following: particles of light, the photons, are associated with the electromagnetic force; photons are bosons that travel at the speed of light; each of the other three fundamental forces also has associated bosons.

The Fermions

The other class of basic particle is the fermion. Electrons, protons, and neutrons — the key constituents of atoms — are the principal fermions. Most of the substance of our familiar world is made from atoms, so most substance is made of fermions. The fermions can in turn be subdivided into two distinct subgroups. The *leptons* are the electrons and their five related but more unusual relatives, including the neutrinos. The leptons are indivisible particles, as far as we know. As it happens, leptons are oblivious to the strong force. A current mystery of significant cosmological import is whether the neutrinos, leptons that are involved in weak-force interactions, have rest mass (like the electron), or not (like the photon). The question is important because the universe is likely to be filled with vast numbers of neutrinos left over from the big bang, and their collective mass may affect the large-scale motion of the universe. Particle physicists used to think that neutrinos had no rest mass, but recent experiments indicate they do have a very slight mass; this discovery will require a rethinking of the standard model of particle physics.

The other group of fermions is the *hadrons*, which do feel the strong force; the two most familiar hadrons are the protons and neutrons. Hadrons are composed of subparticles, smaller units called *quarks*. The name *quark* was given to these fundamental constituents by the physicist Murray Gell-Mann in 1963. He recounts that when he was searching for a name, he ran across the line "Three quarks for Muster Mark" in James Joyce's *Finnegans Wake*. Since he observed that quarks often come in threes, he thought the name was appropriate. (As an aside, there are six basic types, called "flavors," of quarks, with even more, subtler variations on these types, called "colors.") Quarks are especially curious in that they carry only a fraction of an electric charge, and they cannot exist individually, but only in combination with other quarks; as far as we know, quarks exist only when combined in twos or threes. Hadrons that are assembled from three quarks are called *baryons*; this group includes the proton and neutron.

I commented earlier that photons (a type of boson) are produced by the motion, actually the acceleration, of electrically charged particles. These electrically charged particles are, however, fermions. So here is a clue that something interesting is at work to intertwine these two apparently antithetical kinds of particle. We will return to this notion later on.

The baryons are especially prominent particles in the story of the Creation, not least because atomic nuclei are composed of baryons. In the ensuing pages, however, I will use the expression *nuclear matter* to refer to matter composed of atoms, rather than *baryonic matter*, even though there are many three-quark (that is, baryonic) particles besides protons and neutrons. This is not only for simplicity's sake, but also because all of these other, exotic baryons disappear almost as soon as they form.

The points to remember from this section are these: most of the substance in our universe is made of fermions — electrons, protons, and neutrons (but please note the "dark matter" proviso below); one subclass of fermion is itself composed of even more fundamental particles called quarks, which can interact with all four of the forces. The particles of the atomic nucleus, the protons and neutrons, consist of three quarks.

Antimatter

As we probe the processes of the Creation and the behavior of the particles at the very earliest times, we will need to be acquainted with one other exotic property of matter: the aspect that establishes whether a particle is the normal stuff of our immediate environment, matter, or whether it takes the unusual form called "antimatter." Paul Dirac won the Nobel Prize in physics in 1933 for predicting the existence of antimatter. He was attempting to develop a theory of quantum mechanics that was consistent with special relativity, but he faced some formidable challenges. In relativity, the total mass of a particle is not constant; it includes the mass associated with its energy, including its energy of motion, according to $E=mc^2$. This interdependence between energy and mass had to be included in formal expressions for the new theory. Relativity also explains that space and time can mix, and (as we saw earlier) that the size of the time interval between two events, as measured by different observers, will differ according to the observers' different speeds. Finally, Dirac faced one last consideration: the quantum mechanical uncertainty principle (I discuss this in chapter 7) allows for enough "uncertainty" in measuring a time interval that when relativistic effects are included, the "before" and "after" of an event can sometimes appear to be reversed. When Dirac included all of these considerations, the equations he came up with allowed for two possible solutions. The upshot is that while one of the two solutions to Dirac's relativistic equations predicted normal matter, the second seemed to suggest the existence of a particle that "arrived" before it "departed"! Since this is a causal impossibility, Dirac understood that the observer instead sees a similar but distinct kind of particle — an "antiparticle" — moving in the reverse direction. All fermions have a corresponding antiparticle. The antiparticle of an electron, for example, is called a *positron*, and the antiparticle of each type of quark is its *antiquark*. The bosons act as their own antiparticles. Antimatter particles are regularly produced and detected in high-energy particle accelerators.

Matter and antimatter are identical in all respects, except that they have opposite charges. Since there are no other differences between the two forms of matter, calling one of them "normal" is quite arbitrary — in principle, either type might be common. What is significant is that the world (indeed, apparently even the universe as a whole) is almost exclusively made up of "normal matter"; very little antimatter seems to exist. This is lucky. When particles of these opposite types come into contact, they annihilate each other, turning into a short burst of light — two photons — whose combined energy is related to the total mass of the two particles by Einstein's equation $E=mc^2$. The mutual annihilation of matter and antimatter illustrates the essential feature that matter can transmute into energy. We shall see that during the creation of the universe (but also in suitable laboratory situations) the reverse also occurs: energy can transform into matter. The name given to the creation of two opposite particles of matter from pure energy is *pair production*, and this process played a critical role in the early universe.

The reason for the overwhelming predominance of matter over antimatter in the universe was a huge mystery for a long time, because both types are so similar. We now understand the reason in the context of the "inflationary" pictures of the Creation, which I present later in this chapter. Essentially, it is due to a small irregularity (or, asymmetry) in the behavior of the forces. It is worth appreciating how fortunate we are that matter and antimatter did *not* exist in exactly equal amounts in the early universe. If they had, the two might have annihilated each other, leaving the newly born universe brimming with diffuse radiation, but without any matter to gather into interesting objects: stars, planets, or DNA.

The six leptons and six quarks, each with its antiparticle, make up twenty-four fundamental particles. Together with the five force-carrying bosons detected so far, they constitute the twenty-nine basic particle types. (The graviton and one other boson, the Higgs boson, are not counted in this list because they remain undetected.)

Dark Matter

At the beginning of this section I said that most of our world is composed of fewer than a hundred kinds of atoms. More exactly, I should have said that all normal matter in the universe is constituted from about twenty-nine kinds of fundamental particles and their variants. (In this context, the term *matter* means any substance that exerts a measurable gravitational influence.) Astronomers have discovered in the past two decades that — incredible as this might sound — most of the matter in the universe is actually *not* in the form of baryons (protons, neutrons, or anything else made of quarks), or electrons or positrons either. The vast majority of matter, in fact, has not been directly seen at all — it has only been inferred. The first convincing glimpse of the existence of unseen matter came from studying the intricate motions of galaxies as they majestically rotate, or as they move past one another in clusters of galaxies. These kinematic measurements have led scientists to the inescapable conclusion that there is a large gravitational influence on the visible stars and gas in the galaxies from something that is present, but that does not emit light. Astronomers estimate that an amazing 90 percent of the matter in the universe is of this unseen type: this is the so-called dark matter.

The existence of the inscrutable dark matter has been confirmed by at least two other measurements that are completely independent of galaxies' motions. One is the pattern of the cosmic microwave background radiation — the remnant radiation from the big bang. That light appears as speckles of very faint but distinct bright and dim spots in the sky superimposed on a remarkably uniform background. The pattern depends critically on the strength of the gravitational forces present when the radiation was produced, and the observed pattern implies there was more matter present than we can attribute to nuclear matter. The other independent confirmation comes from the relative abundance of the atomic elements in the universe, primarily the relative abundance of the predominant elements, hydrogen and helium. In the section of chapter 5 titled "The Epoch of Radiation" I discuss how these elements were formed in the early universe; for now it is necessary only to establish that all of the hydrogen and helium atoms in the universe were produced during the early moments of the big bang. Calculations predict exactly what the relative abundance of these elements should be, and their measured abundance ratios are in excellent agreement when the calculations include the presence of nonnuclear matter. The inference is that there must be huge quantities of unseen, nonnuclear matter in the universe.

These diverse aspects of our cosmos provide convincing, if astounding, evidence that most of the matter in the universe is dark matter. But aside from its existence, and the fact that it tends to be found predominantly in the halos of galaxies, we know hardly anything about it. There are many ideas, of course, and the most promising ones fall into one of two categories. The *visible* matter

— stars, and the nebulae heated directly or indirectly by stars, and of course the few planets we see — contains less than 2 percent of the matter in the universe. The first suggestion for the remaining 98 percent of matter is that it is normal matter that is very cold or otherwise difficult to detect directly — dead stars, for example, or clusters of wandering asteroids, or black holes, or perhaps reservoirs of subatomic particles. The calculations I just mentioned find that there could be about five times as much of this unseen nuclear matter as there is seen in all of the visible stars and galaxies, but that it is still ten times too small to account for the total amount of dark matter. By far most of the dark matter must be in the second category — a variety of exotic, new nonnuclear-matter particles (that is, particles not made of quarks, and therefore not of atoms) whose properties would nevertheless be consistent with other physical principles. Some of these varieties are associated with a still-unconfirmed property of particles called *supersymmetry*, which we will discuss later in this chapter; it is a consequence of the popular, but hypothetical, grand unified theory.

For the time being, all these speculations are just that — unconfirmed conjectures — and so I will not be able to explain much more about dark matter. The topic is one of those research areas at the forefront of science that I call to your attention — like a theory of everything, or the meaning of quantum mechanics. The only thing that is certain is that someday, the resolution of this puzzle will make our story even more astonishing and miraculous.

A Summary

The world of our experience — the world of light and atoms — is composed of only two kinds of fundamental particles: the bosons and the fermions, characterized, respectively, by tending to aggregate and being indistinguishable or needing to segregate and thus being uniquely identifiable. Particles of light are the most familiar bosons, and they respond only to the force of gravity. Electrons, protons, and neutrons are the most familiar fermions. Fermions fall into two subcategories: leptons (such as the electrons), which are indivisible and feel only three of the four forces (they do not respond to the strong force), and nuclear matter, such as the protons and neutrons, that is made up of even smaller particles, the quarks; nuclear matter responds to all four of the forces. All of these particles originated during the Creation, and they constitute our universe today.

It has taken nearly a century and thousands of technical papers to untangle the physics that I've tried to condense here into a few paragraphs. Many good and easy-to-read books are available that describe in much more detail each of these members of the cast of characters in our cosmos (please see the Notes and Comments for some recommendations). It is not necessary to remember everything in this section, but it is important to recognize that there is a coherent and logical structure at work, one that, at its core, is concise and symmetrical, and which successfully explains nearly everything we need to explore in the Creation. We will investigate next whether these conveniently succinct yet apparently arbitrary categories reflect some deeper level of coherence to the universe.

A UNIFIED DESCRIPTION OF FORCES AND PARTICLES

With that admittedly brief introduction to forces and particles completed, we can ask if and how these two fundamental aspects of the universe — the particles and the forces that govern their interactions — might be related. Jewish mystical tradition asserts that the multitude of forms and relationships in the world all derive from a common source: God's spoken "word" of Genesis that created everything. The scientific picture has arrived at an analogous conclusion about the common basis for forces and particles.

"Action at a distance" refers to a rather peculiar property of nature: particles can interact with one another without coming into actual contact. This feature may not seem particularly strange to us, since it is so familiar (a dropped object falls down even though nothing is touching it to make it do so), but upon reflection it might appear to be odd that things can influence one another without touching. Newton pondered how the force of gravity was communicated from the Earth to the apocryphal falling apple, for example, or to the orbiting Moon. An answer was centuries in coming. Our discussion of general relativity helps restate the question into one more compatible with modern theories: Gravity does not exactly act between things. Rather, gravity deforms space, and does so in a way that basically makes particles in space move closer together. Seen this way, an apple falls not because the Earth pulls it by some mysterious action at a distance, but because the Earth has curved the space around the apple a bit, so that "down" is the natural path for the moving apple to follow. This approach is called a "geometrical" description of gravitation, and it has great analytic and conceptual power. It also illustrates how dramatically a change in imagery can alter the way a problem is approached, or an understanding reached.

A similar analogy applies to the other forces and is formalized through the concept of "fields" — although fields have not (yet) been incorporated into a fully geometrical picture. Fields can be visualized as lines of force that emanate from particles; iron filings, when sprinkled on a piece of paper held over a magnet, will trace the magnetic field lines. When a charged particle (and its electromagnetic field lines) accelerates (for example, is shaken), it radiates light — photons, the particles of the electromagnetic field. Even when the electron is not accelerating, these photons are still visualized as constituting its field but are in what is dubbed a "virtual" state: the photons exist *in potentia*, ready to be emitted if the particle accelerates.

In the strange world of the virtual photons, these particles rapidly appear and disappear around the electron, thus in effect creating the field. When the particles are shaken, virtual photons can escape, become "real," and move through space, but even when the particles are not moving, the virtual photons are buzzing around them. In order to interact with each other, two charged particles swap a virtual photon. In other words, the repulsive or attractive force of electromagnetism is mediated by the exchange of photons — boson particles that are therefore said to "carry" the electromagnetic force. This weird notion of evanescent, virtual bosons that appear and disappear quickly like bubbles sparkling in a glass of soda is actually beautifully elegant. It provides a relatively clear, no-nonsense explanation for "action at a distance" and helps to explain the nature of the relationship between forces and particles.

If the electromagnetic force is mediated by the photons, the strong force is mediated by the gluons, so-called because they "glue" the particles in the nucleus together. The particles that mediate gravity are called gravitons, which (it is thought) are like photons in that they have neither charge nor rest mass. The weak force is mediated by massive particles called the intermediate vector bosons. All of these force carriers are bosons; that bosons carry the forces is related to the fact that they aggregate. Therefore, the dramatis personae of all worldly events, the particles and the forces, are essentially related.

I mentioned earlier the possibility that the four forces might be, in reality, four aspects of a single unified force. Given the kinship between forces and particles, especially during the early moments of the Creation, we need to examine this possible unified force more closely. Since every force is associated with a field, there will also be a field associated with this unified force. Like every other field, this new one presumably has a boson particle counterpart that carries the force between particles. The field is called the Higgs field, and the particle associated with it is called the *Higgs boson*, both named for Peter Higgs, who first developed the theory for this field and its boson in 1964. The grand unified theory, the not quite all-encompassing theory (it lacks a description of gravity) that I have mentioned previously, postulates a Higgs field. Like the graviton, the Higgs boson has never been detected, in part because of the extreme conditions needed to find it. Particle accelerators are urgently being upgraded in an effort to attain the high energies thought essential to finding the Higgs boson. Physicists are hopeful that the particle will either be detected, or its reality disproved, within the next decade. So far its existence is only inferred. The theoretical description of the four forces that "derive" from the Higgs field is well enough developed, however, that many features of the Higgs field are known, even though the Higgs boson itself has never been seen.

One predicted property of the Higgs field is essential to our understanding of the Creation. All fields contain energy. For example, a ball held firmly in your hand against the pull of gravity will pick up energy of motion when it is released. Since total energy can neither be created nor destroyed, but is conserved, the falling ball acquires kinetic energy from the energy that had been stored in the gravitational field and which is gradually transferred to the ball as it drops. The gravitational field in this example has energy. A spring that is stretched and held in readiness also has stored energy. In a pure vacuum, however, the gravitational field has no energy, nor do the fields of the other three forces. The strange exception to this rule is the Higgs field; it is *not* zero in a pure vacuum. The Higgs field is devoid of energy only in a slight non-vacuum. This peculiar (and still thoroughly hypothetical) feature is critical to ideas in the inflationary theory of the Creation: it is thought to have facilitated creation ex nihilo, as we will see in chapter 7, and so I need to introduce it here. There is a second, philosophically reassuring consequence of the Higgs field. The grand unified theory of the three forces that predicts the Higgs field also automatically predicts that the two fundamental classes of particles — bosons and fermions — are intimately related to each other. The variation of GUT that contains this implication is called supersymmetry, which I will return to shortly.

To summarize, the physical universe (at least as far as we know) is described by a combination of four forces interacting via the set of fundamental particles in their myriad combinations. I previously had categorized all known particles as being either bosons or fermions, but there is another way to group them: all particles respond to forces, but some also convey force. The force carriers are all bosons. The laws of physics describe how these particles behave, and the laws of chemistry or biology describe the collective properties of ensembles of atoms and molecules. Physicists suspect that these forces and particles are deeply interrelated and have been able to calculate ways in which the four forces are really different facets of a single force.

STRINGS

A big puzzle remains: why do all of these particles and forces exist with the unique characteristics we observe? Scientists hope (and presume) that one day this question will be answered by a theory that incorporates both quantum mechanics and general relativity. One exciting and currently very active drive to unify all the forces and particles is *string theory*. String theory starts from the presumption that particles may not be the zero-dimensional, pointlike entities we have assumed. Rather, string theory posits that particles are more like waves vibrating on a string, a scenario that enables them to have complex and subtle behaviors not available to pointlike objects. The theory furthermore suggests that strings might have more dimensions than the ones we sense — as many as ten spatial ones, not just the three spatial dimensions we are accustomed to experiencing. More than about this number of dimensions seems to introduce inconsistencies with what we know about the world. If this is true, there is no reason to imagine that nature stops at vibrating one-dimensional strings, or even vibrating two-dimensional surfaces, such as a drum skin. Perhaps elementary particles are vibrations of multidimensional membranes, oscillating in as many dimensions as are needed to explain their observed properties.

It is difficult to imagine what it means to say that an electron or proton is composed of a vibrating multidimensional surface. We have no direct evidence that more than one timelike and three spacelike dimensions even exist. But imagination aside, physicists can nevertheless ask what properties such an object might have if it did exist and can calculate the implications of their theory. (If they couldn't do so, then the theory would not be a scientific one, in that it would have no predictive power, and it would lose its value.) For example, since it takes energy to set something into vibration, we may grasp that more energy is needed to set into multidimensional vibration all the surfaces of a "string," even if these dimensions are not apparent to us.

Remarkably, physicists have known for quite a few years that additional spatial dimensions make a lot of theoretical problems evaporate. By adding just one more spatial dimension to the three we know so well, Theodor Kaluza and Oskar Klein showed in the 1920s that it was possible in principle to combine gravity with electromagnetism in Einstein's equations. These posited extra dimensions are not manifest at the level of our normal world, but are squeezed into minuscule, subparticle-size regions available only to the strings themselves. The extra dimensions are said to be "compactified," effectively unobservable to our direct senses.

String theory also offers a way to calculate the properties of the hypothetical Higgs boson — how massive it is, for example. String theory therefore might, optimistically speaking, be able to explain quite a lot: the Higgs boson and hence the unification of three forces, the relationship between bosons and fermions, perhaps even the unification of the four forces in a quantum gravity theory of everything. One of the recent and most exciting discoveries by the mathematical physicists who explore the complex implications of string theory is that, once all the math is sorted out, string theories may offer a natural origin for the cosmological constant that Einstein injected into his equations, a feature of gravity that may be responsible for the acceleration of the universe that seems to be underway.

String theory actually appears to be able to explain not only the physics of our universe, but also an incredibly vast range of completely different universes with completely different or bizarre physical properties, because it has so many variables in its equations — an attribute that has prompted some physicists to criticize string theory as being useless. We will revisit this feature of string theory in chapter 6.

String theory so far is just a mathematical construction. Scientists take it seriously because, like all good theories right or wrong, it makes predictions that in many cases allow it to be tested against reality. For our purposes, one set of experiments looks particularly exciting: string theory anticipates some features of the bright intensity fluctuations in the cosmic microwave background radiation that astronomy satellites like WMAP, mentioned in chapter 2, might measure. Although we may never be able to probe the additional dimensions, we will be able to compare these cosmic maps with string theory's predictions. So far, this aspect of the research has not reached firm conclusions.

It is exhilarating for everyone interested in the creation of the universe, religious cosmologists included, to recognize that the early universe is one of the few places (perhaps the only place) where conditions were extreme enough to verify many of these extraordinary theories that attempt to unify physics and explain the interconnected nature of the most elemental constituents of the cosmos. The ideas of string theory suggest that the *Resheit*, that essential point of origin, might itself have some still unconsidered multidimensional properties for modern mystics to ponder. Whether or not string theory is proved to provide a better description of the universe, there is a profound significance to the structure of a universe whose forces and particles are harmonious aspects of each other. Deep symmetry, a manifestation of the underlying interrelatedness of all things, is recognized by all mystics, as well as by scientists, mathematicians, and philosophers, as a signpost of truth. Such symmetry was advanced by the Kabbalists in their description of the manifestations of force and matter. If force and matter, the underpinnings of our physical world, are so beautifully and intimately intertwined, might there not be as well — in a world created by the One God — a way to expand such a framework to include the concepts of spirit and soul that are the foundations of the spiritual world? We will find that the Kabbalists thought so. But first, we are nearly ready to consider what the primordial universe was like and how it evolved. The answers to many questions lie in the newest embellishment to cosmology and particle physics: the big bang theory of *inflation*.

THE INFLATIONARY UNIVERSE

I have alluded more than once to the inflationary model of the expanding big-bang universe. At last we have enough background to ponder its revolutionary ideas — ideas that are constructed on the principles of particle physics and cosmology. Edwin Hubble's discovery of the expansion of the universe led scientists to infer, extrapolating backward in time, that in the distant past the whole visible universe was microscopic — the size of a dot tinier even than the nucleus of an atom. It was also correspondingly hotter than it is now, and so dense that the four fundamental forces were then, at least hypothetically, aspects of a single grand force that was not yet dilute enough to allow its four facets to function independently. Likewise, the particles that carry the forces, and also those particles upon which the forces act, were blended.

Two serious problems had been festering since the early days of modern cosmology, despite the remarkable successes of the big bang models. The theory of inflation was proposed by the physicist Alan Guth in the 1980s to resolve them both (along with some others). Since his original work, Guth and many other scientists have continued to refine the implications of inflation. Their newer variations on the original proposal have successfully explained many of the unexpected astronomical observations that have emerged as scientific instruments have become more sensitive and sophisticated. From a spiritual perspective, I think that a firmer understanding of these puzzles can help us better appreciate — and not simply take for granted — some of the subtle, wonderful intricacies of the universe.

The first mystery is isotropy, introduced in chapter 2. Isotropy describes a universe that appears the same in all directions on a large scale. It might seem obvious that the universe would be isotropic, but on consideration, why should it? The Earth is round, but its poles are covered in ice, while the equatorial regions are steamy. Although the processes that govern the evolution of the universe are the same everywhere as far as we know, they might still result, for example, in the part of the universe to our north, say, having many more galaxies than the part to our south: perhaps there was just a bit less matter to the south of us from which to form galaxies. The conventional response is that the universe is naturally isotropic because it has evolved as a single entity, with each part adjusting itself to the others in a way that smooths out large bumps or other nonuniformities. Unfortunately, this scenario is virtually impossible. Any kind of "shared" evolution between separate parts entails communication between those parts; otherwise, one location can't know what is happening elsewhere. The fastest such information can be communicated is the speed of light, and although that's fast, it is not instantaneous. In the earliest blink of the universe there had not been enough time for light to travel even those minuscule distances. Most of the early universe was out of touch with its distant realms. Only as it aged were regions in the expanding cosmos able to communicate with more and more other regions as their light began to arrive. In those early moments, though, there was no way for communication to smooth out the bumps. So the puzzle remains: why are places that are remote from one another so similar?

The second incredible feature of our universe, also much remarked upon, is how unique and precise its rate of expansion appears to be. Since matter pervades the universe, the gravitational attraction of that matter acts to slow down the outward expansion from the big bang. Were gravity strong enough — that is, if there were enough matter in the universe — the expansion should eventually stop and the universe should begin to contract. The rate of expansion is quite well known, and so, therefore, is the required amount of matter. Astronomers have tried to add up all the matter as best they can, but it is not an easy task. The visible matter — the stars, nebulae, and galaxies — constitutes a mere 2 percent of all the matter in the universe. The dominant contribution comes from the mysterious, nonnuclear "dark matter" whose presence is inferred from the movements of galaxies. Whatever that dark matter is, its gravitational pull adds to that of the visible and invisible nuclear matter, and together they all contribute to slowing down the expansion of the universe.

The recent discovery of the apparent acceleration of the outbound motions of the galaxies in the universe contributes a very important additional term to the accounting of all of the effects that control the observed expansion. Recall that this acceleration might be associated with Einstein's cosmological constant — his proposal that gravity may have a repulsive force, in addition to its attractive one — and may therefore be an essential feature of general relativity. In the accounting list of physical effects that contribute to the behavior of the cosmic expansion, the effect of the cosmological constant plays a larger role in the overall reckoning, by a factor of nearly three, than does all of the matter, even including the dark matter. Since matter and energy are equivalent and can be compared, the influence of the cosmological constant is termed *dark energy*. It is called "dark" because it is not yet known whether this energy is actually due to a cosmological constant term in the nature of gravity, or whether instead it might be due to unusual quantum effects of the vacuum, sometimes called *quintessence*. (The vacuum is a region devoid of matter.) Whatever its origin, when measured in comparable units like energy or matter, dark energy is the single largest term in the suite of physical influences just enumerated.

The sum of all the terms that contribute to the cosmological motion of the universe is, to within a few percent, exactly the value needed to achieve balance. Not thousands of times too much (certain collapse), not millions of times too little (certain eternity), but almost exactly the critical amount. Can this be fortuitous? I will speculate more on this fabulous "fine tuning" of the universe and other amazing "accidents" in chapter 6.

The inflationary universe model explains both of these two peculiar features of cosmology — the universe's isotropy and its exactly balanced motion — and a few other puzzles besides, by examining in detail the size and temperature history of the universe at its earliest times. The conditions at that time are calculated from the current expansion rate of the universe and the corresponding rate of cooling, by extrapolating them backward to fantastically early times right after the big bang. The temperature of the universe is the key to modeling the physical processes that were most active during each time period. The earliest moments, hottest temperatures, smallest sizes, or greatest densities that physicists can talk about are the ones in a theory in which all the four forces coexist, sharing that domain as equally influential aspects of a single force with all the many types of particles still unrealized but only the ultimate type of particle present: the Higgs boson. In this mysterious period, less than about 10^{-43} seconds after the Creation, the universe was smaller than 10^{-35} meters across and had a temperature in excess of 10^{32} degrees.

This inconceivable dot of energy, much tinier than an atomic nucleus, expanded because of the prodigious pressure that resulted from its high temperature. As it expanded it cooled, and when its temperature dropped down below about 10^{27} degrees, it was no longer hot enough to keep the strong force united with the electromagnetic and weak forces. This was the moment of inflation, a mere 10^{-35} seconds into the life of the universe. The strong force began to acquire an independent identity. It did so in a transition analogous to the one that occurs to water when it freezes and changes from a liquid with fluid form to a solid with crystalline form. GUT hypothesizes that when the early universe cooled off enough for the strong force to separate into its conventional form, the energy needed to keep it unified with the others was released.

There was a vast amount of this energy, and, like hooking a balloon to a fire hose, it suddenly inflated the universe. In only about 10^{-33} seconds the universe increased in diameter exponentially, growing from an infinitesimal point to the size of a marble. This short interval was the phase of so-called inflation. Afterward the universe resumed the steadier rate of more nearly linear expansion we observe now, 13.7 billion years (about 10^{18} seconds) later. The microscopic *Resheit* inflated and stretched itself — and became our universe.

Astute readers might wonder if such a rapid expansion violated the rule that nothing can move faster than light. Yes, the size of the universe did increase very much faster than the distance light could travel in the same time, but no, it did not violate the basic (observed) law of relativity. The distinction is subtle but important, and worth a short digression. Although nothing can travel faster than light, the inflating universe was not "traveling"; it was just swelling in size. Space itself was being stretched, and there are no known restrictions on this behavior. A similar misunderstanding sometimes arises in the context of Hubble's relationship between the distance and speed of galaxies; that is, the farther away from us a galaxy is, the faster it recedes. Some galaxies we measure today are so remote that we measure their speeds as being apparently six (or more) times the speed of light, and we are confident we will spot even more distant (apparently faster moving) galaxies in the future. The reason for such huge velocities is that the motions we perceive are not properties of the galaxies themselves, but a property of the space in which they are embedded — it is space itself that is expanding in our universe. As it does, it carries galaxies along.

Inflation readily explains why the universe now is so nearly perfectly uniform: before the period of inflation, all of its parts were close enough together that they *could* communicate with one another — at least, all of the parts that today are within the universe we can see. There were small, unsystematic clumps and other irregularities present, but in the same way that wrinkles on a balloon's surface are smoothed out when it is swollen, so too the explosive growth of the universe literally stretched out any such bumps and wrinkles by the same huge factor as the size, rendering them insignificant. That's why the cosmic microwave background radiation appears to be largely uniform, and its irregularities are relatively minute (although important — they are the seeds of future galaxies). The rate of inflation also naturally adjusted so that the current expansion is exactly balanced by the gravitational effects of its constituents and the sources of acceleration. As the universe grew from its marble-size dimension and continued to cool, the more familiar particles, descendants of the Higgs bosons, began to appear. Later still, the bosons called photons — light — came to dominate.

The theory of inflation relies on particle physics to calculate the earliest stages of cosmology. It is therefore worth reemphasizing that the ideas of inflation, like the understanding of particle physics upon which they are based (such as the existence of the

Higgs boson), are still hypothetical. Inflation is not so much a theory as a concept that utilizes, rather than reinvents, the theories of relativity and particle physics, and it is only as good as its constituent theories. Until there is a verified "theory of everything" encompassing quantum mechanics and gravity, it would be prudent to take all these scenarios with a grain of salt. Because the principles and experiments upon which these ideas are based have withstood so many tests, however, it is likely that future variants of the theory of inflation will contain many of the same essential components. They may seem fantastic; they may perhaps become even wilder. We must be open to them, even while holding some reservations. A further caution is in order: our understanding of the holy scriptures, too, can and naturally should evolve as our reading of the book of heaven becomes more sophisticated and new telescopes, accelerators, and computers extend our senses. Still, the theological kabbalistic picture, like the scientific one, may retain its essential components as it develops, and it may elaborate on its view that the universe when young was just an infinitesimal dot, the *Resheit*, about to burst forth.

THE SEFIROT: FORCE AND SUBSTANCE IN THE KABBALAH

Light, say the Kabbalists, is the primary, vital essence of the Creation. According to the textual understanding of the early Kabbalist Nachmanides, light was the first thing to be created, even before the heavens and the Earth. According to Nachmanides' *Commentary on Genesis*, "The Holy One said, 'Let there be light.' If so, then everything else continued after the creation of the light.... Nothing was created during the first stage except light." The *Zohar* echoes the same thought: "Come see! When the Holy One, blessed be He, created His world, He made it from the light that was emanated from above, and He created the heavens from the first firmament... [which] produced all the lights from the light it received from above."

The term for the creative Divine light is *sefirot*, a word that derives from the Hebrew word for "enumeration" (*sfr*) and the related word for "declare." "Why are they called the sefirot? Because it is written, 'The heavens declare [*sfr*] the glory of God' [Psalm 19:2]" (*The Bahir*). Isaiah Tishby, the distinguished scholar who anthologized the *Zohar* texts and translated them into Hebrew, describes the sefirot in the following way:

> The God who reveals Himself through His attributes and powers is depicted [in the Kabbalah] in a system of ten sefirot.... In this symbolic system the sefirot are seen as spiritual forces, attributes of the soul, or as means of activity within the Godhead, that is to say, as revelations of the hidden God, both to Himself and to that which is other than He. The fundamental element in this revelation is His emergence from the depths of limitless infinity. The sefirot become specified, limited areas within the Godhead, not, of course, limited in the sense of tangible objects, but as displaying a spiritual pattern of categories, both of content and of character.

Together with the twenty-two letters of the Hebrew alphabet, the ten sefirot constitute the thirty-two paths by which the world was made (discussed in *Sefer Yetzirah*), perhaps evocative of the roughly twenty-nine elementary particles. The ten sefirot are described as being "without concreteness" (*b'limah*, literally, "without anything"), a descriptive expression that may be associated with the words of Job 26:7, "He hangs the world on nothing [*b'limah*]." In the words of the thirteenth-century Kabbalist Moses de Leon,

> The ten sefirot are the secret of existence, the array of wisdom by which the worlds above and below were created. Corresponding to this secret are the ten utterances by which the world was created" — that is, the ten times God speaks in the Genesis creation narrative, from Genesis 1:1 to 1:31 [if you are counting, note that the list embraces the indirect association of speech with the first word, *B'Resheit*] — "and the ten commandments, which epitomize the holy Torah. Indeed the ten sefirot constitute the secret of divine existence; they comprise above and below, every single thing. They are ancient and concealed. From them emerges the mystery of the supernal chariot — a matter concealed and sealed for those who discover knowledge.

An extensive literature, developed over at least a thousand years, deliberates over the complex nature of the sefirot. We will touch here on just a tiny sample of this rich theological and metaphorical material. The discussions are intricate and obscure, not least because God's transcendental unity allows for no "other" in creation, much less ten anthropomorphic others, and so explaining the relationship of the sefirot without drifting toward heresy makes for many indirect analogies. The Kabbalah fully appreciated these difficulties, and as a result the viewpoints of the numerous kabbalistic teachers are often ambiguous and occasionally at variance.

The light of the sefirot, a manifestation of Divine attributes and activities, was not only the first thing to be created; it was also the indispensable vehicle by which the rest of the cosmos was created. In *The Bahir*, the sefirot are explicitly called forces: "What is 'His hidden force?' [The term referred to in Habakkuk 3:4.] This is the light [of Creation, that is, the sefirot] that was stored away and hidden." According to the *Sefer Yetzirah*, the sefirot are also the origin of the substance of the cosmos: "There are ten sefirot.... The first is the Breath of the Living God.... The third is 'water' which was hewed from Breath.... Material substance was created from this 'water.'" The sefirot thus comprise both the "forces" and the "particles" of the Creation, playing a role as physical entities and as enabling forces for the creation of all material things. As we saw earlier in the chapter, the fundamental physical forces and particles of the scientific picture are not disjointed entities — they are interwoven: the forces are mediated (or, transmitted) by particles of light or other bosons in a refined and relatively natural picture. The Kabbalah reaches a similar conclusion about the role of the sefirot, the mystical lights of Creation.

The sefirot also provided the enabling means of creation. In the words of Nachmanides again, "The world was created by means of ten sefirot." They provide the mystics with an answer to the enigmatic problem of how a perfect, infinite, and spiritual God could interact with and create an imperfect, finite, and corruptible universe. In a sense, the sefirot are an extension of Divine potency. Lest there be any misunderstanding, the *Sefer Yetzirah* quickly clarifies that God is unconstrained: "There are ten sefirot without concreteness; their measure is ten which have no end.... The One Master, God the faithful King, rules over them all from His holy place forever."

The sefirot created and then shaped the newly expanding universe, enabling it to differentiate, consolidate, balance, and evolve into the world we inhabit. Furthermore, the ten sefirot continue to permeate the universe and sustain it. The sefirot are light; that much is clear from the first two quotes I presented from Nachmanides and the *Zohar*. They are associated with the declaration "Let there be light." But they are certainly an exceptionally unfamiliar kind of light, at once Divine and corporeal, primordial and contemporary, incomprehensible in their essence and explicitly metaphoric. In the *Etz Hayyim*, Isaac Luria teaches that:

> At the beginning of everything the whole of existence was a simple kind of light called the 'light of the *Ein-Sof*' [Infinite].... The name *Ein-Sof* indicates there is absolutely no way to comprehend Him, either by thought or contemplation, because He is completely inconceivable.... It should be clear that... as for all the images and pictures we use, they are not actually so, God forbid, but only [used] to propitiate the ear so that one can understand the higher spiritual things that cannot be grasped or comprehended at all.

"Light" is usually construed to mean optical electromagnetic radiation — in other words, optical photons, the bosons that mediate the electromagnetic force, and in particular the photons whose wavelengths put them in the visible portion of the spectrum where we can see them with our eyes. But as we have learned, most of the electromagnetic spectrum is invisible to our eyes, and furthermore there are other bosons that mediate the other forces: gravitons for gravitational force, gluons for the strong force, and the vector bosons for the weak force. I suggest that all references to "light" in the Kabbalah (which uses the Hebrew word *ohr*) may be taken more generally to allude to any bosons — those particles, not only photons, that convey force. One of the key philosophical issues with which the mystics struggle is whether the sefirot are the essence of the Divine or instead are the vessels of the Divine; the scientific treatment of forces and particles is helpful by demonstrating that bosons (or, "light") play just such a dual role.

ONE FROM MANY: THE REVELATIONS OF SYMMETRY

Sometimes all it takes for a flash of insight is a change of perspective. Imagine driving down a road past a dense wood, its trees thick and seemingly impenetrable. Suddenly, at a particular curve along the road, the same forest reveals itself to be organized in strictly ordered lines and columns — it is a meticulously planted orchard whose trees are spaced uniformly. When viewed from this angle even the distant horizon, previously obscured, is plainly evident between the receding rows. When symmetries are present, the proper point of view can transform the murky into the obvious, and the chaotic into the simple. Moreover, as this example of an orchard illustrates, the right perspective can provide much more than just a new insight into geometry — it can lead to a deeper understanding of what's really going on.

We learned earlier in the chapter that the physical particles can be classified according to their nature as segregating (the fermions) or aggregating (the bosons). They also can be broadly grouped according to their function, as being either material substance (for example the leptons), or as the carriers of the forces that act upon substance (for example the photons or gravitons). There are still other ways of grouping the particles. For example, particles can be grouped according to whether they are normal matter or antimatter, or by the value of an internal quantum mechanical property they possess, called spin. In essence, however, all of the seemingly diverse ways of categorizing the particles are in reality just one way: the particles are classified according to their *symmetries*. In our physical world, all of the meaningful collections of fundamental particles (called "groups") are consequential because of the physical symmetries they share and that interrelate them.

The principles of symmetry are sophisticated and profound in their details and their mathematics, but straightforward in concept.

They are an appropriate conclusion to this chapter on the "cosmic cast." The physicist Richard Feynman explained symmetry by quoting the mathematician Hermann Weyl: "A thing is symmetrical if there is something that you can do to it so that after you have finished doing it, it looks the same as it did before." Some forms of symmetry are obvious to us because the congruencies they display are in space. For example, a snowflake is symmetrical (that is, unchanged) in space when it is rotated about its center by one of its essential angles (a multiple of sixty degrees), or when it is viewed in a mirror (parts are swapped left for right), or for that matter when it is moved sideways by any distance.

The comprehensive symmetries of the particle world are much more profound, for two reasons. The first is that there are many more different kinds of things you can do to particles besides move them around in three-dimensional space. Here is just one example to provide a flavor of the unexpected and hidden symmetries in nature, and to illustrate their power to simplify our descriptions of reality: The two basic particles constituting an atomic nucleus are the proton and the neutron. It turns out that these particles share a symmetry that results from a curious internal property called *isospin*, which in their case can have only one of two values: plus one unit of isospin, or minus one unit. According to this assessment, a proton is actually the same particle as a neutron except that it has a different value of isospin: when the particle's isospin value is plus one, it behaves like a proton (that is, it has a positive electrical charge), and when the value is minus one, it behaves like a neutron (that is, it has no electrical charge and slightly more mass than a proton). The two particles are symmetric with respect to this internal property. The existence of this symmetry helped lead to the realization that the proton and neutron are not two strangely disparate things; they are the *same* thing, appearing in different ways.

They are united by their internal substructure, which, for each of these baryonic, or nuclear matter, particles, is composed of three quarks.

Symmetry not only determines how some particles exhibit their properties of charge and mass, it also determines whether the particle is a boson (and aggregates) or a fermion (and segregates). Bosons by their nature are symmetric, and fermions by their nature are antisymmetric; everything falls into one of these two categories. Because this symmetry is an intrinsically quantum mechanical feature of matter, not appearing in the classical descriptions, we will need to wait until the discussion of quantum mechanics to properly define *antisymmetric*, to understand what it means for something to be symmetric or antisymmetric, and to show why nature behaves this way. For now, I simply emphasize that this property of matter is yet another way that symmetry governs in the universe.

I have mentioned several times the ongoing search for confirmation of a grand unified theory in which the three forces (excluding gravity) are facets of a single force; this theory is the basis for the big-bang inflation scenarios. A GUT will almost certainly contain another symmetry for particles, called *supersymmetry*. A consequence of particles being supersymmetric is that every particle — bosons and fermions alike, and even the Higgs boson — will have a supersymmetric partner particle identical to itself except in two ways: the partner will have a much larger mass (that is why none have been found yet: they are massive, and the task of measuring them requires energies beyond the capability of current elementary-particle detectors), and it will have the opposite symmetric "nature," meaning that partners of symmetric particles will be antisymmetric, and vice versa. If this truly super symmetry accords with reality, every boson will therefore have a (nearly) identical fermion partner, and every fermion will have a boson partner. Many astrophysicists suspect that dark matter is made up of the still-unconfirmed supersymmetric partner particles. And, not least, the existence of supersymmetry will imply that there is some natural way for bosons and fermions to transform into one another.

Come see! For several thousand years, philosophers and theologians of science embraced the picture of a natural world composed of four basic and distinct "elements": earth, water, fire, and air. These elements mirrored the four different combinations of solid or liquid, hot or cold. Jewish and kabbalistic sources also generally presumed the fundamental nature of these four elements. But today, with the realization that matter and energy are interrelated and that the constituents of matter and force are (probably) supersymmetric, we understand that four elements are three too many. There is an underlying sense in which the world is composed of only one sort of thing.

The second remarkable feature of symmetry is that in nature it applies not only to the particles but to the forces as well. The force of gravity works exactly the same way, for example, if it is moved sideways — you will weigh the same amount whether you stand on a scale over here or over there. Indeed, symmetry is thought to be a foundational principle for all the laws of the universe. Einstein's theory of relativity, as we saw in chapter 3, is grounded in the assurance that the laws of physics appear the same to all observers — that is, all observers use the same expressions — regardless of whether or how the observers are moving. It is easy to understand that simple rules of motion follow this kind of behavior in ordinary situations. It is not much harder to see that when things move very fast, something odd must happen to them, because, as discussed in chapter 3, the speed of light is a universal constant. Instinctively, one might expect that the speed of light measured by a stationary observer would be different from the speed measured by a rapidly moving observer. It isn't. Relativity reformulates the laws of physics to express the equality (that is, the symmetry) of all reference frames. The mathematician Amalie (Emmy) Noether proved a famous and important theorem in 1918 which shows that each fundamental symmetry corresponds to a conservation law of nature. A conservation law expresses the fact that a physical quantity — energy, momentum, angular momentum, and others — is neither created nor destroyed by interactions, but is transferred in such a way that its total value stays the same. For example, the conservation of momentum is not a mysterious or arbitrary law; it is the consequence of the fact that the symmetry of an object (think of that snowflake) is preserved under sideways translation. The fundamental role of symmetry in the natural world also encourages scientists to think that the four forces really are aspects of a single force, and that a theory of everything will be possible to formulate. As you might expect from the intimate interrelatedness of particles and forces, the symmetries of the particles are an ingredient of the symmetries of the forces.

The sefirot can be grouped together in symmetrical categories in very much the same way as the physical particles and forces. In fact, the primary kabbalistic texts devote extensive efforts to describing the multifold symmetries of the sefirot, and then relating these symmetries to other aspects of the Divine system or to the natural world (although they don't say so in quite these words). Three kinds of symmetries, or pseudo-symmetries, are manifest in the sefirot and are particularly worthy of comment. Two are fundamental and relatively easy to understand: a sexual symmetry of male and female, and geometrical symmetries in which the sefirot are described as being either in a linear or spherically concentric relationship. The linear spatial symmetry is echoed in the widely depicted Tree of Life, or ladderlike talisman, of the sefirot (see p. 220), in which the left and right sides of the pattern have complementary symmetrical properties.

The third pseudo-symmetry is derived from an association of the sefirot with the letters of the Hebrew alphabet, the vowel marks, and the marks that are used for punctuation, decoration, and musical notation for the Torah. These symbols are in turn aligned with symmetries of the human body. Since symmetries lend themselves to a mathematical description, the kabbalistic explorations even sometimes slip into a pseudo-mathematical framework. Words are explored and extensively manipulated both individually and in combinations and permutations that reflect aspects of the sefirot. The symbols are sometimes rotated, rearranged, and combined to illustrate how they can transform into one another. Hebrew letters are also assigned numeric values (*gematria*), so that apparently unrelated words (and therefore concepts) become associated by their mathematic equivalences or other mathematic relationships. God's ineffable four-letter name is also explicated with numerous substitutions and inversions, some of which build on principles of symmetry. In the Kabbalah, many symmetries follow as a natural result of the dialectical pairing of sefirot, while the qualities of symmetry itself can be thought of as resulting from the distinctive beauty of *Tiferet*, the sixth of the sefirot, whose radiance results from the convergence of the open plenitude of *Hesed* (the fourth sefirah) with the constraining regularities of *Gevurah* (the fifth sefirah). For readers familiar with the kabbalistic hierarchy, the mathematical and physical notions of symmetries and groups can provide new insights into the structure of the sefirot.

The sefirot can also be collected in distinctive combinations. One such grouping is called the *partzufim* (personifications), a family of five archetypal figures, each one being a combination of one or more of the sefirot. Each *partzuf*, because of its particular composition and relationship to the others, unveils a new set of attributes of its sefirot. Although they are important and interesting in their own right, I will not say more about these particular symmetries and groupings. There is, however, one further category that will be pertinent to our inquiry. This is the set of four "worlds" (*olamot*), which I will explain and use to group the stages of the physical creation in the next chapter.

There are two important observations to make before closing this chapter on the cosmic cast: There were no magical or inexplicable processes involved in the Creation. No unknown forces participated in the big bang, only to disappear from the universe once that work was done. No strange or mysterious particles were needed in the Creation. The power of the sefirot radiated from the *Resheit* and continues to sustain and permeate our own existence today. The cast of the Creation is the cast of the present. God "renews every day the workings of the Creation."

In the Kabbalah, the sefirot are often depicted in a linear form, as suggested by the Tree of Life image, each unfolding from the last. The *Etz Hayyim* is particularly emphatic in explaining, however, that the sefirot simultaneously have circular as well as linear aspects and may be imagined as shells nested each within the next. People tend to think of process, history, and even the cosmic narrative we are about to examine as linear, flowing from *then* to *now* or from *there* to *here*. But the cosmic light created *then* surrounds you *now*, and the *Resheit*, the point of the big bang's *there*, resides at the very space you occupy *here*. Such are the lessons of modern science.

5 MOMENTS OF CREATION

We are about to begin a detailed comparison between scientific and kabbalistic creation models. Before we do, it seems worthwhile to reflect on the aims of such a comparison. The physical picture is rich, specific, complete, and satisfying. Even its puzzles (neutrino mass, quantum gravity, the rate of cosmic expansion) seem ready to yield to the scientific method with a little more time and effort. What do we stand to gain from wandering into the imprecise, metaphoric, obscure imagery of the Kabbalah? For that matter, what about the reverse? What possible relevance can a scientific, formulaic, and esoteric mathematical construct have to our spiritual lives? For me, there are at least two answers. First, some of the kabbalistic concepts included in the picture of the sefirot cast insight into the quantum notions of reality, and kabbalistic imagery provides some perspective that is lacking in scientific descriptions. The physical picture, in turn, is invaluable to a sophisticated understanding of kabbalistic concepts of space, time, and process. Both the scientific and the kabbalistic pictures of the Creation involve an expansion and evolution of the universe, allowing crude analogies to be drawn between the developing physical stages and the corresponding sefirot. By making such associations, it is neither my intent to imply any kind of distinct physical form to the sefirot, nor to suggest any mystical import to the cosmological forces, but I do suggest that these radically disparate models of cosmogenesis are not so different in their worldviews, and that we can benefit from their combined imagery. Isaiah Tishby writes: "[The Kabbalist] is not an introspective mystic who denies and effaces the external order of nature as he draws near to the Godhead, and crosses the final bridge by communing only with his own soul. He is, on the contrary, the type of mystic who searches for and discovers the divine light in the innermost recesses of Nature." As the Bible explains, "It is not bread alone that sustains the human being, but rather everything that proceeds from the Divine sustains a human being" (Deuteronomy 8:3). It is my premise that even in the most intricate pictures of creation there should be complementarity as well as compatibility.

My second answer has been one of my primary motivations for writing this book, namely, the importance of recognizing that, in the words of Rabbi Abraham Isaac Kook, "One of the great afflictions of man's spiritual world is that every discipline of knowledge, every feeling, impedes the emergence of the other. The result is that most people remain limited and one-sided.... This defect cannot continue permanently. Man's nobler future is destined to come when he will develop to a sound spiritual state so that instead of each discipline negating the other, all knowledge, all feeling will be envisioned from any branch of it. This is precisely the true nature of reality."

THE SEFIROT IN CREATION

The sefirot, "the secret of existence," are envisioned as encompassing all known properties of reality in natural and human domains, but a few dozen rather general features are frequently prominent, including wisdom, beauty, balance, order, and majesty, with some qualities framed as contrasting pairs, such as attraction or separation, grace or rigor, opportunity or stability. The sefirot relate to a wide range of archetypical qualities of human nature and the human world and correspond, for example, to physical attributes, human emotions, levels of consciousness and the subconscious, parts of the body, or archetypal biblical personalities. The Tree of Life on p. 220, the sefirot, identifies a few of the most common characteristics. Kabbalistic language relies heavily on analogy to describe complex or subtle ideas. Despite the possibly dangerous misunderstandings such analogies may introduce, the poverty of linguistic descriptions sometimes leaves no other option.

The Kabbalists recognized that, although the universe was created ex nihilo, it did not suddenly appear completed — it evolved over time, at least in the sense that some stages preceded and others followed. The early processes, however, unfolded within the Divine, where our normal notions of time are inadequate. According to the Kabbalists, the Creation was the ontological process of passing from the absence of being, the "*ein*" or no-thing, to the "*yesh*" or state of being. The sequential unveiling of the ten sefirot in ten well-defined stages is a manifestation of this order and correlates with the seven days of creation plus three key preliminary mystical phases. As the *Zohar* explains, in reference to *Hokhmah*, the second of the sefirot, "Here the six great supernal extremities [the next sefirot] are engraved... from which six fountains and streams are made so that they might be poured into the great sea." The *Sefer Yetzirah* continues, also in reference to *Hokhmah*, "Next came substance from spirit [literally, "water from wind"]. He engraved and carved in them twenty-two letters [of the Hebrew alphabet] from chaos and void [*tohu vavohu*], mud and clay, engraved them like a garden, established them like a wall, covered them with snow, and it became dust." (Compare Job 37:6, which says, "To snow He said, 'Become earth.' ") The *Etz Hayyim*, while elaborating in great detail on the sequential order of Creation, explains, however, that each sefirah subsumes attributes of all ten of the sefirot.

Each sefirah has a name that encapsulates its most essential quality. The first of them, *Keter*, or "Crown" (sometimes referred to as Highest Crown), comprises the ontological, or philosophical, basis for existence. Moses de Leon writes, "*Keter Elyon* (Highest Crown) is called the pure ether that cannot be grasped. It is the sum of all existence, and all have wearied in their search for it. One should not ponder this place. It is secretly named *Ein-Sof* [Without-Limit] for it engenders everything that is." *Keter* is followed by *Hokhmah* (Wisdom, or Thought), the conceptualization of reality, and then by the setting up of a framework for reality's actualization in *Binah* (Understanding). *Binah*, the "mother" of Creation, completes the first three preeminent segments that precede the actual creation of substance. Rabbi Arthur Green recently described this initial triad as "constitut[ing] the most primal and recondite level of the inner divine world. It is a reality that the Kabbalists regularly claim to be quite obscure and beyond human ken."

The translation of the ideas embodied in the philosophical framework of the first three sefirot into a real cosmos begins with the second triad of sefirot. The starting point is characterized by encompassing unity, *Hesed* (Grace), followed by the individualization and separation into different parts, *Gevurah* (Rigor), and then by a harmonizing between these opposite tendencies in *Tiferet* (Beauty).

Instead of bringing these now differentiated and balanced systems forward to the final level of reality, the Kabbalah introduces a third and final hierarchical set of three, which echoes the symmetries of the first and second triads. This next set begins with *Netzah*

(Victory), the unity of possibilities, which again emphasizes the unity in all creation. Then comes *Hod* (Glory), in which potentialities separate from one another to become manifest, and finally *Yesod* (Foundation), a basis for the world derived from the balance between the now realized possibilities. The tenth and last sefirah, *Malkhut* (Kingdom), corresponds to the palpable universe of the present: our world that is the consequence of the preceding nine sefirot, filled with structures, life, complexity, and beauty.

Jewish mysticism, especially as developed by Isaac Luria and others in Tzefat, emphasizes the existence of four levels of reality, the four worlds, or *olamot*, introduced at the end of chapter 4. Although there are other consequential groupings of the sefirot, the four worlds are particularly valuable to our inquiry, because they are readily associated with temporal phases and group the sefirot and their complex set of associated concepts into a coherent structure. The names of these four worlds are *Atzilut* (Emanation), *Briyah* (Creation), *Yetzirah* (Formation), and *Assiyah* (Doing); the last three terms are taken from the verse in Isaiah 43:7 that says, "I have created [*brh*] him for my glory, I have formed [*ytzh*] him, indeed I have made [*assh*] him." Like the sefirot, these worlds are multifaceted and simultaneously describe both cosmological phases of evolution (marking stages in the process of physical creation), and spiritual levels of existence that in the post-Creation universe characterize different aspects of reality. The worlds subsume the ten sefirot, which unfold in ten identifiable stages. Each stage after the primal first three corresponds approximately to a day in the Genesis narrative.

The kabbalistic literature over time presented numerous variations on the relationships between the four worlds and the sefirot. Indeed, the sources posit variant arrangements of the sefirot themselves, even some different names and characteristics. I have not followed any particular school in the ensuing discussion but prefer an arrangement which seems to me to be the most useful for our purposes of comparing the scientific and mystical traditions. The next sections attempt to encapsulate in just a few paragraphs a sophisticated and complex schema in order to provide a basis for our own limited discourse. These esoteric concepts can be easily misunderstood in the best of contexts, and my highly abbreviated explanations can be all the more misleading; I urge interested readers to continue their study with one of the many excellent popular books available on the Kabbalah and the sefirot, some of which are listed in the notes. Bearing all this in mind, we should proceed with caution as we tackle the meanings of the sefirot, recognizing that the scientific description (general relativity, quantum mechanics, etc.) faces the same problem of explicating nonintuitive ideas with language that sometimes carries with it misleading connotations.

The physical creation of the universe occurred in a series of consecutive stages. Astronomers calculate the conditions and processes in each stage by applying a unified theory of particles and forces to the general relativistic, quantum mechanical model of the unfolding universe. Each stage is defined predominantly by its temperature, because temperature reflects the energy of the constituents and, therefore, their prevailing behavior.

As the universe expanded in the big bang, it cooled, and as the temperature of the universe decreased, the four forces gradually differentiated from one another. The various elementary particles condensed out of the hot plasma in a sequence depending on what might be thought of as their "freezing points"; as they did, the interactions between them, for example their mergers into other particles (or, ultimately, atoms) became steadily less and less energetic. Approximately speaking, there are four broad hierarchical periods of time in the history of the cosmos. The earliest time, at least the earliest one that physicists can model with any confidence, is called the *Planck time*. It is named after Max Planck, the founder of quantum mechanics, who realized that energy was quantized (or, subdivided) into small but finite packets, and who estimated the size of the smallest quanta. Physicists suspect that at some early time, possibly earlier than the Planck time, gravity assumed an identity separate from the other three forces, but they can't say much more about this first, enigmatic period.

The second period spans from the end of the Planck time through the dramatic moment about 10^{-35} seconds later, when the strong force became distinct from the weak and electromagnetic forces. This event, called the "symmetry breaking" between the forces, led to the exponential inflation of the universe and the eventual production of matter.

The third period began with the end of inflation and lasted for about three hundred thousand years. It featured the sequential preeminence of quarks, leptons, radiation, and finally atomic nuclei.

The final period is characterized by neutral matter and commenced when temperatures in the universe had cooled to only a few thousand degrees, allowing neutral atoms to exist. This era has lasted 13.7 billion years so far. It is distinguished by the production of galaxies, stars, and finally — life. Each of these four hierarchical periods corresponds to one of the four kabbalistic worlds. We will consider each of them in turn, beginning with the first, *Atzilut*.

BEFORE THE BIG BANG: THE WORLD OF ATZILUT

The very earliest moments of the universe, the ones even before the episode of inflation, are the most mysterious because we still lack a theory of quantum gravity essential to understanding the extreme

> *environment of that time. Nevertheless, important general characteristics can be inferred from what happened later.*

The universe began as a hot, dense, and intensely energetic embryo. Originally the four fundamental forces were simply different aspects of a single force: the chaotic blaze was so intense and so dense that gravity and the electromagnetic forces were just as significant as the strong or the weak forces. As the universe expanded, it also cooled, and as it did, the interactions between particles decreased in frequency and vigor. During these primordial moments each of the forces began to acquire its own distinctive properties. The first force to become disentangled was gravity itself.

The Sefirah of Keter

The most remote level of the mystics is *Atzilut*, the World of Emanation. The name itself comes from the Hebrew word for near, *atzl*, because this world is so closely tied to the highest, most intimate, limitless aspect of God, the *Ein-Sof.* In his book on Isaac Luria and the early Kabbalists, Lawrence Fine writes:

> According to kabbalistic theology, divine life has two aspects, the first of which is known as *Ein-Sof* (literally, "Infinite" or "Without-End"). *Ein-Sof* is the ultimate source of all reality, the divine Mystery from which all else derives. It is regarded by the kabbalists as a dimension of God that is utterly unknowable, concealed beyond all human comprehension. As the hidden and perfect root of all reality, it can neither be positively named nor imagined by the human intellect.... However, the kabbalists go far beyond the ["negative theology" of the] philosophical rationalists by means of their concept of the sefirot, ten aspects of the divine that *emanate* from within the wellsprings of *Ein-Sof*.... Together, *Ein-Sof* and the ten sefirot constitute what the kabbalists

> refer to as the upper world.... Creation takes place simultaneously on two levels, the material world constituting a visible, physical manifestation of a process that occurs in a concealed manner in the realm of the sefirot.

In *Atzilut* the preliminaries of the Divine creative process were gathered, including the philosophical principles for that which was to come. A force of gravitation was probably one such ideal principle, as was a quantum mechanical process to trigger the Creation and expansion, and also the mathematical underpinnings that would enable us to use numbers as the language of reality. Perhaps there were other principles that originated in *Atzilut* as well.

In contemplating this highest of levels, Lurianic Kabbalah directly confronts the difficult question of how there can have been a "place" for creation if God is omnipresent; it offers a striking image based on concepts found in one of the oldest kabbalistic texts, *The Bahir*. In Isaac Luria's picture, God withdrew Himself from a part of Himself, as it were, in a process called "*tzimtzum*" (contraction), to make room for the created world to come. The *Etz Hayyim* presents Luria's conception: "Know that before the emanations emanated, or the created things were created, there was a pure, supreme light that filled the whole of existence. There was no vacant place, space or void, but everything was filled with the simple light of the *Ein-Sof*. It had no beginning and no end, and was completely simple and uniform. When it arose in His simple will to create worlds... then the Infinite contracted itself... and left an empty space, a void."

Contraction was an act of Divine self-exile. It is echoed in the exile of the Jewish people and became a powerful concept both for its philosophical imagery and its attestation that human history echoes cosmic history. While the language is metaphoric, it is easy to see that the process of *tzimtzum* has an intellectual counterpart in the force of gravity, the physical mechanism for contraction. General relativity provides us with invaluable insight into the limitations and implications of the meanings of "place," or "space," in the kabbalistic picture, while quantum gravity holds the secret to the initiation of the Creation.

Keter (Crown), the highest of the sefirot, is, in this scheme, gathered in the world of *Atzilut*. *Keter* represents the esoteric concepts of the highest order, the "All-Enlightened and All-Enlightening Source," the primal rousing of Divine will and desire. In the famous biblical passage where God answers Moses' question about his nature by saying, "I am that I am" (Exodus 3:14), *Keter* is the aspect of being that is that first "I am." There is little in *Keter* that connects with current physical principles.

Atzilut, the highest of worlds before creation took root, was characterized by God's perfect unity and may therefore be distinguished by the quality of unity —*yichud*.

THE BIG BANG THROUGH THE GREAT INFLATION: THE WORLD OF BRIYAH

The period from the initiation of the Big Bang through the end of inflation corresponds roughly to the world called Briyah, *the World of Creation, and encompasses the sefirot of* Hokhmah *and* Binah. *Here at last, modern physics, astronomy, and cosmology can begin to hypothesize, measure, and even model what the mystics were striving to comprehend.*

In the beginning the universe was ruled by quantum effects and unified physical laws we do not yet completely know. The earliest time physicists can confidently model, the Planck time, is about 10^{-43} seconds. At this time, the size of the universe was about 10^{-35} meters — much, much smaller than the size of an atomic nucleus. (Many of the fabulously large or small numbers we are about to encounter are model dependent, and the precise values of the exponents are uncertain, although in all cases the numbers are still very large or small.) The three forces (excluding gravity) and their fields, and all of the particles, were merged into one field and one kind of particle: the enigmatic Higgs field and Higgs boson. In the extraordinarily hot conditions of these very early moments, all that existed was energy.

Under the tremendous pressure of this hot mix the universe grew larger, and as it swelled it cooled further. When the temperature dropped to about 10^{27} degrees, about 10^{-35} seconds after the big bang, the universe had cooled just enough for the strong force to "freeze out" — to dissociate itself from the weak and electromagnetic forces. The dissociation of forces happened in a manner roughly analogous to the changes of phase of a substance. Most substances can assume several forms. Water, for instance, can be either a solid (ice), a liquid, or a gas (water vapor). Temperature is the primary physical parameter, along with the pressure, that determines which form water takes. Water can smoothly transform from one of these "phases" to another as the temperature of the water varies. We see it happen all the time in our everyday lives. However, these phases are different from one another in structure, and some energy is exchanged in order for water to change from one into another. For example, as the temperature of liquid water gradually decreases to the freezing point, the molecules of water in the fluid configuration vibrate less and less briskly, and with each subsequent drop in temperature they decrease their motion a bit more. When water reaches zero degrees Celsius (32 degrees Fahrenheit), it is still not ice. Some additional motion of its molecules — some additional energy — must be removed so that the molecules move less freely. With this added cooling, water changes its structure from an amorphous liquid into a regular crystalline solid — it freezes. The water morphs from something that was very symmetric (that is, it looked the same from any direction) into something with a regular structure that is much less symmetric (the alignment of the ice crystals appears the same only when viewed along specific angles). The essential point is that energy is released at the "phase change" from water to ice.

A similar process is thought to have occurred when the forces changed their phase in the early universe. Physicists do not know when or how gravity froze out, but it was the first force to do so. The strong force was second, and because the quantum mechanical theory of this force is relatively successful, a much more detailed picture of what happened emerges. When the strong force disengaged from the remaining two (the electromagnetic and weak forces), like water freezing into ice, the symmetry of the system was decreased and energy was surrendered — a vast amount of energy. The release of this energy inflated the size of the universe by an incredible amount — a factor of 10^{25} or even vastly more, depending on the theory — to approximately the size of a marble, in only about a billionth of a trillionth of a trillionth of a second. This is the miracle called inflation. By the time the inflation ended, about 10^{-33} seconds after it began, the universe had stretched out to an almost perfectly uniform density and was undergoing a more normal, linear expansion, more or less doubling its diameter with every tripling of time — the stage in which it remains today.

The Sefirot of Hokhmah and Binah

The second of the sefirot is *Hokhmah* (Wisdom). At the limits of normal physical reality, *Hokhmah* encompasses active thought and the first glimmers of the being of everything that is to exist. *Hokhmah* engenders the point from which the cosmos sprang, the *Resheit*. *Hokhmah* is therefore considered the beginning of being, the essence of existence, and although it is itself pictured as unbounded and undifferentiated, it contains the archetypes of all distinct things and their potential for being.

The third of the ten sefirot is *Binah* (Understanding). In the description of the Kabbalah, the big bang expansion of the universe from the *Resheit* originated from *Binah*; it therefore includes some things that are knowable by the scientific method. *Binah* is treated in the kabbalistic sources as the "mother" of Creation, encompassing the feminine aspect of the sefirot. (*Hokhmah* encompasses the masculine aspect.) *Binah* is the source of the differentiation and actualization of *being*. Within *Binah* lie all the qualities of the archetypes of things, those entities that were the ideal manifestations of what would become reality. What *Hokhmah* imagines, *Binah* articulates. With the expansion of the *Resheit*, *Binah* gives birth to the physical Creation.

In the kabbalistic literature the sefirot of *Hokhmah* and *Binah* are nearly always grouped together with the first esoteric sefirah, *Keter*. They are obviously intimate partners of *Keter*, but because they begin to include that which *can* be known, and because they are the sources of the *Resheit*, I have placed them here in the World of Creation — *Briyah*. Our physically driven arrangement associates this stage with the Planck time and the fecund process of inflation. The Kabbalists emphasized the many complex interrelationships between the sefirot; the Tree of Life (p. 220) diagrams many of the linkages. Typical is the association of *Binah* with the first two sefirot in a triad of philosophical principle, and yet also with the next two sefirot, which emanate from it and which begin to manifest reality. In a similar fashion the final sefirah, *Malkhut*, stands both alone as the manifestation of the current world yet is also closely tied to its predecessor, *Yesod*, the foundation of stability. I chose the groupings here as the most productive for a comparison with the scientific picture and to simplify the discussion while still taking advantage of this complex of relationships; these groups do not necessarily adhere to one particular school of thought.

The act of Creation was an act of Divine love. The world of *Briyah*, and the sefirah of *Binah*, the motherly, are therefore characterized by Divine love (*ahavah*).

FROM INFLATION TO ATOMS: THE WORLD OF YETZIRAH

The World of Formation, Yetzirah, *is the first of the kabbalistic worlds that encompasses a universe with the familiar characteristics of our own world.* Yetzirah *spans the transition from an exotic universe filled mostly with bosons to one containing protons, neutrons, and electrons. Scientists think they understand the operative rules of physics beginning with this epoch. As our knowledge grows and a theory of everything (which includes a quantum mechanical description of gravity) develops, our grasp of the very earliest moments will no doubt be recast, but a revised theory is unlikely to alter significantly our picture of what happened during* Yetzirah, *the period spanning about three hundred and eighty thousand years, from the end of the great inflation to the production of neutral atoms. The World of* Yetzirah *is characterized by awe,* yirah.

The Epoch of Quarks

Our familiar universe is characterized by the atomic matter it contains: protons, neutrons, and electrons — fermions. This may seem obvious, but that is only because in our own epoch, that of the last sefirah, *Malkhut*, matter dominates our lives. We gaze up into a dark night sky filled with glowing stars and planets, nebulae and other galaxies — all made of matter. But the universe just after inflation was not like this at all. The temperature after inflation was still more than 10^{25} degrees, and the density of that marble-size universe was 10^{73} grams per cubic centimeter, numbers to notice not because of their impressive magnitude, but because even under such extreme conditions the physical models work relatively consistently. One might think that very little can be known about such an extreme environment, but the opposite is the case, because this seething mix was dominated by the statistical processes of thermodynamics. Individual interactions can be neglected for the average behavior of the whole collection, for which we need to know only the general properties of matter, radiation, and the rules that govern their interactions.

Our universe started as an infinitesimal dot, much tinier than nuclear dimensions, and even after the inflation its size was still only centimeters in diameter. It was so fantastically hot that subatomic particles could not have survived in the heat, and all substance was in the form of radiation — bosons. The universe was born in light, created with light.

Space continued to expand and cool after the inflation, although at a much more leisurely and steady pace than in that burst of exponential growth. Gradually, by processes of quantum mechanics whose rules were somehow already in place, the energy of light began to turn into matter consistent with the relationship $E=mc^2$. The radiation transmuted spontaneously, by the process of pair production, as photons converted into particle-antiparticle pairs, primarily as quark combinations — familiar ones like protons and neutrons, and also more exotic combinations of quarks. The environment was still far too hot, however, for these particles to survive for any significant period. They quickly collided with and annihilated each other, transmuting back into light, only to form again from the radiation. The result was a cauldron of radiation and matter, bosons and fermions: an energy-matter stew.

As the cosmos distended and cooled, the simmering transformation between matter and energy, back and forth between these dual forms, slowed. Quarks and the particles they constitute began to consolidate and linger. Cosmologists therefore refer to the period immediately following inflation as the quark-dominated universe, or the epoch of quarks. As the universe continued to expand and cool, other types of particles sequentially assumed roles as the principal players in the unfolding drama, and by convention each epoch subsequent is named for that group.

Sometime during this period, the quark matter became more abundant than the antiquark matter. Rather than the two types being exactly equal in number, fewer than about one particle in one billion was antimatter. This difference was possible thanks in part to a physical phenomenon discovered in modern particle accelerators. A slight asymmetry, or difference, exists between the way the strong and weak forces interact with particles and with antiparticles. While the physics is not well understood or settled, it is likely that this asymmetry led to the resultant preponderance of matter over antimatter, with two sweeping consequences. During this period, as the quarks and antiquarks collided with each other and transformed into energy (photons), they might have obliterated each other completely, leaving none to assemble into atoms. The imbalance in their numbers, however, meant instead that our universe ended up today with some net amount of nuclear matter in it — only about one-billionth of the total quantity it had during the epoch of quarks, but still enough to make all of the atoms in the universe today.

A related implication of the unbalanced annihilation of antiparticles is that our universe is constructed almost completely of only one kind of matter, with little of the opposite kind, the antimatter.

Even the minute amounts of antimatter that once existed are now thought to be mostly gone, annihilated by subsequent chance encounters they had with normal matter long ago. If we ever travel to planets around other stars in our galaxy, our spacecraft, upon landing, will not risk being vaporized in a burst of gamma ray photons. Or, if our Milky Way galaxy ever collides with another galaxy (as probably happened before, and which is likely to happen again — galaxies frequently collide in the cosmic plan), the two will just crash together — but not annihilate. These fortuitous results — that our universe contains nuclear matter, and that it will not ultimately self-immolate — are attributable to the asymmetry produced in the early moments of *Yetzirah*, and the fact that this asymmetry was very small.

The universe continued to expand and cool under the influence of the tremendous pressure of the light. About one picosecond (10^{-12} seconds) after the big bang, when the temperature fell to about 10^{15} degrees, the last two of the original four forces, the electromagnetic and weak forces, disentangled and became distinguishable from each other. This event marked the end of the unification of the electromagnetic and weak forces, and therefore the end of the unification of any of the forces. Each of the four forces of our universe acquired its distinctive character during these early moments and remains distinct to this day.

The primitive cosmic broth continued to stew as radiation transmuted into particles, particles annihilated with their antiparticles back into radiation, and each was constantly recast into the other. After some tens of microseconds had elapsed, the universe had cooled enough that some of the growing number of lingering quarks could stick to one another when they collided, fashioning composite particles of nuclear matter: the protons, neutrons, and other particles made of quarks. Most of the particles continued to transmute into radiation and back again, but not all of them did. Some exotic quark-composite particles formed and did not collide with their antiparticle and disappear. These exotic species have intrinsically short lifetimes, however; they are unstable to decay and soon dissolved into other particles. By then the universe was too cool to replenish them, and they played no further role in cosmic evolution. The more familiar, long-lived particles that formed, most notably the protons, neutrons, and also some leptons like the electrons, did not decay. These stable particles persist today as the familiar constituents of our world.

These interactions continued until the temperatures dropped to about a trillion degrees, at which point the energies were finally no longer adequate for even the lightest and most easily made of the quark-blended particles (the *pions*) to continue dissolving and re-forming. They formed, persisted, and marked the end of the epoch of quarks: the time was 10^{-4} seconds after the Creation. Less than a millisecond after the big bang, nearly all particles of nuclear matter in the universe had been produced. The stage was set for the class of leptons and its most well known particle, the electron, and the electron's antiparticle, the positron.

The Epoch of Leptons

The epoch of leptons was characterized by the same processes of pair production and annihilation that dominated the epoch of quarks, but since the universe was no longer hot enough for the more massive quarks to collide reactively, the dominant processes instead involved the less massive electrons, positrons, neutrinos, and the other leptons. The adventures of the nuclear particles, however, were not over. Indeed, the story of protons and neutrons is starting to become more interesting.

A short digression: A neutron, you will recall, is the counterpart to a proton, having about the same mass but no electric charge. Neutrons are key constituents of atomic nuclei, ensuring the stability of nuclei by binding together the normally self-repelling, positively charged protons via the strong force. The protons and neutrons that were produced from quarks during the epoch of quarks were then able to couple with one another. The mechanism that enables this coupling interaction was discovered in the 1940s by particle physicists who noticed that a free neutron (one found outside a stabilizing atomic nucleus) would spontaneously decompose into three other particles: a proton, an electron, and a neutrino. The process occurs because of the weak force and was named "beta decay," because at the time of the discovery, electrons in the decay product were called "beta particles." All reactions have an inverse, and so does this one: inverse beta decay allows a neutron to be created out of a proton, an electron, and a neutrino when the three coalesce. Calculations based on the well-known properties of these basic building blocks of matter reveal that, as we pick up the story of matter, the balance between the beta-processes of creating new neutrons and destroying existing ones had resulted in there being approximately one neutron for every five protons in the universe.

The abundance of neutrons was critical to the formation of the atomic elements because neutrons allowed the atoms more complex than hydrogen to exist. (The hydrogen nucleus has one proton and no neutrons, but all other atomic nuclei, starting immediately with the next element, helium, have sequentially increasing numbers of protons, plus neutrons to bind them.) Alone and outside of a nucleus, a neutron can survive for only about fifteen minutes before it spontaneously beta-decays into a proton, electron, and neutrino; inside an atomic nucleus, neutrons are stable and live indefinitely.

A seminal moment in the epoch of leptons was the time when the temperature of the growing universe dropped down to about ten billion degrees, low enough that the energies no longer enabled the neutrinos to coalesce with the protons and electrons to make new neutrons. This event is referred to as the decoupling of neutrinos — the effective dissociation of neutrinos from the rest of matter. After this moment, virtually no new neutrons could be made.

As was the case determining the end of the epoch of quarks, the epoch of leptons did not end until the temperatures dropped far enough that the processes involving leptons could no longer be sustained. Annihilation reactions between electrons and their antiparticles, the positrons, ceased, bringing to a close the epoch of leptons a few seconds after the big bang. Matter at that time existed predominantly in the form of relatively stable subatomic particles. The neutrons had begun to combine with protons to make new elements, but were quickly vanishing.

The Epoch of Radiation

With the relative cessation of the reactions transmuting the neutrinos and other leptons, our attention turns to the newly predominant constituent of the universe, radiation. The observable universe at this time was about the size of the distance between the Earth and the Moon, vastly larger than it had been at the end of the inflation period only seconds earlier, and its temperature had fallen to a few billion degrees — which is still very much hotter than the interior of the Sun. In this environment the photons, although individually not energetic enough to form new particles via pair production, were nonetheless abundant; there was nearly a billion times as much energy in the form of radiation as there was in the form of matter. Therefore this next period of time is called the epoch of radiation, and it persisted for about three hundred thousand years, until the universe had cooled down to a temperature of only about 3,000 kelvin.

Cosmic history at the beginning of this period commenced and soon completed, once and for all, the assembly of the atomic elements. The process of synthesizing elements is called nucleosynthesis. At the end of the epoch of leptons the balance between neutrons and protons had been roughly one-to-five. Those neutrons that then collided with a proton were able to form a stable atomic nucleus. Neutrons that did not combine into atomic elements, however, decayed and disappeared in about fifteen minutes, and since no new neutrons were being produced, their total numbers quickly dwindled to nothing, thereby ending after about fifteen minutes nearly all subsequent element production. Ninety-nine point nine percent of the atoms we see today were formed during this early era, when the neutrons and protons combined.

Primordial nucleosynthesis first made *deuterium*, the simplest atomic nucleus after that of hydrogen. Consisting of one proton and one neutron, deuterium is actually not a new element. It is an isotope of hydrogen, meaning that it is chemically identical to hydrogen but has an additional neutron in its nucleus and so is physically distinguishable. (Electrons had not yet bound to the deuterium nuclei to form neutral atoms of deuterium — that would not happen for another three hundred thousand years. Such a nucleus is therefore more precisely referred to as a deuteron, not deuterium, but I will usually adopt the more familiar term of deuterium.) Once sufficient deuterium had been created, pairs of deuterium nuclei began to collide and fuse together, resulting in nuclei with two protons and two neutrons: helium, the lightest element after hydrogen.

The free neutrons were living against the clock. In the fifteen minutes allotted to them, they either collided with protons to produce deuterium, helium, and the lightest elements, or they dissolved away into protons, electrons, and neutrinos. At the same time, the universe was still expanding, and as it did, the density of matter plummeted, and with it so did the frequency of those formative collisional encounters between the neutrons and protons. If the universe had been expanding much faster, the conditions for frequent encounters might have lasted only for seconds or less. Very few neutrons would have been able to join with protons to form new elements, and then all the remaining neutrons would have decayed. But fortunately the expansion did not proceed too fast, and in these fifteen minutes many of the neutrons did stick to protons. The first stable atomic nuclei were assembled.

Cosmologists know how fast the universe was expanding, as well as the rate at which deuterium tends to form from a proton and neutron. Using basic nuclear physics, they calculate that about 25 percent of the nuclei in the universe should have been converted into helium, while the bulk of nuclei, 75 percent worth, should be hydrogen. Aside from minor traces of deuterium and tritium (hydrogen isotopes) and lithium (the next element after helium in the periodic table), only hydrogen and helium could have been created in the beginning.

Collisions between helium nuclei and other particles or nuclei were common. One might have expected that these collisions would produce even heavier elements — perhaps even some like carbon or oxygen, with twelve and sixteen nucleons, respectively. That did not happen. Curiously — accidentally — there are no stable atomic nuclei with five or six nucleons. Every combination of protons and neutrons might be imagined, but it just so happens that the basic character of the nuclear forces does not permit stable light nuclei containing just five or six particles. Any of these that happened to form in a collision decayed immediately. As a consequence of this extraordinary gap in stable nuclei at five and six nucleons, all the heavier elements — from beryllium to plutonium — were inhibited from forming in the cumulative, iterative cosmic process of atom assembly. At the conclusion of the era of cosmic nucleosynthesis, according to our best understanding, there was virtually nothing atomic except hydrogen and some helium — no carbon or oxygen, no sodium or nitrogen, no silicon or iron, nothing but hydrogen and helium, a few traces of their isotopes, and an even smaller amount of lithium.

It is a stunning fact that when we actually measure how much of the universe is hydrogen, helium, carbon, oxygen, and the rest of the approximately one hundred known elements, we find nearly perfect agreement with these modeled results: nearly all the universe is hydrogen and helium. The question must be asked, Where did the carbon, oxygen, nitrogen, and other elements so essential to life come from? They were *not* created during the Creation, but much, much later in the life of the universe, inside stars or supernovas, where temperatures can be hotter than the temperature of the universe during the epoch of radiation. Many diverse kinds of observations confirm this amazing story and these remarkable predictions of big bang cosmology. The correct value of the relative abundance of hydrogen and helium is one of the primary touchstones of supporting evidence for the big bang, and less directly also for the existence of nonnuclear dark matter (discussed in chapter 4).

The Sefirot of Hesed, Gevurah, and Tiferet

The fourth of the sefirot is *Hesed* (Grace, or Loving kindness). It is the first of the sefirot in the World of *Yetzirah* and the first that unfolds from the mysterious depths of the *Ein-Sof* into the apprehensible world of forms. This sefirah is traditionally seen as corresponding to the first day of the biblical creation narrative. The newly forming world could not have continued to exist without God's purest grace and blessing. *Hesed* reveals the essential unity of all the archetypes now forming in a continuous process of emanations. While each of the newly created things in this multitude appears to be unique and disconnected from the other, in truth they are all rooted in the unity of the Divine. *Hesed*, by manifesting this coherence, displays its nature as grace.

Gevurah (Rigor, or Justice) brings order into the cosmos, counterbalancing the unadulterated forbearance of *Hesed*. *Gevurah* corresponds to the second day of biblical Creation. Just as the world has an underlying unity, so too it has a creative potential that naturally introduces distinctions by designing limitations, thus enabling the wide variety of different structures seen in the universe. But constraints and limits, even in the beneficent form as "justice," are fundamentally qualities of negation. In the Kabbalah, evil in the world is traced to the qualities of this essential sefirah of *Gevurah*. *Hesed* and *Gevurah* are a pair, together supporting the tension that enables the real world to be on the one hand filled with distinct, individual entities, yet on the other to be at its deepest levels linked to the unity of the Divine. These two sefirot are often associated with the qualities of love and awe, *ahavah* and *yirah*.

The Bahir describes *Tiferet* (Beauty, Splendor, or Mercy), the sixth sefirah, as follows: "The sixth [of the sefirot] is the adorned, glorious, delightful throne of glory, the house of the world to come. Its place is engraved in wisdom, as it says: 'God said, "Let there be light," and there was light.'" *Tiferet* resolves and blends the contrasting qualities of *Hesed* and *Gevurah*; it mediates and balances the tension between the two prior sefirot and brings a peace and wholeness whose strength develops from the energy in these opposites. *Tiferet* is the ideal balance that the Kabbalah designated as the root of perfection and the source of blessings. *Tiferet* is also the mirror of the spiritual life. Rabbi Arthur Green explains, "The struggle to integrate love and judgment is not only the great human task but a reflection of the cosmic struggle. The inner structure of psychic life *is* the hidden structure of the universe; it is because of this that humans can come to know God by the path of inward contemplation and true self-knowledge." In *Tiferet*, the analogue of the biblical third day, the archetypes of reality become revealed, finally, in their principal forms. *Tiferet* brings to a close the epoch of radiation, a period whose most important achievement was, at least from our point of view, the production of atomic nuclei, but which was characterized not by matter but by the abundance of intense radiation that established the environment in which everything else transpired.

Come see! Astronomers recognize that the universe was filled with radiation *from its birth*. As in the biblical description of the Creation, light, or more technically the panoply of bosons, was created eons (about nine billion years) before the Sun. For centuries this apparent discrepancy in the biblical account, which places the creation of the Sun on the fourth "day," has been the source of concern and speculation by literal readers of scripture, but modern discoveries enable us to understand that in any reasonable scientific description it is certain that light was created, and filled the universe, long before the creation of the Sun and stars.

THE PARTING OF RADIATION AND MATTER TO THE FORMATION OF GALAXIES, STARS, PLANETS, AND LIFE: THE WORLD OF ASSIYAH

The fourth and last of the worlds is Assiyah *— the World of Doing. It begins about three hundred eighty thousand years after the big bang, when electrons united with naked atomic nuclei to form neutral atoms, thereby allowing the fog of scattered light sustained by the free electrons to evaporate and releasing the cosmic background radiation that still envelops us. This era continues to the present day, almost fourteen billion years later. The intervening time is of considerable consequence: neutral atoms formed and gathered into the first stars, while stately, rotating galaxies developed and populated themselves with these self-luminous entities. Nuclear reactions in stars synthesized the elements beyond hydrogen and helium in their nuclear cores and then expelled them, enriching the cosmos and enabling stars more characteristic of our Sun to form, some with families of planets, until finally: life.* Assiyah *comprises the fantastic drama that culminates in the creation of humanity, and by implication, the range of possibilities and challenges that constitute the human task of rebuilding a world whose birth was necessarily intense. The World of* Assiyah, *the epoch in which humanity lives, is characterized by* tikkun olam*: the kabbalistic responsibility to complete God's handiwork by caring for one another and the Creation.*

The Epoch of Matter

As the universe continued its inexorable growth and cooling, matter gradually became more important than radiation in the simple sense that there just was more of it per unit of volume. Today, much later on but still in the epoch of matter, it is the matter in the universe, and not the radiation, that determines what happens for most intents and purposes. When we pick up our story, matter in the universe did not yet exist in the form of neutral atoms. It consisted, instead, of a plasma of positively charged atomic nuclei, with electrons also present but unattached to the nuclei. Because they were free to move, these electrons *scattered the light* that permeated space, as a fog of water droplets will redirect and diffuse light into an opaque haze. The practical effect of this cosmic mist was to block us from peering though its veil to see directly into the happenings of the universe earlier than the epoch of matter.

But eventually — when the universe was about three hundred eighty thousand years old — the relentlessly expanding universe cooled to a temperature of a mere 3,000 kelvin. At last the negatively charged electrons could bond to the naked, positively charged atomic nuclei, producing neutral atoms: the chemically active elementary building blocks of our familiar world. The process whereby electrons bind to atomic nuclei is generically called *recombination*. Even though these particles in the early universe were combining for the first time ever, this phase is still by convention called the time of "*re*combination." Virtually all of the nuclei present at that moment were of hydrogen and helium, and so now true *atoms* of hydrogen and helium formed as electrons swarmed around the nuclei. In the moments after recombination, the light of the Creation was free to propagate without the constant bouncing and redirection by the fog of electrons. It *decoupled* and has forever after traveled unhindered through space. The veil was lifted.

That first unhindered light, still traveling from its last reflection off the mist of electrons nearly fourteen billion years ago, even now fills the universe. It is the cosmic microwave background radiation. But it has aged. When it started out, the light was characteristic of a hot furnace whose temperature was about 3,000 kelvin, just the temperature of the universe at the time of recombination. Like all electromagnetic radiation from warm bodies, this light contained radiation with a comprehensive range of wavelengths from the very short X-rays to the longest radio waves. Most of the energy, however, was in the swathe of optical wavelengths characteristic of its 3,000 kelvin environment. Today, cooled and stretched out to longer values of wavelength by the expansion of the universe in which it travels, the light has been transformed into radiation whose peak energy is at radio wavelengths, not optical ones. The night sky, without the Sun's bright scattered light, appears black to our eyes, but it started out looking like radiation from a hot oven. When scientists peer into the sky with sensitive modern satellites whose "eyes" respond to radio wavelengths, this light appears everywhere, bright and present in all directions, but now its temperature corresponds to only about 2.7 kelvin, or a Celsius temperature of about minus 270 degrees. It has been stretched in wavelength and corresponding temperature by a factor of a thousand from then until today, in exact correspondence with the dramatic growth in the size of the universe since the era of recombination. Since its intensity today is by far strongest in the microwave portion of the radio spectrum, this light is called the "cosmic microwave" radiation, although it has photons at all wavelengths. Invisible to our eyes, this bright light contains nearly as much energy as there is in all the other kinds of radiation in the universe produced from stars and galaxies combined.

The big bang took place *everywhere*, as we saw in chapter 3. The 2.7 degree kelvin radiation is therefore also everywhere. It surrounds us today. Its ubiquity makes it very hard to detect, because there is nowhere to look for a reference blank point, no black sky for comparison. Its omnidirectional, pervasive presence makes it the practical background, and so the light is most often referred to as the "cosmic microwave *background* radiation." Cosmic — because it was produced in the cosmic birth; microwave — because most of the energy lies at these wavelengths; background

— because it is everywhere; radiation — because it is electromagnetic waves. Astronomers must take meticulous care when studying this radiation to ensure a signal is not the result of a mistake or residual instrument noise. The successful landmark detection of this light was made in the 1960s by two scientists, Arno Penzias and Robert Wilson, using a sensitive radio telescope, and they received the Nobel Prize for their discovery. In 1989, NASA launched the Cosmic Background Explorer (COBE) satellite to study this radiation thoroughly. COBE measured the radiation's temperature and spectral character precisely and found that it looks just like it should if it were born as a result of the big bang. COBE also peered intently to spot any differences in the brightness coming from different directions in the sky, searching for any deviation from perfect isotropy. In fact, images of the cosmic microwave background radiation did show some variations, only a few percent of a few percent of the total brightness, but nevertheless more than had ever been perceived before, and of incredible significance: the faint images capture the structure of the universe at the earliest time we can clearly see, the moment of the decoupling of radiation and matter.

COBE also helped resolve a long-standing mystery. Recall that inflation was so fast and so effective that it smoothed away all the structural variations present in the chaos of the first moments, much the same way the surface of a wrinkled, deflated balloon will become smooth when the balloon expands. How was it, then, that the universe ended up with the many distinct structures we now see: stars, galaxies, and even clusters and superclusters of galaxies? What provided the skeletal framework for gravity to build upon? These modest, wispy filaments and clumps first revealed by COBE are all that were needed. Gravity, in its single-minded fashion, steadily built upon these seeds of nonuniformity until, eventually, the great web of galaxies precipitated. Finding out exactly how this happened, and how the first stars formed, is part of the active quest in which our species is currently engaged. In 2001, NASA launched another satellite to study the cosmic microwave background radiation: the Wilkinson Microwave Anisotropy Probe (WMAP). As its name suggests, the goal of WMAP is to map the differences in the relative cosmic microwave background temperature (the anisotropies) over the entire sky with an angular precision more than twenty times finer than that of COBE, and a precision better than one part in one hundred thousand. The detail WMAP has discovered so far not only helps to explain the origins of galaxies, it also provides amazingly intricate diagnostics on what the universe was really like only a few hundred thousand years after the big bang, and by implication earlier than that as well. The best results so far measure the temperature of the cosmic microwave background as 2.725 kelvin with a formal precision of less than one-tenth of a percent, the age of the universe as 13.73 billion years with a formal precision of 1 percent, and the time of recombination as about 380,000 years (although this process did not occur in one instant everywhere, and I have sometimes used an approximate value of three hundred thousand years).

Immediately after the recombination, gravity began to build galaxies from the primordial filaments and clumps of neutral matter, almost entirely hydrogen and helium atoms. Gravity condensed the cosmic clumps of atoms into giant clouds and then shrank these clouds further, squeezing and heating them until their temperatures finally triggered nuclear ignition. In this way the first stars were born. It is thanks to gravity, the *least* of the forces in strength, that the strong and weak forces, which had been comparatively inactive for eons, began again to play a cosmic role, creating new and more complex atoms inside these stars. These new atoms were the products of the sequential, nuclear fusing of smaller nuclei into larger ones. Hydrogen and helium, almost alone since the early moments of creation, now had company as the new elements were assembled.

The formation of galaxies and stars was, of course, the prelude to the formation of planets once the universe had been sufficiently enriched in these more complex elements. Astronomers think that a portion of the natal cloud material of a star is not gravitationally captured into the star but remains around it, spread into a thin, circumstellar disk. At some point in a star's early development, dust in this disk begins to nucleate around seeds that grow larger and larger, mutually coalescing and eventually assembling into planets. The asteroids and comets that are also produced sometimes collide violently with new planets, leaving as evidence their characteristic marks, craters. If conditions on a planet — temperature, chemistry, and who knows what else — are exactly right, perhaps life can form there.

The Sefirot of Netzah, Hod, Yesod, and Malkhut

In a manner analogous to the physical processes of the Creation, the final four sefirot in the World of Doing transmute the primordial spiritual and material structures — still fresh from their creation but blended and not yet gathered into shapes — into the structures and forms of the rich and complex world in which we live.

Netzah (Victory, Dominance) represents the possibilities of all the newly revealed archetypes and is therefore considered the traditional wellspring of prophecy. *Netzah*, the fourth day of biblical Creation, is the first sefirah in the last hierarchical triad of sefirot, a set that mirrors the preceding two triads (*Keter-Hokhmah-Binah*, and *Hesed-Gevurah-Tiferet*) and their dialectical mixing and balancing. *Netzah* leads ultimately to the production of all the manifested worlds and is the flow of pure life to all beings. As such, it embodies a limitless condition, similar to *Hesed*'s unrestrained benevolence.

In our physical world *Netzah* dominates at the formation of neutral atoms (the moment of recombination) as the cosmic veil lifts and the cosmic microwave background radiation is set free.

Hod (Glory), by analogy the fifth day in the Genesis story, generates the complex, multifaceted forms of the universe by transforming the more elemental world of *Netzah*; it is also, like *Netzah*, a source of prophecy. In a universe dominated by matter in the epoch of matter, gravity impels this conversion by attracting and accumulating the slight irregularities left after the inflation into structures of ever larger size. The steady development of structures, via their gravitational coalescence, is possible now because the electrically charged particles have merged into neutral atoms. Gravity can play an unhindered, authoritative role. In the phase dominated by *Hod*, the hydrogen and helium atoms aggregate into a magnificent web of matter, filamentary cosmic strings that gradually develop dense beads destined to become the first generation of galaxies and stars. *Hod*, then, is indeed glorious in its ability to bring things together in new forms.

Gravity is the force that ultimately binds the universe together, and as we have seen, gravity is the force that powered the gradual coalescence of matter into larger and larger forms. But gravity is simultaneously the source of *separation* in the universe, because it took the (nearly) uniform distribution of matter and amplified its minute differences, enabling each small, slightly thickened condensation of matter to grow separately into a star or a galaxy. Just as the two prior sefirot of *Hesed* and *Gevurah* represent the contrasts of unlimited potential versus constraint, so *Netzah* and *Hod* contrast the symmetric qualities of unrestrained expansion versus condensation into specific entities.

The ninth sefirah is *Yesod* (Foundation), and it corresponds to the sixth day of Genesis. Like its analogue *Tiferet*, *Yesod* is the last in a triad and balances the effects of the previous two sefirot. *Yesod* mediates *Netzah* and *Hod*, producing an equilibrium between full and empty, expansive and restrictive. It reveals and reintegrates what has come before and is the juncture where all of the prior energies combine and flow into the material world. It is seen as the basis for sexuality, in particular male sexuality, because of its ability to combine opposites in a productive union and its role as the source of flowing energy. In our physical description of *Yesod*, physical structures — galaxies, star clusters, solar systems — settle into a lengthy and normative period governed by relatively unhurried timescales, as the forces reprocess the primitive matter of the big bang nucleosynthesis into the richer diversity of elements and structures needed for life.

Malkhut (Kingdom), the tenth and last of the sefirot, is often portrayed in the Kabbalah as the only sefirah in the World of *Assiyah*, but as noted before, a slightly different grouping fits the cosmological picture more closely. *Malkhut* takes its name from its being symbolic of the establishment of God's "kingdom" in our reality. It is not so much a process in the creation drama, as were the other nine sefirot, as it is the current state of our being. God's Divine worldly (and female) presence is called the *Shekhinah*. *Malkhut* is the *Shekhinah*, the well of blessings for our world. *Malkhut* is effective because of the existence of humanity: our consciousness, awareness, and free will. Containing as it does consciousness, *Malkhut* is quintessentially the present — the now — but it also spans the long times needed in the creation process to arrive at consciousness from a random mix of matter and light.

The seven final sefirot transform the newly born cosmos from pure radiation into material worlds filled with life. Like the four physical forces, the sefirot are not phenomena peculiar to the Creation. The universe was not fashioned by unique forces that faded long ago. The influence of the sefirot continues to permeate and dominate the universe today, at every level of being. The same principles that dominated during that early time are manifest now, although in a more modest way. The *Zohar* says, " 'By understanding He continually established the heavens' [Proverbs 3:19]. What does 'continually established' mean? He goes on establishing [the sefirot] every day, and does not cease. They were not arranged at one particular time, but He arranges them daily...because of the great love and pleasure that the Holy One, blessed be He, feels for them, and their preciousness in His sight."

The world was born in an explosive, chaotic cauldron, with precision as well as division, with coupling as well as disrupting. The Kabbalah describes the birth as a commingling of opposites like these. The presence of negativity in the Creation is regrettable but necessary; it results in imperfection, but raises concomitant needs and opportunities. Kabbalists call the process of repairing and perfecting the imperfect world *tikkun olam*, and humanity's task is to engage in *tikkun olam*. The World of *Assiyah* is characterized by this concept. I will discuss it at length in chapter 6. As envisioned in the Kabbalah, the consciousness, awareness, and free will that we human beings possess empower us to complete the process of creation as conceived by the One.

From the moment God thought to create until the formation in *Malkhut* of creatures themselves capable of creative and conscious thinking, ten steps and about 13.73 billion years were required. *Malkhut* is also the seventh day: the Sabbath, described by the Bible and traditional Jewish texts as the source of all potentiality, a time for harmony and rest, a flavor of paradise and the world to come.

For us, each moment — the *now* — is filled with the spirit of the seventh day in the same way that each place — the *here* — is filled with the cosmic microwave background light. We are constantly bathed in their figurative and literal glows. It is for us, God's vehicles of free will and consciousness, to come together somehow with the will of that pretemporal consciousness.

6 COSMIC WISDOM

THE AWESOME UNIVERSE

The preceding chapters are filled with incredible facts and profound ideas. They will take time to digest. This is an opportune moment to step back, reflect on what it all means, and try to broaden our sensibilities.

The heavens are more than just fascinating and beautiful. They evoke emotions of wonder, appreciation, and thanksgiving to the Creator. The night sky, that "mystical, moist night air" of Walt Whitman, is a source of inspiration like other profound majesties of nature. As an astronomer, I know the names of many stars, recognize the constellations, and even have an understanding of how stars are born and die, but nevertheless I am moved by the visual and imaginative power of the whole. Such feelings are important to evoke because they are in a deep sense themselves a part of the creation story. In the words of Psalm 19:2–5, "The skies declare God's glory; the heavens describe His handiwork. Daily they elaborate a story, and nightly they reveal knowledge. There is no speech, no words, no voice — yet their message is heard throughout the world."

Reading a book like this one is no substitute for experiencing the night sky: the pitch-black air, a cool breeze, and as your eyes adapt to the darkness, the heavens gradually revealing themselves as abounding in stars too numerous to count. Recall and meditate on this vision as we journey outward for perspective.

The Moon orbits the Earth at a distance of roughly 180,000 miles. It is only the first step in the cosmic voyage we now embark upon, but already it is farther than we can easily comprehend or appreciate. The circumference of the whole Earth, after all, is only about 25,000 miles at the equator. As we travel beyond the Moon and across cosmological distances, the number of zeros after the "one" in our imaginary odometer will increase dramatically. We need a unit of distance measure that is more manageable than the kilometers or miles of the human scale. Astronomers use time to measure a length — the time it takes for a beam of light to traverse it. Since the speed of light is a constant at about 186,000 miles (or 300,000 kilometers) per second, the Moon by this metric lies about one light-second away. The Sun, which is 93 million miles away, is 8 light-minutes from Earth. (These and other measurements are not given precisely but are close approximations.) The planet Mars, when its orbit brings it to the same side of the Sun as Earth's, is 4 light-minutes away, while Pluto, the last planet in the solar system, is 5.3 light-hours out. (Its orbit, however, is highly elliptical, and this planet is sometimes even closer to us than Neptune is.) If the Sun were the size of a basketball, then the Earth would be the size of a poppy seed twenty-five feet away, and Pluto would be an imperceptible speck a third of a mile away. The star nearest to us is of course the Sun; the next closest star is Proxima Centauri. On our scale with the Sun as a basketball, Proxima Centauri would be the size of a cherry and would reside about 4,000 miles away. In real distance it is 4 light-years away; it takes light from that star four years to reach us. If we could travel at the speed of light, it would take us four years to reach Proxima Centauri, but of course the laws of physics preclude our moving that fast. A more reasonable maximum speed for a spaceship (though this technology is infeasible at the moment) might be about a tenth that of light, constraining a physical journey to at least a few decades of Earth time — each way.

Our Milky Way galaxy has more than a hundred billion stars arranged in a giant spiral disk and luminous spherical halo stretching about three hundred thousand light-years from edge to edge, with our Sun residing about two-thirds of the way out from the center. The Milky Way is but one galaxy. Andromeda, a nearby spiral galaxy rather like our own, is more than two million light-years away and is itself filled with hundreds of billions of stars and who knows how many planets, nebulae, and other celestial bodies. Galaxies cluster into groups. The Milky Way and Andromeda are the largest members of the local group of galaxies, together with more than 40 other smaller galaxies of varying types. Groups of galaxies cluster into larger units called "superclusters" that are linked collectively by gravity into stupendous filaments and strands, permeated by vast, relatively empty hollows that stretch as far as we can see to the edges of the known universe. The light from the most remote of these galaxies, light that has been traveling toward us since the early infancy of the universe nearly fourteen billion years ago, shows us what the universe looked like back then, billions of years before life, before the Earth, even before the solar system was formed. "O Lord, what is a man, yet You acknowledge him? Or a child of humanity, yet You think of him? . . . Still, teach us to measure, that we may be wise" (Psalm 1). "And all the inhabitants of the Earth are considered as nothing." (Daniel 4:32).

Stop reading for one moment, please. Notice where you are and sense the warmth of your skin. Remember that you are surrounded by the radiation of the Creation, the cosmic microwave background radiation, and although it is far too gentle to feel, it fills your room, and you are bathed in its glow. The ground on which you stand is holy ground (Exodus 3:5), the very location of the big bang. True, the universe today is much bigger, much cooler, and much changed since its birth, but your place is here with the *Resheit*.

If you have been able to suspend the internal dialogue in your mind for a moment, and to simply appreciate the majestic scale of the universe, then perhaps you have also tasted that sense of wonder, or even of transcendent being, that comes with the mystic's sense of *awareness*. Knowledge and appreciation can stimulate this feeling, which has a name in Hebrew: *yirah*. Jewish mystics call *yirah* the awe, or fear, of God; in Hebrew the word can be used for either and has both verbal and nominative forms. For example, David's psalms say, using two constructions of the word *yirah*: "I will fear [*irah*] no evil" (Psalm 23:4), and "Taste and see that God is good.... Nothing is lacking to those who are in awe [*y-irah-v*]" (Psalm 34:9–10).

"Awe-wareness" captures in English some of the multiple meanings of the Hebrew *yirah*. I believe that the more we know (and are aware), the more we can appreciate God's handiwork and become capable of wonder and awe. This is why a tour of the sky, and a description of its dimensions, its age, its motions, and its varied content, is so conducive to a greater sense of amazement and wonder. The sense of *yirah* involves both perception and understanding. In contrast to *ahavah*, the Divine love that enhances feelings of closeness and comfort (the sefirah of *Hesed*), *yirah* brings with it a sense of self-awareness, separation, and distancing (the sefirah of *Gevurah*). The universe is itself the paradigm for the tension between these two qualities: it may have been created because of

God's love, but as we saw, the process of creation is essentially also one of separation. It should not be surprising that the connections between science and religion, cosmology and Kabbalah, go far beyond the technicalities compared in chapter 5. The ontological wellspring extends as well to sensibility and intellect. The *Zohar* acknowledges the connections between the stars and wonder:

> Rabbi Elazar and Rabbi Abba were staying together one night. When night fell they went out into the garden by Lake Tiberias. As they did so they saw two stars moving from different directions collide with each other and then disappear. Rabbi Abba said, "How great are the works of the Holy One, blessed be He, in the heavens above and on the Earth beneath. Who can possibly understand the significance of these two stars that have come together from different directions and collided with one another and then disappeared?" Rabbi Elazar said to him, "But we did actually see them! We have witnessed this and witnessed many other things that the Holy One, blessed be He, performs continually."

Psalm 111:10 teaches about the *yirah* we have been contemplating: "The beginning of wisdom [is] the *yirah* of God." [ראשית חכמה יראת ה transliteration: *Resheit hokhmah yirah[t] hashem.*] Solomon's Proverbs 9:10 and 1:7 reiterate this sentiment. The Hebrew word for *beginning* is the usual one, the same as the word for "[In the] beginning" in the Creation story — *resheit.* Note that Hebrew has no word for *is*; in the present tense it simply juxtaposes the subject and predicate, allowing for some useful ambiguity. The plain meaning of Psalm 111:10 is that the beginning of true wisdom comes from first having a fear of heaven. The Hebrew also allows it to be understood the other way around, that the first fruits of wisdom lead to a fear of heaven. "The beginning of wisdom? It is the *yirah* of God," because the more that is known, the more that is appreciated. As we gain in wisdom, we deepen our sense of *yirah*.

A mystical observation from the *Zohar* is that *yirah* and *resheit* are effectively equivalent. The following passage exploits the fact that the prefix *b'* in *B'Resheit* can also mean "for the sake of."

> *Yirah* [awe or fear] is of three types. In two there is no proper principle; only in one is the real principle of *yirah*. A man may fear the Holy One, blessed be He to have compassion on his children... or for physical or material punishment; or, because he is afraid of punishment in the World to Come. These two do not demonstrate the basic principle and root of fear. Real *yirah* comes when a person fears his Master because He is the great Ruler, the basic principle and root of all worlds, compared with whom nothing is of any consequence, as it is said [in Daniel 4:32], "And all the inhabitants of the Earth are considered as nothing."... Therefore it is written [in the opening word of scripture]: B'Resheit [or, *for the sake of Resheit* ראשית] — that is, for the sake of *yirah* God created the heavens and the Earth.

The towering vision of Abraham in Genesis 15:1–6, which occurred before his name was changed from Abram, describes the first instance of *yirah* in the Bible:

> After these events the word of God came to Abram in a vision saying, "Fear not Abram [literally: have no *yirah*], I am a shield for you; your reward is very great." And Abram said, "My Lord God, what can you give me seeing that I am childless, and the steward of my house is Eliezer of Damascus?"... Suddenly the word of God came to him saying, "He will not inherit from you. Only him who shall come forth from you shall inherit from you." And He took him outside and said, "Gaze now at the sky, and count the stars — if you can!"

In this passage we see all three types of *yirah* mentioned in the previous passage from the *Zohar*. Of the unsuitable first two kinds (fear of harm or childlessness, and fear of punishment in the next world), God reassures Abraham not to worry: God will protect him (be a shield), grant him children, and reward him in the next world. As the *Zohar* explains, the first two kinds of *yirah* are not the authentic forms. Instead, God tells Abraham to go outside and "count the stars — if you can!" By leading Abraham outside to meditate on the unbounded vastness of the cosmos, God leads him toward the deepest and truest level of *yirah*, in which, as the *Zohar* explains, a person fears his master because his master is the great ruler, the basic principle and root of all worlds compared with whom nothing is of any worth, as it is said (in Daniel 4:32), "And all the inhabitants of the Earth are considered as nothing." This type of *yirah* is the level of *self-awareness* from which derive the senses of isolation from God and the awe of God.

WISDOM (HOKHMAH) AND THE UNIVERSE

There is a deep underlying association between *yirah*, in all of the senses we have just discussed, and the Creation. The connections are alluded to in Psalm 111:10, which we can further explicate in the way of midrash. "The beginning of wisdom [is] the awe of God [*resheit hokhmah yira(t) hashem*]." The Kabbalists derive a lesson from a word association between the three words *beginning* (*resheit*), *wisdom* (*hokhmah*), and *awe* (*yirah*) in this passage, and the fact that the same word, *beginning* (*resheit*), opens the Bible: "Rabbi Yudai said: 'What does "In the Beginning/With the *Resheit*" mean? It means, "With Wisdom/*Hokhmah*." This is the Wisdom upon which the world relies.' " Rabbi Yudai uses the passage from Psalms to equate *Resheit* (Beginning) with wisdom (*hokhmah*), and associates wisdom (*hokhmah*) with the second sefirah, *Hokhmah*. *Yirah* is thereby also associated not only with the *Resheit*, but also with the second of the sefirot, *Hokhmah* — the one that predates the inflation of the universe and marks the start of our conventional reality. The *Zohar* teaches that the *Resheit/Hokhmah* is the link to the initial stage of the big bang, as the universe expanded and creation began ex nihilo during the period of inflation:

> In the beginning [*B'Resheit*] — At the very beginning the king made engravings in the supernal purity. A spark of blackness emerged in the sealed within the sealed from the mystery of *Ein-Sof* [Without-Limit], a mist within matter, implanted within a ring, no white, no black, no red, no yellow, no color at all. Within the spark, in the innermost part, emerged a source.... It was not known at all until, from the pressure of its penetration, a single point shone. Beyond this point nothing is known, and so it is called *Resheit*, the first word of all.... Then afterward *B'Resheit* comprised Resheit and *Hokhmah* [Wisdom].

Resheit (the big bang); *yirah* (awareness); *Hokhmah* (wisdom and the unfolding sefirot): these three are all manifestations of the same creative process. Chapter 7 will consider how these insights of the Kabbalah on awareness lend a novel perspective to the physical processes of the Creation. First, though, I want to enhance your own levels of appreciation and awareness of the universe even further by considering not just the majesty of the cosmos, but the fabulous precision with which it is endowed.

THE ANTHROPIC PRINCIPLE

A Miraculous World?

The universe is vast, complex, and composed of many remarkably varied and wondrous things, from quarks to deoxyribonucleic acid, from peanuts to galaxies, from black holes to people. We can appreciate it. We may be awed by it. Surely it is worthy of notice that we — here, and today — are also able to describe and understand it, complex and diverse as it is, even if our knowledge is still incomplete. Considering that it took about 13.7 billion years for such an astonishing ensemble of forms to be created, is it not also striking that with only a few decades of study, creatures like us can learn enough to comprehend it, and even to model it well enough to make amazingly accurate predictions (for example, of eclipses), and to contribute to a further improvement in our own understanding? Humans, uniquely among all the forms of life on Earth, have the ability to discover and understand those laws and to unravel the basic nature of matter. (Although in fairness, it is worth considering if we are just deluded by hubris.) As far as we can determine, we have made amazing progress in genuine understanding, and that is very likely not by accident. I think that it is therefore incumbent upon us to use our utmost talents to study these basic governing principles. In so doing, we praise the Creator. After all, might not the world be so miraculous (that is, unpredictable) that rational comprehension is impossible, or so complex that it is beyond a human life span or a human brain to grasp?

Yet the universe *is* both logical and relatively straightforward: it does lend itself to understanding by the rational scientific method, even while being remarkably ordered, considering that it began from an explosion with all of the randomness and chaos one normally associates with anything blowing up. (See also the "formlessness and void [*tohu va-vohu*]" of Genesis 1:2.) While certainly sophisticated and complex, the essence of the world appears to us to be of the kind that is amenable to mathematics and other rational tools we can master in a lifetime, suggesting that we are somehow well positioned.

Consider the scale of structures in the universe, for example. Human beings, at about two meters in size (about 10^0 meters), are roughly mid-range in orders of magnitude (that is, exponents of

10) between the very smallest measurable things fifteen orders smaller, protons (about 10^{-15} meters), and the very largest thing twenty-six orders larger, the visible universe (about 10^{26} meters). The mass of a human is also roughly mid-range in orders of magnitude between the extremes of a proton (about 10^{-27} kilograms) and the visible universe (crudely about 10^{55} kilograms). As we contemplate the universe today, 13.7 billion years after it began to expand and diversify, many of its features appear to be incredibly and delicately tuned to our advantage. The *anthropic principle* was advanced to explain the precision with which the universe is suited to the existence of intelligent life. Before probing the principle itself, it would be worthwhile to look at some examples of it, coincidences that span the disciplines of cosmology, astronomy, physics, and chemistry, to illustrate how striking the anthropic argument can be.

The first coincidence implicates the big bang itself. Recall that if the expansion of the universe had been more modest, with galaxies receding at small velocities, then, like a rock tossed gently upward from the ground, the universe would eventually slow down and stop expanding because of the gravitational pull of all its contained mass, and would then begin to collapse. On the other hand, if the initial rate of expansion had been large, like a rock hurled fast enough to escape the Earth's gravitational pull, then the universe would never stop growing, but would continue getting forever larger simply because it had started off at such a high rate. In this oversimplified scenario, the fortunes of the cosmos depend only on the rate of expansion from the big bang and the amount of matter in the universe available to pull it back together — both of which are quantities that scientists can measure. Had the first situation been the case, then the universe would have collapsed after a short time — much shorter than the 13.7 billion years we measure — and there would have been no time for life to evolve, because evolution takes billions of years. Perhaps there would not even have been enough time for complex biological molecules to form. If, on the other hand, the expansion had been very rapid from the outset, then during the very early universe, neutrons would have decayed before they could combine with protons to form the stable atomic nuclei on which life is based. Later on in the development of the cosmos even that matter, still as particles, would have been so dispersed that the filamentary clumps needed to form the first generation of galaxies, stars, and planets would never have formed. In fact, our universe happens to be built exactly between these two extremes, with the density of matter lying dramatically close to the so-called critical density (the boundary value between these options) — so close that today it is measured to be within about 10 percent of that density.

Let me remind you of a further remarkable fact. Inflation models of the big bang predict that for the density of the universe to be so close to the critical density today, after 13.7 billion years of expanding and stretching, the equivalent tendencies to expansion and recollapse must have been balanced much more closely in the first seconds of the universe. When the universe expands, the density of matter naturally drops as the volume increases. Since the inward pull of gravity depends on the average distances between the matter, as the universe ages the balance between gravity (inward) and expansion (outward) gets progressively weaker. For the balance between them to be about equal today, in the very early universe the two tendencies had to be the same to about one part in an incredible 10^{52}. Why should the universe be so carefully tuned? From the anthropic perspective it is because we are here to measure it: in any other kind of expanding universe there can *be* no intelligent life. We might say, using a kabbalistic framework, that only the careful horizontal balance between *Hokhmah* and *Binah*, contextual framework and expansive birth, enables the vertical balance between *Hesed* and *Malkhut*, the structure of this world and its realization.

Astronomy provides many other examples of the anthropic principle. The Sun is the ultimate source of energy for life on our planet. Its stability over billions of years was necessary for life to evolve. Should we take for granted such a wonderful gift, a star whose life is long enough to enable evolution to proceed? By no means. The details of stellar atmospheres and nuclear physics are among the best understood aspects of modern astronomy. The Sun is powered by atomic fusion, in which four hydrogen nuclei (four protons) fuse in a series of three steps to form helium (the atom having two protons and two neutrons) in stages that release energy. In the first step, two particles collide to form a deuteron (a proton plus a neutron — the nucleus of the deuterium atom) with the release of a positron and a neutrino. This step requires the weak force. The deuteron has the simplest atomic nucleus after that of hydrogen, with its two particles bound together by the strong force but only just barely. Most atomic nuclei are spinning. If the deuteron were to spin around, the centrifugal force would overcome the strong force's binding attraction, and the deuteron could not exist. This is one of two fortunate coincidences regarding two-particle nuclei. The other one recognizes that two protons could also (like one proton and one neutron) be bound together by the strong force. They would form something that might be called the "di-proton." This happens to be impossible, though, because in reality the strong force is not quite strong enough to manage it against the electromagnetic repulsion. So, to within a mere few tens of a percent, the strong force is so finely tuned that on one hand the deuteron can exist, but on the other the di-proton cannot. This is indeed lucky for us. If the strong force were a bit stronger and the di-proton existed, nearly all of the protons in the early universe would have combined together (during that early phase associated with *Gevurah*) to form helium from di-protons instead of making hydrogen from deuterons. Stable, long-lived stars, which need to burn hydrogen and its isotopes, would have been impossible. If the strong force had been a tad weaker, then the deuterium nucleus (the deuteron) would not be stable, and the process that powers our Sun and stars would fail.

The elements that follow helium in the periodic table — that is, the ones with consecutively more protons in their nuclei, up to iron — are assembled in the fusion furnaces of stars; the more massive nuclei from iron to uranium (and beyond) were made in nova outbursts and supernova explosions that frequently mark the evolution and death of stars, and in some exotic interactions between the dense remnants of stars. Practically none were made in the early moments of the Creation. These elements, though, enable the existence of life — carbon is an obvious example. The precise recipes used by these stellar factories to assemble specific blends of elements from simple nuclei are critical, and the end products are by no means a foregone conclusion. Fusion is controlled in part by the strong force, and as we have seen, were this force only slightly more powerful, stars would not burn hydrogen, nor live very long. But on the other hand, were the strong force about 50 percent *weaker*, yet a different catastrophe would ensue. The nuclei of more complex, massive atoms would not be able to hold themselves together against spontaneous breakup (fission). The heavy nuclei of elements essential to life could not exist were the strong force much weaker than it is — they would break apart. The amazing thing is that the strong force is carefully tuned in favor of allowing life to exist, being neither too strong nor too weak. All of life, which needs starlight to thrive, depends on the strong force having a value perfect to a few percentage points. The electromagnetic force is also rather sensitively tuned, albeit not as precisely as the strong force. Were the electromagnetic force only three times stronger than it is (that is, having three times the repulsive power it now has between like-charged particles), even the relatively lightweight carbon nuclei that make up all organic life would spontaneously decay.

A final example of the anthropic principle comes from chemistry. All life, as far as we know and regardless of how extreme the environment is, depends on liquid water. Water is an unconventional chemical, however. Unlike most other liquids or solids, which shrink when they cool, water expands when it freezes. This is why ice cubes float, a vital, life-preserving quality that allows fish to survive in the winter below a lake's protective blanket of ice, instead of being frozen to death as the ice layer gradually thickens upward from the bottom of the lake to the surface, encompassing everything in it. If life evolved from primitive organisms in water, then it is hard to imagine how they (like fish) could persist if their world froze solid occasionally, allowing them no escape. Water also is peculiarly adept at dissolving other substances, another essential feature enabling it to support life and carry nutrients, but an unusual feature for a liquid nevertheless.

The reason why water has all these wonderful properties is well appreciated by scientists: water is made from two hydrogen atoms and one oxygen atom. Because of the way in which the electrons circle the hydrogen atom, bound to the proton at the nucleus by the electromagnetic force, the combination of these three electrically bound atoms gives the water molecule a strong "hydrogen bond" — the ability to link electromagnetically to other nearby molecules: other water molecules, for instance (to form crystalline ice when cold), or other chemicals (to pull them apart and dissolve them). It is by no means evident that the one proton–one electron pair that composes hydrogen necessarily will lead to the "hydrogen bond." It depends on how tightly the electromagnetic force binds these two particles, and this fundamental force has a strength that, like the strong force, can in principle take any value (at least as far as we know). It happens that the strength of the electromagnetic force is exactly right to produce the hydrogen bond. Were it stronger or weaker by even a few tenths of a percent, water would not exist with these properties essential for life.

In fairness, we do not know of any kind of life except one: the organic (that is, carbon-based), water-dependent life forms of Earth, nor do we know exactly what life is, or even what is required to give it vitality. It may be that some other, weird form of life exists somewhere, in which case these anthropic examples have overstated the argument for fine tuning. Although this is a logical possibility (one that is impossible to disprove if we have to search every distant place in the universe to be certain), it is also one that is so speculative that, without some kind of new information, we ought not to use it to undervalue the anthropic observations.

Of course, we may be deluding ourselves about all these matters — that is, about the significance of the remarkable suitability of the universe for life. A suitable universe may not necessarily imply anything. Furthermore, the universe could perhaps be suitable to life, yet not develop beings who can calculate the physical processes of the Creation.

A Purposeful World?

Philosophers, scientists, and mystics have long speculated that natural coincidences like the ones in the preceding section may not be the result of random luck, but the consequences of physical processes with specific goals. In their comprehensive book *The Anthropic Cosmological Principle*, John Barrow and Frank Tipler trace the earliest variations on this theme to Aristotle, who, unlike many other Greek philosophers, argued that it was not really possible to understand a natural phenomenon without understanding its "final cause" — that is, the reason for its existence. This notion is the *teleological* argument: order must have a purpose. To use a famous example, the mechanical perfection of a clock is purposeful — it exists in order for the clock to show the time. Our world, by the teleological argument, is ordered and so therefore must have a purpose. Theologians extended this idea to argue not only that the order (perfection) of the universe implies a purpose, but also that the purpose implies a conscious Designer.

There is a difference, however, between saying that order has a cause, and saying that order has a purpose. By the time of the Renaissance, natural philosophers such as Francis Bacon and René Descartes were objecting to teleological arguments on exactly this basis, and also because a teleological approach did not seem to offer a productive, scientific way forward. An increased interest in teleology followed Isaac Newton's discovery of a universal law of gravitation, because laws suggest Lawgivers, but Newton himself thought that the perfectly ordered laws of motion were themselves a suitable goal of nature. Although a firm champion of religion ("This most beautiful system of the sun, planets, and comets could only proceed from the counsel and dominion of an intelligent and powerful Being"), Newton also wrote: "Hitherto I have not been able to discover the cause of these properties of gravity from phenomena, and I frame no hypotheses; for whatever is not deduced from the phenomena is to be called a hypothesis, and hypotheses, whether metaphysical or physical, whether of occult qualities, or mechanical, have no place in experimental philosophy. . . . And to us it is enough that gravity does really exist and act according to the laws which we have explained."

With Darwin's discovery of natural selection, and as other branches of science (electromagnetism, for example) proved that the world is beautiful, complex, very old, and naturally comprehensible, arguments based on teleology became correspondingly more sophisticated. The anthropic principle is the current name for the teleological argument, and in the context of cosmology it has been advanced to explain the precision with which the universe was created as ideal for the existence of intelligent life (at least as we know it on Earth). The principle is formulated in several useful variants. The three most commonly stated alternatives are: (1) The universe just happens to be right to have produced life, and so life exists — in another, slightly different kind of universe, intelligent life would not be present; (2) the universe is the way it is *because* only this kind of universe can produce and nurture intelligent life, although why this should be the case is debated; and (3) the "strong" anthropic principle, which holds that the universe was *designed* to produce life.

The term *intelligent design* has come into vogue recently. It means the same thing as the strong anthropic principle, except that its name makes use of two familiar words that are more readily understood by the general public, and so it emphasizes a point that is somewhat veiled in the definition of the strong anthropic principle, namely, that there is a Designer. The term *intelligent design* is sometimes invoked by antagonists of science education, who advocate the teaching of scripture in the classroom to counter scientific explanations of how the Earth and humanity evolved as the result of understood natural physical processes. Needless to say, I think this attitude sadly misunderstands both the Bible and science. Nevertheless, examples of the anthropic principle itself offer other opportunities to contemplate and appreciate our remarkable world. All of the earlier illustrations, for example, are to my mind spiritually uplifting, and for this reason alone they are worth contemplating. The anthropic principle serves to familiarize us with the remarkable fine-tuning of the world in which we live. Cosmic nature is *not* necessarily favorable to life. Our world would be quite a different place if the physical constants differed from their current values even slightly. But for some reason, in our universe these constants are nearly exactly right for life to evolve and thrive. "Come see!" exhorts the *Zohar*. "Everything in the world came into being only for the sake of man, and all created things continue to exist only for his sake." Similarly, the Talmud states, "The whole world was created only for the sake of [the person] who fears God."

A quasi-scientific explanation — an entire set of them, actually — has been advanced to explain the many coincidences identified by the anthropic principle. The essence of these explanations is that there are (or were) *many* different universes. It does not matter how rare or balanced conditions must be for life — intelligent life arose only in those universe(s) in which the conditions were perfectly suited for it (the first formulation of the anthropic principle). This explanation is called the "many worlds" solution to the anthropic puzzle. The physics motivating these alternative solutions is extravagant, but not demonstrably incorrect. Inflation theory, for example, predicts that many universes with differing conditions, even an infinite number of them, will arise naturally from the vacuum. String theory, which has been dismissed by some for containing so many possible variables in its equations that it can predict practically anything, has turned this defect into an asset by showing that it can actually predict so many different, physically possible kinds of universes — about 10^{500} of them in the "landscape" — that intelligent life is almost certain to develop in some of them even if the conditions for life are very, very unusual accidents. In short, conditions for life may be rare, but with virtually limitless universes and opportunities, life arises in the ones that permit it. In chapter 9 we will return to explore some of these notions. Before we do, we return to the ideas of awareness introduced at the beginning of this chapter and consider the last of the essential theories of physics, the mysterious quantum mechanical nature of the world.

7 A QUANTUM OF SENSE

Why should the physical properties of the world be the way they are, so fantastically balanced as to enable intelligent life to evolve and thrive? Is this circumstance one of statistics and luck, many universes, or physical fundamentals, or is it perhaps about purpose in the universe? If it is the last, and if the strong anthropic principle is at work, dare a scientist wonder about the *purpose* that intelligent life serves in the universe? Although science does not address "final causes," to use the terminology of Aristotle, the purpose of a thing is not independent of the way it functions, and as science discovers new levels of order it simultaneously uncovers new constraints and insights about purpose. As the physics Nobel laureate and inventor of the maser and laser, Charles H. Townes, has observed, "Understanding the *order* in the universe and understanding the *purpose* in the universe are not identical, but they are also not very far apart.... Thus we readily and inevitably link closely together the nature and purpose of our universe."

The twentieth century's physical theory of nature — quantum mechanics — contains within its framework some revolutionary principles that allow radical scientific speculation about purpose. Quantum mechanics permits the suggestion that human thought (*hokhmah*, associated with the eponymous sefirah), by means of human observing (although more akin to witnessing than observing), was vital for the Creation. John Wheeler, an eminent professor of physics, a colleague of Einstein, and among the most creative and speculative thinkers in quantum mechanics, writes:

> We find that nature at the quantum level is not a machine that goes its inexorable way. Instead what answer we get depends on the question we put, the experiment we arrange, the registering device we choose. *We are inescapably involved in bringing about that which appears to be happening*.... [My emphasis.]
>
> In every elementary quantum process the act of observation or the act of registration or the act of observer-participancy or whatever we choose to call it, plays an essential part in giving "tangible reality" to that which we say is happening.... In what other way does an elementary quantum phenomenon become a phenomenon except through the act of observer-participancy? To what other foundation then can the universe itself owe its existence except billions upon billions of such acts of registration? What other explanation is there than this for the central place of the quantum principle in the scheme of things, that it supplies the machinery by which the world comes into being?

Of all the topics we have examined so far, the meaning of quantum theory is the most hypothetical, and its implications are among the most outrageous. In this chapter we will investigate quantum mechanics succinctly and try to clarify what Wheeler meant by the "tangible reality" conferred by "the act of observation."

It is essential to grasp some of the counterintuitive physical insights of quantum mechanics before we can appreciate the curious role an observer plays. Unlike the classical mechanics of the nineteenth century, which quantified our visceral, commonsense understanding of physical behavior, quantum mechanics asserts that nature has some very peculiar, almost nonsensical characteristics.

They are all traceable to the unexpected but incontrovertible observation that matter sometimes behaves like waves rather than like hard, tiny balls. Quantum theory accounts for this property of matter, with revolutionary implications.

Consider how normal ocean waves behave. The crests and troughs of two overlapping waves combine either to make their crests larger and troughs deeper (add), or to do the opposite when crests and troughs cancel each other out (subtract). This feature, wave *interference*, is said to be either constructive or destructive, respectively. A second key aspect of wave behavior is *diffraction*. If a wide wave front of moving water encounters a seawall with a narrow opening, when it emerges from the other side of the opening it will spread out — diffract — with a nearly semicircular wave emerging on the far side of the wall. The wave passes through the opening and radiates in all directions even though, on the incident side of the hole, the wave front was originally moving only in one direction — straight ahead. (Some of the wave is reflected backward, too.) Light waves (photons) similarly interfere with each other, adding or subtracting their intensities, and diffract — spreading around edges or through apertures. Two beams of pure light, like the kind that shines from a laser, will produce an interference pattern of alternating bright and dark stripes when they overlap on a wall, or will produce a "diffraction pattern" when they pass through a narrow opening. Another noteworthy property of a wave is its ill-constrained dimensions. A wave stretches out both before and behind its crest, and efforts to contain it only make it diffract, causing it to spread even more. Thus although a wave may be found mostly in one place, it will also have some presence well away from that spot. A wave cannot be confined to one specific place.

In the last century, experiments with particles of matter —

beams of electrons, for example — uncovered an astonishing property of matter: it behaves like waves, or packets of waves; matter interferes with itself, diffracts, and cannot be confined to one specific place. Today, beams of electrons are employed routinely to measure the dimensions and structures of substances by using the wave property of electrons to diffract around the crystalline structures of rocks or proteins, for example. A beam of electrons can produce interference fringes just like light, and it will produce a fringed shadow, not a simple, straight-line shadow, when passing a sharp edge. When beamed through a narrow slit onto a wall, electrons will strike not simply at one spot; they will produce a complex diffraction pattern in which they are completely absent from some places and bright elsewhere, just as light does when it diffracts. The wavelike behavior of particles benefits us daily and directly, in devices ranging from computers to superconducting wires, performing feats that a collection of classical particles could not emulate. Yet in the macroscopic world of our normal environment the wavelike nature of atomic matter is usually blurred. Billiard balls do behave like classical bouncing balls because they are each assemblages of more than a trillion trillion atoms whose wavelike properties when averaged over the large ensemble in the ball blend into classical behaviors.

Quantum mechanics successfully describes and predicts all these features. The mathematical description of a wave is provided by what is called its *wavefunction*. Quantum mechanics is the physical and mathematical description of the behavior of wavefunctions. Elementary particles, and people, are physically not so much a collection of little molecular balls as they are a complex of wavefunctions, the superposition of the many waves of their constituent particles.

Now we can finally complete the discussion of bosons and

fermions. Recall that everything in the universe — all particles, whether of matter or radiation — are either bosons or fermions. Atoms, molecules, people, substance in general, are made of fermions; particles of light (the photons) are bosons, as indeed are the corresponding particles that transmit the four forces: gravity, electromagnetism, strong, and weak. Each of these two fundamental types of particle has a corresponding character: bosons tend to aggregate, fermions must segregate. (Put another way, there is no limit to the number of identical bosons, but the Pauli exclusion principle, named for the physicist Wolfgang Pauli, who discovered it, specifies that no two fermions can be exactly alike.) In the section on symmetries in chapter 4, I remarked that bosons aggregate because they are symmetric in nature, while fermions are antisymmetric. Now I can explain what that means. It means that the *wavefunction* of bosons is symmetric in appearance, which is to say that when features describing a boson's wavefunction are flipped (in the sense of symmetry, for example left-right), nothing changes. The wavefunction looks the same: where the wave went up (or down) before the swap, it goes up (or down) after the swap. For fermions, the wavefunction is antisymmetric in appearance, meaning that when a feature of a fermion's wavefunction is swapped, the wavefunction changes its sign — where the wave went up (or down) before, it now goes down (or up). Electrons, for example, although they are basically the same, can be distinguished by where they are located, by how they are spinning, or in other ways. Bosons cannot be so distinguished. Because particles are waves, they can interfere with one another. Symmetric wavefunctions are indistinguishable, and when they interfere the waves are higher in amplitude in a way that causes them to aggregate. When antisymmetric wavefunctions interfere, the inverse happens: the opposing ups and downs of the waves cancel each other out, and in the case of nearly identical (and thus co-spatial) fermions (two protons, for example) they cancel completely; hence there cannot be two totally identical fermions. The simple, twofold nature of substance in the universe, and these corresponding characteristics, are a direct consequence of quantum mechanics. The classical picture of particles that existed before the 1920s conceived of nothing at all like this.

As a consequence of quantum mechanics and the wavelike behavior of matter, several other important physical consequences can be derived. Most famous is the Heisenberg uncertainty principle, named for the German physicist Werner Heisenberg, which explains that we cannot know precisely the position of a particle *and* its complementary velocity (actually, its momentum), because constraining one parameter, such as trying to force a wave to fit into a small space, causes its complement to increase. The product of the spread in uncertainty in a complementary pair is set by a universal constant: Planck's constant, a very small but fundamental constant of nature. (The speed of light is another fundamental constant.)

The Heisenberg uncertainty principle applies to other pairs (or, "conjugates") of physical properties of waves besides position-momentum, the most notable other pair being that of energy and time. The time interval over which the energy of a particle can be specified cannot itself be known precisely; rather, the product of the two must be less than Planck's constant. In the discussion of forces and fields, and then in the description of the early universe, "virtual particles" were shown to play an important role. Virtual bosons act as the mediators of the forces, for example. As long as a particle of a certain energy does not live longer than the allotted time (approximately equal to Planck's constant divided by that energy), its existence is permitted. These so-called virtual particles are constantly appearing and disappearing from within the vacuum.

Even in the classical descriptions of physics a measurement will slightly disturb a system and in this sense prevent our knowing exactly the position, momentum, or energy of a particle. It is important to realize that Heisenberg's uncertainty principle is completely different. It describes a thoroughly quantum mechanical phenomenon — a property of reality — not simply the practicalities of doing an experiment. More subtle equipment or sophisticated calculation techniques will never be able to improve our ability to know certain things beyond the limits set by Planck's constant.

There is one last aspect of quantum mechanics to introduce. It is even weirder than the consequences of the uncertainty principle. It relates to the composition of matter waves. Water waves are composed of the water itself moving. Sound waves are pressure waves carried by the molecules in the air. Light waves (photons) are made of vibrating electric and magnetic fields; this was part of the great discovery of James Clerk Maxwell, when he realized and described the relationship between electric and magnetic forces. But matter waves are totally different. In striking contrast to water waves or sound waves or electromagnetic waves, matter waves are not exactly waves *of* anything. Instead, matter waves express a *probability distribution* — the probability that an experiment will find the particle in one place or another. Remember that a wavefunction is not narrowly restricted in space, but is spread out. The probability of finding a particle in a place depends only on how large its wavefunction is at that place (that is, the amplitude of the wave at that location). Like other kinds of waves, probability waves oscillate up and down in space, acquiring larger values when the wave is at a crest, smaller values elsewhere along the wave, or even zero at some points. Although a particle is most probably localized to the general place where its wave amplitude is largest, the particle need not actually be found there — this is, after all, only its probability of being there. The particle retains a finite chance of being anywhere in the broad range of locations that its widespread wavefunction covers, with the likelihood of its being in *some* place at 100 percent.

If you are still with me, let's consider an electron in an atom, bound to the nucleus by the electromagnetic force between its negative charge and the positive charges of the protons in the center. In a quantum picture, the electron surrounds the nucleus as a distorted cloud of probabilities. The shape of that cloud — perhaps spherical but more likely a combination of symmetric, elongated lobes — can be calculated exactly by its physical properties and quantum mechanics. In contrast, an electron that is not bound to an atom but which can move freely interferes, diffracts, and spreads out like any unbound wave. When quantum mechanics describes how the *probability of a particle's being somewhere* interferes, diffracts, or spreads.

There is one final leap to make. Just as an electron, a proton, or an atom is extended broadly but is most likely to be found where its wavefunction probability is largest, so it is with collections of electrons, protons, and atoms: people, planets, and the universe itself are described by their probabilities. "In the experiments about atomic events we have to do with things and facts," Werner Heisenberg wrote, "[that is to say,] with phenomena that are just as real as any phenomena in daily life. But the atoms or the elementary particles themselves are not as real; they form a world of potentialities or possibilities rather than one of things or facts.... Atoms are not things."

QUANTUM MECHANICS AND AWARENESS (YIRAH)

If matter is described as a "wave of probabilities," then the crux of the puzzle for quantum mechanics is, what in the world does that *mean?* How do we reconcile this ghostly mathematical construct of matter moving through space and time with the corporeal world we experience? The abstract idea of an object as being spread simultaneously over many locations at once (as precisely described mathematically by its wavefunction) is an eerily counterintuitive notion. The picture becomes more bizarre when we realize that the same transcendental imagery persists even as that particle or body interacts with other particles or bodies, and even as it changes and evolves. It continues to develop, that is, until something existential happens to the object: it is *measured*.

The resolution of this thorny and still controversial question about the meaning of probability waves comes from how physicists understand the meaning of measurement. According to the most conventional traditional understanding of quantum mechanics, measurement — the sensing of a thing by a *conscious observer* — is the event that inalterably changes the wavefunction from possibility to reality, from being a dispersed set of probabilities of being simultaneously here and there to being not a probability at all but an actuality. Upon measurement, its being is realized in some specific place. This event is therefore marked by what is termed "the collapse of the wavefunction," meaning that the many possibilities of the wavefunction have now been reduced (or, collapsed) to only one.

The microscopic world of atomic particles is remote from our everyday experience. Perhaps, you might ask, the arcane ambiguities of probability wavefunctions become insignificant or irrelevant at human scales, where many atoms are involved? A frequently cited "thought experiment" to show that this is not the case is the example of Schrödinger's cat, named for Erwin Schrödinger, the physicist who first wrote down the equation that describes the quantum mechanical behavior of a wavefunction. The thought experiment perfectly illustrates the outlandish situations that arise when quantum probability effects manifest themselves in the macroscopic world. The argument goes as follows: Professor Schrödinger has locked his cat in a cabinet, along with a vial of poison gas rigged to topple and shatter if a Geiger counter detects the decay of even a single atom in a radioactive sample placed alongside the vial. The wavefunction of the atom, indisputably a quantum system, includes a combination of the probability that the atom will decay and the probability that it will not decay. The wavefunction for Professor Schrödinger's cat, which is causally determined by that same atom, therefore must also include these two options, and so the combined wavefunction of the whole system of cat plus vial plus radioactive sample must incorporate a cat that is possibly dead and possibly alive. The wavefunction of this combined system (or any complex system) continues to evolve and interact with other wavefunctions. But surely when we look in the cabinet we will see that the cat is either dead or alive — not a mathematical wavefunction in both states. We must have collapsed its wavefunction, but what does this superficially nonsensical quantum interpretation mean? The equations for the behavior of particles in the cabinet (or their ensemble as a cat) give the correct predictions (answers), but we ponder their meaning.

These next brief comments are a summary to provide a bridge to the upcoming discussion of human awareness. I particularly want to highlight the abridged nature of our quantum discussion here, because the arguments are sophisticated, important, and still controversial, and interested readers will want to take a closer look for themselves. Laypeople acquainted with the concepts of quantum mechanics may find these words familiar, but their meaning no doubt is elusive; even to practicing scientists the meaning of quantum mechanics is bizarre and uncertain. Readers unfamiliar with the ideas of quantum mechanics are strongly encouraged to consult the many excellent books that explore this miraculous feature of the physical world in greater detail.

Everyone agrees that Schrödinger's cat is a superposition of wavefunctions, and everyone agrees a measurement will record either a live cat or a dead one and not some half-and-half phantom. The disagreement centers on the meaning of the wavefunction and the meaning of the observer whose observation collapses it. These questions of *meaning* are at the heart of modern debate on quantum mechanics, and it is here that quantum mechanics merges with the deepest realms of philosophy and religion. The predominant view — the one traditionally cited by most physicists — is the "Copenhagen interpretation" of quantum mechanics from the school of Niels Bohr and is the basis for the capsule statement in the first paragraph: that the sensing of a thing by a conscious observer inalterably changes its wavefunction from a set of possibilities to a single reality. It explains that Professor Schrödinger's cat is indeed a wavefunction that is a superposition of a dead and a living cat... *until* a conscious being, by virtue of its consciousness and awareness, observes the cat and thereby forces the wavefunction into either one or the other of its possibilities. This act of measurement, effected only by a conscious observer, collapses (or, fixes) the wavefunction, and transforms it from having many possibilities to being a single actuality. The physicist Eugene Wigner noted, "The result of an observation modifies the wavefunction of the system.... It is at this point that the consciousness enters the theory unavoidably and unalterably."

Arguments have raged between the giants of quantum theory — Bohr, Einstein, Schrödinger, Wigner, John von Neumann, and others — and continue today over how, and when, the observer can effect this seemingly magical ability to collapse the wavefunction, a role that seems to place the conscious being outside of the quantum system. The most popular variant of this basic interpretation argues that it is the *complexity* of the human system, not consciousness, that really collapses the wavefunction in a measurement. Other recent, very speculative arguments suggest that still-to-be-demonstrated quantum gravity effects in certain brain cells are responsible for the collapse. Since consciousness itself is not understood, it may or may not be associated with either of these suggestions.

A possibly less exotic explanation, developed over the past decade, has won increasing support within the physics community and presents a serious challenge to the Copenhagen interpretation. This approach calculates that any quantum system — an atom or a cat — will naturally and quickly interact with its complex environment in a way that dramatically focuses the wavefunction into a relatively small subset of its most probable choices. The interactions happen in a way that reduces the interrelatedness (or, "coherence") between different parts of the wavefunction. The theory that models this behavior is termed "decoherence theory." In the words of one of its chief proponents, Wojciech Zurek, "Decoherence is a process of continuous measurement-like interaction between the system and an (external or internal) environment. Its effect is to invalidate the superposition principle," the principle that enables the wavefunction to interfere like probability waves.

A subtle implication of this approach is that questions of meaning about the wavefunction are immaterial; only that which is knowable is real, and the only knowledge possible about the wavefunction is that which is obtained by measurement. As Zurek explains, decoherence "settles these questions [of meaning] operationally," by limiting knowable reality to that which can be measured. He terms this the "existential interpretation" of quantum mechanics. Supporters of the Copenhagen interpretation object that all of the interacting particles in the environment of the quantum system are themselves quantum wavefunctions and therefore are incapable of altering the fundamental picture of the *combined* quantum system as a probability wave. Sophisticated new laboratory experiments, capable of configuring and manipulating specific quantum systems, are now testing subtleties of quantum theory and promise to shed light on these and other philosophical quantum mysteries.

The insights that the Kabbalah might bring to the issues of quantum mechanics are, in contrast, not widely considered, and the remainder of this discussion, my own speculations, must be recognized as very much more conjectural. I adopt a form of the traditional Copenhagen interpretation. I suggest that the measurement of a thing, in the quantum mechanical sense of fixing its wavefunction, is embedded in that sense of awareness of a thing — the paying attention to it — which is encompassed by the sefirah of *Hokhmah* and the principles of *yirah*. This kabbalistic interpretation of quantum interpretation (others may also be possible) posits that human awareness "collapses" the wavefunction and fixes the perceived reality. (Here, *reality* is used with its conventional meaning, since wavefunctions also have reality of their own.) Our awareness of Professor Schrödinger's cat transforms it from probability to certainty. Our attention to whether the cat is alive or dead collapses its wavefunction into one or another of its possibilities, and were we not to notice, the ghostlike mix of cat possibilities would continue to evolve. Not only does our awareness resolve the state of the cat, but it also fixes that which made the cat a cat.

Consider an even more fantastic implication. If we view a cat in a galaxy ten million light-years away (or, more likely but just as pointedly, some atomic process in that galaxy) through a powerful telescope, we are viewing a cat that must have lived, or an event that must have occurred, ten million years ago, since it has taken that long for the photons to travel to us, given their finite speed. Yet according to the Copenhagen interpretation, our measurement *now* immediately collapses the wavefunction *there*, in the distant galaxy. Recent laboratory experiments probing such quantum mechanical effects give results consistent with the notion that collapse occurs instantaneously. This kind of action at a distance is called a "non-locality" effect, because the effect is not local to the observer. The forced collapse of the wavefunction does not violate the rule that nothing can travel faster than the speed of light, because in this example nothing has so traveled. Non-locality seems to be a general property of quantum systems and is not restricted to features of the Copenhagen Interpretation, as far as we know.

What about the existence of our universe itself? What is it that measures and fixes the meta-wavefunction (the combination of all the wavefunctions of all the constituents in the universe) that makes *it* real? Could it be that the reality of the universe is somehow fixed only by *our* observations of it? If you accept the principles of the Copenhagen interpretation, is there any way to avoid this dramatic implication? According to John Wheeler:

> These considerations lead us at the end to ask if the universe is not best conceived as a self-excited circuit: Beginning with the big bang, the universe expands and cools. After eons of dynamic development it gives rise to observership. Acts of observer-participancy — via the mechanism of the delayed-choice experiment [that is, collapsing the wavefunction] — in turn give tangible reality to the universe not only now but back to the beginning. To speak of the universe as a self-excited circuit is to imply once more a participatory universe.

The Creation itself was a thoroughly quantum mechanical process. The evolving, expanding complex of matter and energy that is our universe comprises an unimaginable, complete, universal wavefunction whose probabilities multiplied and diversified for fourteen billion years until — according to these ideas — a being arose with conscious awareness capable of collapsing it (or part of it) into a real state of being. Some physicists have suggested that, even though special relativity constrains the parts of the universe we can affect by our observations (other parts are too far away from us to be seen), still the universe in its early moments was so small that there was ample time for its wavefunctions to be firmly connected. In that case the collapse of a part of the wavefunction today might limit, by nonlocality properties, the possibilities in remote parts of the universe whose wavefunctions back then were entangled with ours. Thus not only the universe but even aspects of its very creation were determined (or at least selected from myriad possibilities) by our awareness. The physicists Menas Kafatos and Robert Nadeau write in *The Conscious Universe:*

> What this means, in short, is that non-locality can be assumed to be a fundamental property of the entire universe.... And yet all that we can say about this reality is that it appears to be an indivisible whole whose existence is inferred where there is an interaction with an observer, or with instruments of observation.... If we assume that this reality is also a property of the entire universe at all times and scales, then we can infer that an undivided wholeness exists on the most primary and basic level in physical reality.

Although our own awareness, *hokhmah*, comes much later in space-time than the events of the Creation, in this approach our awareness is actually related to the cause and purpose of the *Resheit*, the point of the Creation, whose alter ego, as we have seen, is *Hokhmah*. The elaborate, intricate web of wavefunctions and interactions leading to the realities of our world is, in this quantum sense, fixed by human awareness.

How much of this incredible description corresponds to physical reality, and how much is hypothesis and speculation? Quantum mechanics has been one of the most successful theories ever developed. It is verified constantly in our own lives in the solid-state circuitry of our computers, cell phones, and CD players, at laser-scanning checkout counters, and in the light from the Sun, to name but a few examples. The limits of its predictions continue to be probed, tested, and confirmed. Quantum mechanics is extremely reliable so far, and further improvements to the theory will not change the way the world behaves, but only refine our mathematical descriptions of that behavior. The role of what I call *Hokhmah* is much more problematic. If decoherence theories and laboratory experiments lead to the abandonment of the Copenhagen interpretation and concomitant ideas about collapse via measurement, or even if it turns out that much simpler mechanisms than consciousness can effect wavefunction collapse, these ideas about *Hokhmah* are wrong. The debate about the meaning of quantum mechanics is not close to being settled, and controversy is very much alive. Some physicists adamantly advocate decoherence and its variants; others dismiss them as dodging the deeper philosophical implications of quantum mechanics. Progress is being made, but for now quantum mechanics remains as deeply puzzling as when Nobel laureate Richard Feynman made the following observations:

> I think it is safe to say that no one understands quantum mechanics. Do not keep saying to yourself, if you can possibly avoid it, "But how can it be like that?" because you will go down the drain into a blind alley from which nobody has yet escaped. Nobody knows how it can be like that.
>
> What I am going to tell you about [in quantum mechanics] is what we teach our physics students in the third or fourth year of graduate school.... It is my task to convince you not to turn away because you don't understand it. You see my physics students don't understand it.... That is because I don't understand it. Nobody does.

PURPOSE AND THE KABBALAH

The Lurianic Kabbalists emphasized that the process of the Creation, which originated as a formless expansion, necessarily involved the aspects of shaping, constriction, and limitation. The *Zohar* says, "When the most secret of secrets sought to be revealed, He made first of all a single point, and this became Thought. He made all the designs there; He did all the engravings there, and He engraved within the hidden holy luminary an engraving of hidden design... the beginning of construction."

The sefirot are not simply processes that were once active in the earliest moments of the Creation; they are continuous channels of Divine influence to the world. *Gevurah* was not only the dominant sefirah functioning during the epoch of leptons, but also the sefirah, channel, or process that the Kabbalists associated with constraining and shaping the uniformly expanding material into galaxies and stars. According to kabbalistic doctrine, the great pressures that such constriction and separation produced in the universe led inevitably to the introduction of negativity into the world, the result of what they term the "breaking of the vessels," the "containers" for the light of the sefirot as the evolving world took form. The rupturing of these metaphoric vessels represents the world's imperfection.

The Kabbalists place immense importance on the process of *tikkun olam*, repair. Personal *tikkun* is the path we traverse to return ourselves to spiritual wholeness. Cosmic *tikkun*, *tikkun olam*, is our effort to return the world to a perfect condition. Judaism emphasizes the importance of behavior. God's commandments, the *mitzvot*, are the guides to moral and holy actions. Jewish mysticism likewise emphasizes behavior in this world versus the rewards of the next one and adopts a fundamentally cosmic perspective: humanity is actually God's *partner* in the Creation. Indeed, this is our purpose. The *mitzvot* are steps to improving a world born with imperfection, the "vessels" shattering as the form of the universe took shape. *Tikkun olam*, repairing the world, is humanity's cosmological purpose to perfect what was begun 13.7 billion years ago. In the Kabbalah, the process is accomplished with good deeds that serve not only as goals in themselves but also as tools to deepen our sensitivity and appreciation. Action is enhanced by deep attention, which the rabbis call *kavvanah*, from the word meaning "to be focused." *Kavvanah*, or attention, can be associated with the kind of *yirah* I argue is required to collapse the wavefunctions of the world we view. Perhaps it is not such a great stretch of imagination finally to associate the idea of humanity's *tikkun olam* with the quantum mechanical notions of awareness and the bringing of the universe from probability to reality. From the *Zohar*: "One must direct one's heart and one's will so that both the upper and lower realms may be blessed.... The end of all is particular knowledge: to know Him in particular. And the general and the particular are the beginning and the end."

God creates, and by virtue of creating introduces separation. This is the resonant significance of *yirah*, the fear-awareness that comes from being separate, and from being aware of being separate (or, self-aware), yet which is essential for the ability-power to transform what is only *possible* into what is *actual* through quantum measurement. The Talmudic sage Rabbi Akiva ben Joseph (50–135 CE) expressed the thought this way: "Beloved is humanity who were created with free will [literally: in God's image], and even more beloved are they that this [gift] was made known to them."

Religion addresses the question of human purpose. The Copenhagen interpretation of quantum mechanics, and the Wignerian approach to consciousness, offer a bridge from physics to purpose (even without a kabbalistic framework). Should decoherence or other theories dispose of this particular link to meaning, quantum mechanics would continue to be inspirational, but unable to contribute in this way to an explanation of the human situation. Even if consciousness does play a unique role in quantum collapse, it is not certain that awareness (as distinguished here from consciousness) is necessary, nor is the role of religion clearly necessary; these are only possible roles. But what we must admit is that these two superficially different approaches, science and religion, have many deep issues to wonder about together, and that as our understanding increases and descriptive language expands, they can provide important, alternative, mutually respectful perspectives from which to ponder the questions.

FROM NOTHING, EVERYTHING: CREATION EX NIHILO

Aristotle had no concerns about creation ex nihilo, because the universe was eternal and unchanging in its essence — there was no creation. Some Jewish commentators also believed that the opening sentence of the Bible describes not an ultimate creation, but rather how the current Earth and heavens were formed from preexistent matter. The rationalist Jewish philosopher Maimonides disagreed and wrote in his *Guide for the Perplexed* that not only Aristotle, but all the philosophers he knew, argue that it is impossible for God to produce "anything from nothing," or to completely destroy matter either. This is not seen as a defect in God, but simply a logical impossibility, even for those who, like Plato in the *Timaeus*, disagreed in part with Aristotle by thinking that the heavens were "transient," in the sense that they could change in form and might have been fashioned out of something else. Maimonides, to the contrary, asserted that the Bible holds "the heavens have been formed out of absolutely nothing." Not only that, he contended that "even time itself is among the things created." The Kabbalist Nachmanides, who disagreed with Maimonides on many other issues, agreed on this one, in conformance with basic kabbalistic doctrine. In the words of the *Zohar*, "When the Holy One, Blessed Be He, created His worlds, He created them from nothing, and brought them into actuality, and made substance out of them." Nachmanides explains in *Commentary on Torah* that the creation proceeded from "absolute, certain nothingness." He also adds, as we saw earlier, that the first thing to be created was not matter, but only the light: "Nothing was created during the first stage except light." It is a curious development that today all of the major proposed theories of cosmogenesis, even alternative ones like the now doubtful steady-state theory of Hoyle, Bondi, and Gold, invoke creation ex nihilo. (The steady-state theory posits that the universe is expanding today because it has always been expanding, and that new matter is being created in some unknown way to fill the voids and maintain the cosmic density of matter.)

A remarkable and unique feature of gravity enables creation to proceed ex nihilo in the inflationary picture. The property is best grasped by contrasting it first with the properties of a force without this particular character, the electromagnetic force. When two opposite but equally charged unconstrained particles move toward each other, as they will because they are attracted by the electromagnetic force, they will speed up, moving together faster and faster as they approach each other. Their kinetic energy — that is, their energy of motion — increases. Since energy is conserved, where does this new kinetic energy come from? As described in chapter 4, the electromagnetic field contains potential energy, and it is the energy from the field of the two particles that is converted into their energy of motion.

In the same way, as two masses are attracted together by gravity, the energy in their gravitational field is also converted into the energy of motion of the masses. But there is one essential difference: in the electromagnetic case the attracting charges are *opposite* in nature; in the gravitational case they are the *same*. (Indeed, there is only one kind of gravitational "charge.") Were the two approaching electrically charged particles to merge, the *net* charge would be zero (positive and negative exactly canceling), and so of course their field, and their field's energy, would also disappear. It would be swapped for the total kinetic energy (the motion) of the merged particles. For approaching masses, however, the conjoined object is twice as massive, with twice the field, and so it has twice the field energy. This example makes it clear that gravity has a curious property: the energy stored in a gravitational field is described by *negative* energy, which gets larger as more is subtracted.

The negative energy of the gravitational field energy has fantastic implications, as Alan Guth, the founder of the inflationary theory of the Creation, realized when he calculated the effects of his inflationary universe model. An *expanding* universe will release stupendous amounts of *positive* energy from the vacuum as it undergoes inflation. When the gravitational field expands to fill new space, its energy decreases while other energy is released — the total [net] energy of the universe before and after the Creation remains the same: zero. This gravitational energy, spontaneously released in the Creation, is the source of the matter and energy that produced particles as the universe cooled. As Guth put it, "Inflation is the ultimate free lunch." Until a theory is developed that combines the gravitational force with the other three in a quantum mechanical framework, many of these scientific ideas should be considered speculative, but at least creation ex nihilo has some basis in current physical concepts.

This explanation of creation in the language of modern physics helps to clarify the Kabbalah's imagery of the Creation. The Living God Who Is Blessed created the universe and life from the principles of gravity, a manifestation of Divine love. Divine love (*ahavah*) is subsumed in *Keter*, the highest of the sefirot, the source of self-attraction and gravity. It is withheld by *Hokhmah* until the "spontaneous symmetry breaking" of the strong force releases energy in the inflation during the sefirah of *Binah*. This freed energy of attraction then cools and condenses during the phases of *Hesed* and *Gevurah*, generating the first stable particles of matter and initiating our new world. The Kabbalah of course does not put things this way, but it does use metaphors of attraction followed by phased expansion that lend themselves to this physical interpretation. And why was the world created at all? Arguments from the strong anthropic principle and quantum mechanics suggest one answer: the purpose of the existence of the universe is intelligent life, whose free will and awareness ground the universe.

8 MIRACULOUS WILL

INTELLIGENCE AND SELF-AWARENESS

If life is a significant feature of the universe, we may wonder whether there is any distinction to be made between amoebas and people. *Intelligence* seems like a useful differentiating criterion, with intelligent life being defined as life capable of thought and reason. I suggest an important proviso for our discussion: true intelligent life is that form of life capable of achieving awareness in the sense of the previous chapter, that is, an ability to collapse the wavefunction of the universe or its parts. It is not yet known how — or even whether — these two definitions are related.

What is it about intelligent life that enables it to make such powerful, wavefunction-anchoring observations? Is it something about the brain alone, or might it also involve other organs or bodily systems? How might such a process or processes work? For example, if intelligence is a function only of brain power, animals with complex brains must also be intelligent. Similarly, a digital computer might someday have enough calculating power to acquire this kind of awareness. On the other hand, perhaps this ability is not limited to a complex brain or to any other bodily functions. Were something else required, then perhaps a soul might be defined in the same functional context as I have defined intelligent life, namely, that aspect of life which enables it to collapse a wavefunction. For the Kabbalists, the soul is an obvious part of humanity's makeup, a facet of Adam's being that God designed into the Creation. (The Kabbalists actually portray the human soul as having five hierarchical levels, related to the four worlds and the sefirot and called, respectively, Unity, Vitality, Breath, Spirit, and Soul — of which only the last three are obviously related to functions of the mind.) For the scientist the existence of a soul, or the less controversial nature of intelligence, remains largely a question of philosophy, although one that, like cosmology itself, is gradually yielding to the scientific method.

Computer scientists commonly espouse the view that intelligence (so-called artificial intelligence, or, "AI") can indeed be achieved with computers. How to tell whether or not a computer actually has AI is a little tricky. The usual method proposed is the famous "Turing test," proposed by the British mathematician Alan Turing (1912–1954). The premise of this test is that a machine is intelligent, by definition, if it cannot be distinguished from a human by its response to any series of questions. An obvious trick question because of its great difficulty, for example, would be to ask a computer, "What is the fifth root of two?" It would reveal itself to be a computer if it gives the correct answer, so a machine with real AI would be programmed to recognize this stratagem and instructed when to lie or evade. It would also be programmed to learn from experience and modify its behavior accordingly. These arguments are based on the reductionist principle that intelligence, like anything else in the world, can be gradually built up from the simpler components we understand, acquiring qualitatively new properties as it becomes more complicated. It is hard, but presumably possible in this way of thinking, to prepare a computer with all the trick questions accounted for, and to program it to evade them. A minority of scientists and philosophers disagree — Roger Penrose and Hubert Dreyfus, for example. They argue that the Turing test will never be genuinely passed, because human intelligence and experience go beyond the simple "yes or no" logic of digital electronics.

My thesis is that the working premise of artificial intelligence is misleading: intelligence is not determined simply by an ability to answer questions in a Turing test. Intelligence in the sense we need for quantum mechanics involves a sense of awareness. This may or may not be linked to the ability to appear intelligent to human interrogators. Similarly, it is not clear how consciousness — and especially self-consciousness — relates to awareness. A common view holds that consciousness is a prerequisite for awareness. Animals may be conscious, for example, and they may be aware, but as far as we can tell they do not have an abstract language and so are neither intelligent nor aware in the senses I use here. One might even adopt the reverse thinking for the case of computers: they might be aware, or intelligent, but not really conscious. Penrose and others address the quantum mechanical facets of intelligence as well, even attempting to link it to an eventual theory that will include gravity, but these speculations are so far only preliminary musings.

FREE WILL

The brilliant first-century Talmudic personality Rabbi Akiva ben Joseph was also famous as a mystic, the student of mystics, and an early Kabbalist. He is reported to have ascended to paradise and returned safely. Rabbi Akiva formulated a bold epigram that addresses the mystery of awareness in the sense we have discussed, and coupled it to another key concept, that of free will. Free will is the control we all believe we have to decide to do something, and then to do it. Free will is a persistent mystery, however, because we not only believe that we have free will, we also believe that every event occurs as the result of some earlier causal event — indeed, is the necessary result of that causal event. But in that case there is no role for genuine free will. The riddle of free will is particularly acute because it involves issues of the mind, consciousness, causality, and probably some other things as well.

Rabbi Akiva captured an essential Jewish acceptance of the paradox of free will when he declared in his epigram, "Everything is foreseen, yet free will [literally, *permission*] is given." In a subsequent generation, Rabbi Hanina bar Hama (c. 220 CE) reformulated the epigram as follows: "Everything is in the hands of Heaven, except the fear [*yirah*] of Heaven." From Rabbi Akiva and Rabbi Hanina we understand that *yirah* — awareness, the attribute that in our speculations about quantum mechanics may bring about the collapse of the quantum wavefunction — is related to free will. Free will appears as a prerequisite for awareness, a Divine gift to humanity paradoxically granted by an omnipotent and omniscient Creator. Like the paradoxes encountered in general relativity, this self-referential one also seems less illogical when considered in the light of modern science. The reality of the universe depends in some way on having a subset of its many quantum possibilities selected by an intelligent observer. Selection is an act of choice, not one of mechanistic determination. An intelligent observer with free will is necessary for a universe whose very reality depends on that being's conscious ability to notice it.

Rabbi Akiva may have asserted the paradoxical principle of free will, but other religious thinkers, even Jewish ones, have not been so certain. Disputes about free will have developed into bitter controversies between and within many religious circles. The clearest statement of the alternative Jewish view is the one of the nineteenth-century Hasidic rabbi of Izbitz, Mordekhai Yosef, known by his nom de plume, the Mai-Hashiloah. He states, twisting Rabbi Akiva and Rabbi Hanina's dictum on its head, " 'Everything is in the hands of Heaven except for the fear of Heaven.' So it seems, because of the limited capacity of human understanding. But, in truth, everything is in the hands of Heaven, *even* the fear of Heaven. It is just that in *this* world God has hidden His ways."

Science has many pertinent insights to offer on free will, providing yet another instance where science and religion can converse. First, of course, is the classical view of physics. The laws of physics are known, and even were they not known, they nevertheless would still exist. They specify with precision how a system, even a very complicated one with vast numbers of particles, will evolve over time. All that is needed to predict what will happen is to stipulate the initial conditions of the system, and then the laws themselves, through simple cause and effect, will propagate the system automatically to determine what happens next. In essence, Rabbi Yosef is right: we may not be smart enough to figure out the future, but in truth everything is predetermined by the rules. Free will is an illusion.

In my view there are four modern ideas that make this classical approach much less assured and more interesting: quantum theory, complexity, chaos theory, and computing. The first, quantum theory, refers to those quantum mechanical ideas about the conscious observer that I have already discussed. Quantum mechanics is strictly causal in the sense of classical mechanics, in that quantum objects are governed by laws that can predict precisely what happens to them as they evolve in time. The hitch is that the predictable, evolving quantum objects are probability distributions — the wavefunctions we encountered earlier. Only the final observation determines which of the possibilities has been actualized. In this Copenhagen-interpretation sense, it may be that free will exists as a consequence of our quantum world, which requires an aware observer to turn potentiality into actuality.

The world is a place of complexity, the next concept to consider. Every single handful of matter has more than a trillion trillion atoms. It is even more complex to our perception because our brains have about one hundred billion neurons, and between them are a vastly larger number of interconnections. Even if every atom moved in a predictable way, and even if every neuron (and the neighbors that help it decide) were to "fire" in a predictable manner, it is far from obvious that the ensemble of atoms and neurons would also be predictable. The possibilities are too numerous and too complex. According to one currently popular analysis, free will is what is called an "emergent phenomenon," one that is not an obvious part of the fabric of the rules but rather a property that turns up when systems become complex. An example of an emergent phenomenon is the apparent majesty of a waterfall, whose behavior is completely governed by known laws of science, but whose intricate beauty those laws cannot themselves infer. Life itself is regularly cited as another example, because life is certainly governed by the rules of molecular chemistry, but its wondrous essence is just as clearly more than unadorned chemistry. Free will and life may somehow emerge from the physical world as a consequence of the world's complexity. The strongest objection to this approach is that it is not at all clear that emergence can establish qualitatively new phenomena, such as life or free will, that are not already latent in the basic system.

Chaos theory introduces a variation on this theme. Even in relatively simple situations, objects can behave and interact with one another in ways that make their futures fantastically sensitive to the exact conditions of their past. Chaos theory describes this behavior. The precise positions of the planets in our solar system, for example, though governed entirely by the well-known law of gravity, are not predictable to arbitrary precision, because the system of mutual gravitational interactions is complicated enough to be chaotic. It is impossible in principle to predict the location of even an asteroid arbitrarily far into the future. A famous, if somewhat exaggerated, example is the so-called butterfly effect, in which the climate in South America can be affected by a butterfly in North America flapping its wings. Physical principles like the conservation of energy, however, restrict the range of possible chaotic outcomes; not everything is possible. In short, a chaotic system follows clear rules of cause and effect, but the evolution of the system is unpredictable in detail. Free will might entail some kind of chaotic unpredictability.

There is one final take on the origin of free will. It is possible to object to these previous assertions about complexity or chaos. Computers, after all, have changed the way we think about complicated calculations. So what if there are astronomically many subtle interactions at play in our human drama? Several decades ago the first computers, such as ENIAC (the Electronic Numerical Integrator and Computer), weighed thirty tons and managed about five thousand calculations per second. Today we talk about "petflops," calculations trillions of times faster, and computers vastly more powerful might someday do as many as 10^{18} operations in a second. Perhaps in another fifty or one hundred years, or maybe in another thousand, computers will be able to keep track of every one of these atoms, neurons, and their pathways, even in systems that are complex or chaotic, in the sense that they will be able to predict outcomes far enough ahead — say, one lifetime — with acceptable accuracy. Prophecy might be risky today, but routine in another century. In this case, classical physics could be right about free will — there is none. All we need is more computing power.

The counterargument is that more than just computational power is required for certain well-defined calculations corresponding to processes that are called "noncomputable." For these problems no amount of computation can ever arrive at an answer. Even a fully deterministic physics could not use computers to calculate a result of the noncomputable process. Clear but familiar examples of these processes are rare. One is the case of deciding whether or not a particular small set of polygonal tiles of specific (but not simple) shapes can be fitted together and laid down on a floor in a way that fully covers an arbitrarily large area without leaving any gaps *and* in a pattern that never repeats itself exactly. These tiles are obviously not hexagonal in shape, since such symmetric tiles, and all other commonly shaped tiles, do repeat their patterns rather obviously. These special ones have quite nonintuitive geometries. Nevertheless, sets of such tiles have been designed by the physicist Roger Penrose, who also proved they satisfied the condition that they never repeat their pattern, and that no computer computation could ever figure out that they never repeat. If the world has within it, perhaps at the quantum level, some noncomputable processes, then in principle no computer will be able to predict its complete future. At the moment it is not known whether there are such physical processes operating, but neither do we have a theory of everything. Perhaps such an ultimate theory will have embedded within it a noncomputable component. If it does, perhaps such a theory will offer a mechanism for free will.

While professional philosophers, biologists, neurologists, physicists, and others ponder the nature of free will, or the meaning of free will, or even the existence of free will, most of us simply take it for granted that we somehow do possess this wonderful privilege. It exists, but it's complicated, and we don't understand it. In conclusion, then, science and religion seem to agree at least on this: it is not obvious whether there is free will or not, or (perhaps more important) if there is free will, exactly what that implies. The theologian John Polkinghorne has observed that if we are generous enough to allow ourselves the benefit of the doubt in regard to this mysterious power, which we sense but do not comprehend, perhaps we should be prepared to grant the same thing to a deity who exists and who can likewise express free will, although in a sense that we may perhaps never understand.

It strikes me that there are two lessons to be drawn. By now you can guess the first: the topic of free will is another area for mutual discourse and the respectful exchange of thoughtful ideas between science and religion. The second is that we cannot avoid taking responsibility. Neither religion nor science offers us absolute assurance about our fate. On the contrary, taken as a whole they are in broad agreement that the case is quite open, even though particular approaches can, and do, disagree. Even were a conceptual breakthrough to someday prove we do not actually have free will, we may still need to *act* as though we do. Taking responsibility by acting as if there is free will, whether proven or not, is part of being aware. Acting responsibly is part of that purposeful awareness that helps to make the world a better place, part of what the Jewish mystics call *tikkun olam*: repairing the world.

INTELLIGENT LIFE IN THE UNIVERSE

Is humanity unique in being intelligent, in the quantum mechanical sense of observing? The Bible certainly avouches humanity's singular nature on Earth. In the midst of the luxurious richness of life forms that God called into existence in the six days of Genesis, only the creation of human life was deliberated in advance (Genesis 1:26); only humanity commanded God's *attention.* Furthermore, only humanity was created with a soul (Genesis 2:7), in a passage that incorporates three of the five kabbalistic levels of soul. God's attention endows every human with a feature that in turn enables our own capacity for attention, namely *yirah* — awareness. Animals may also have souls, in the sense of an eternal aspect of their being, and Genesis certainly uses two of the terms for *soul* when discussing animals, but not in the sense that animals are capable of *yirah.* Computers, although smart and perhaps even capable of passing the Turing test, likewise do not have awareness. On this Earth, only humans have a soul capable of *yirah*-awareness.

The dramatic revolution in cosmology during the past few decades is echoed by an equally dramatic one in biology. The miracle of genetics is now unfolding to our comprehension. These revolutions join in speculating about the possibility of life, even intelligent life, elsewhere in the universe. Perhaps the universe was created to be ideal for life; perhaps it was even created for the sake of life. To the extent that we understand biology, however, it seems possible that carbon-based life like ours could exist elsewhere. If life is common, then what is the role of Homo sapiens?

The advances of modern science have allowed astronomers to estimate rather closely the number of galaxies in the universe, the number of stars in a galaxy, and even the number of possible Sun-like stars. More than 150 variegated planets have already been discovered orbiting stars other than our Sun, and in the coming decades this number will without doubt grow by hundreds or thousands. Surely, many scientists believe, hospitable planets in the universe must number in the millions, although none of the ones found so far could sustain Earthlike life. Furthermore, astronomers have detected water, carbon, and more than a hundred other complex molecules — from formaldehyde to complex "polyaromatic hydrocarbons" — floating in interstellar space, some of them composed of chains of hundreds of carbon atoms. Carbon is the backbone for life as we know it. Considering that life on Earth exists under an extreme range of conditions, from the ocean depths to the tops of mountains, life is certainly resilient. With abundant carbon, chemicals, and locales, life may be common in the universe. There is, however, one overriding uncertainty: how easy is it for *intelligent* life to form? For if it is a rare occurrence, say a one-in-a-ten-billion chance, then even if there are billions of attempts, we could be alone.

Despite all the science fiction, fantasy, and wonderfully creative special effects of movies, we have to acknowledge that life in space — of any kind — is certainly not *very* common. Although there are interesting, even tantalizing, hints from meteorites, there is still no life known anywhere in the universe except here on Earth. Enrico Fermi, one of the insightful founders of modern physics, asserted that the very absence of unequivocal evidence of extraterrestrial life is proof that life is not common in the universe. He argued that, since there are apparently so many suitable planets for life, if intelligent life were easy to form, there should be many advanced civilizations in the galaxy — cultures technologically advanced, willing, and interested enough to travel to Earth to visit us now, even while other civilizations might choose not to. That we know of none — zero — suggests strongly that life is *not* easy to make; intelligent life does not exist anywhere in our galactic neighborhood except here on Earth.

We do not know what, if any, special properties are required to form life. Neither do we know whether some additional special quality is needed to enable intelligence in the sense I have been using. Computers can be made to be very smart but maybe not intelligent; perhaps in a laboratory, life can be created but might not have the capacity for intelligence — amoebas do not have souls. An equally noteworthy observation is that despite the sophistication of modern chemistry and biochemistry, life has never been created from chemicals in the laboratory. I suspect that were life easily generated, we would create it here on Earth before we located it elsewhere in the cosmos. Again, the fabrication of life from chemicals in a test tube by no means implies it is possible to fabricate *intelligent* life in the laboratory, nor would the discovery of simple life forms in space demonstrate that intelligent life exists in space.

It is worth highlighting four underappreciated facets of this question. They are reminiscent of the discussion of the anthropic principle, in that they emphasize the rather specific conditions on Earth that made intelligent life possible. The first is the felicitous environment with which our planet is blessed, and which makes Earth almost certainly the only place in our solar system capable of intelligent life. As far as we know, or even can imagine, intelligent life requires a sophisticated chemistry. Recall that in the creation of the early universe, only hydrogen and helium were produced, with virtually no other kinds of atoms. It took generations of stars, novas, and especially supernovas to manufacture the elements essential to life in their nuclear furnaces, and to disperse those atoms into the cosmos to be recycled into planets and their denizens. Iron, for example, is the critical element that enables the hemoglobin in the blood both to carry oxygen to the cells and then also to release it for burning (the source of our energy). Iron did not exist until it was created in the final stages of a dying massive star, and so only those stars that formed from the debris of earlier explosions had the iron-enriched material needed for life in the planets that ring them. Precisely the need for the rich broth of heavy elements could make intelligent life rare, even if life is otherwise easy to germinate, because many stars in our galaxy are deficient in these heavy elements. Not all stars become supernovas; only very massive stars do. It is not fully understood what prompts these uncommon giants to form from enormous clouds of gas and dust in space. Observations of other galaxies where clusters of giant stars are seen suggest at least one circumstance that can encourage such formation — the collision between two galaxies. These stupendous interactions are thought to be common in the universe. If intelligent life was a "goal" of the universe, in the sense of the strong anthropic principle, it must be that the existence of the vast and intricate dance of colliding galaxies, the dramatic birth and death of stars, and the eons of processing atoms in nuclear cauldrons, all were necessary, purposeful parts of the long process required to produce the conditions that made life — us — possible.

A second undervalued contributor to the evolution of life on Earth is the Moon. In all of the solar system, only our Moon is large enough, compared to its parent planet, to produce substantial tides. The daily stirring of the shoreline, and the washing and refreshing of the primitive Earth's life pools, may have been essential to enabling simple single-celled creatures to evolve. The Moon is certainly an oddity, created from a tremendous collision between the Earth and a Mars-size object that nearly obliterated our home planet — but didn't quite. Instead, this catastrophe led to the tides. Very likely it was also responsible for tilting the Earth's spin axis by $23\frac{1}{2}$ degrees, thus providing for our salubrious seasonal variations.

Our lives depend on a world where liquid water is abundant. In fact the only absolute requirement for life in the varied places where it is found on Earth is liquid water. Earth is the only planet in the solar system where liquid water is known to exist, although it once existed on Mars and may perhaps still lie under the putative ice sheets of Europa (a moon of Jupiter); future space exploration will find out. The Earth's surface temperature is an elaborate function of solar illumination, natural underground heating, and the planet's atmosphere, but for its temperature to stay in the narrow range where most of its water is liquid, neither frozen nor boiling, requires all of these parameters to be just right. If the Sun were much hotter or colder, or if the Earth were much closer to the Sun or farther away, liquid water might not exist. For that matter, recent models suggest that, were it not for the stabilizing presence of a giant planet in our solar system, Jupiter, the Earth might never have ended up safely in the orbit it has, or if it did, it would have been bombarded by a deluge of deadly comets and asteroids, which were instead swept aside by Jupiter's gravitational field. All these calculations show that even in a universe where stars and planets are ubiquitous, Earthlike planets may be rare.

The fourth and final example illustrates that even an ideal chemistry and climate are not enough to create intelligent life on Earth. Life formed quickly on the young Earth, in less than about half a billion years. But then it took nearly another 3.5 billion years to evolve beyond the simplest organisms. Intelligence sprang up only in the most recent few moments of the cosmic clock. It took three times longer to make intelligent life after the Earth formed than it took to make the great webs of galaxies and stars after the Creation. We understand how those galaxies and stars formed, as gravity slowly drew together the great clouds of gas until they coalesced into nascent stars, and we know why (or at least we think we are making good progress toward knowing why) it took about a billion years for this to occur. Was an analogous process needed to produce intelligent life, some complex chemical reactions that for some reason needed 3.5 billion years to complete? We don't know. Not only do we not know of any such process, we realize that during the long wait for intelligence, many accidents occurred that were antithetical to its emergence. The Earth suffered disasters, the formation of the Moon being just one. Over billions of years the Earth endured numerous collisions with meteorites. One notable collision sixty-five million years ago, the now infamous Chixlub event, killed off the dinosaurs, leaving behind the eponymous crater off the coast of Mexico. These successful creatures had dominated the Earth for a hundred million years — far, far longer than humanity has been around — and they might possibly have continued to dominate the Earth, except for that collision, which filled the Earth's atmosphere with black dust and led to their extinction, thus clearing the way for other species to fill the biosphere and introduce true intelligence to the planet. Perhaps life on other worlds, if it exists, is dinosaurlike, and only in the extremely unlikely case of a massive (but not too massive) meteorite collision might intelligent creatures there stand half a chance of succeeding and evolving.

And what of evolution itself? Scholars, using the latest tools of biology and paleontology, assert that there is no convincing evidence for an evolutionary drive toward intelligent life. To the contrary, and in harmony with basic Darwinian ideas, the fossil record shows that species evolve in response to local, randomly changing conditions that might not even favor increased complexity. These scientists have argued that the human species cannot be seen as either particularly successful or favored, much less the inevitable consequence of an evolutionary drive toward progress. As Stephen Jay Gould put it when considering what might happen were the story of evolution on Earth to be replayed with a new set of creatures emergent: "The chance that this alternative set will contain anything remotely like a human being must be effectively nil, while the probability of any kind of creature endowed with self-confidence must also be extremely small.... We are glorious accidents of an unpredictable process with no drive to complexity."

This line of argument calls into question, at least from an evolutionary perspective, the teleological implications of the strong anthropic principle. While humbling humanity's feelings of superiority toward other life forms, these evolutionary biologists simultaneously demonstrate that even were life to develop elsewhere in the universe, intelligent creatures would by no means be the guaranteed outcome. We are indeed special. The evolutionary debates, like the physical ones, are still ongoing. The technical arguments rely on specific physiological criteria such as complexity, size, or neurological flexibility, all of which I would challenge as too restrictive. We will have to keep listening.

In the end, the fact remains that we know of the existence of no other life, intelligent or otherwise. All this talk is perforce only educated speculation. Perhaps we will not know one way or the other for a very long time whether life is unique or ubiquitous, although from our understanding of biochemistry, we should have a much clearer sense of the statistics in a few decades. If we are alone in the universe, or at least alone in that portion of the universe we can observe, then the awe we feel upon looking at the night sky surely should be tempered with humility. If we are not alone, then just as we join with our neighbors in the Creator's task of completing the universe, so too perhaps our task of *tikkun olam* will benefit from the creative energy of many different species of intelligent life.

MIRACLES

An essential aspect of awe-*yirah* is the appreciation of the miraculous, wonder-full universe God has created. The word *miracle* comes from the Latin word *mirari*, with its meaning of "to wonder at." The more the scientist or seeker learns, the more he or she grows in appreciation and wonder at the beauty of the world. Far from being contrary to nature, miracles are embedded in nature in a way designed for us to discover the patterns. As Einstein famously put it, "The most amazing thing about the universe is that we can understand it."

Most people, however, think of miracles as events that occur *contrary* to nature's (that is, God's) normal laws. There are numerous ways to consider miracles, and I will mention two mainstream Jewish approaches. The first one candidly accepts the fantastic nature of miracles. The second, expressed by some of the early rabbis who were uncomfortable with the notion that God sometimes had to undermine eternal laws with one-time fixes, tries to finesse the difficulty. These rabbis postulated that one-time miracles were really part and parcel of the original plan and were built into the governing laws of physics at the Creation. A classical example of a biblical miracle is the ground opening up to swallow the rebellious Korah and his associates when they challenge Moses' authority during the Israelites' forty-year wandering in the desert (Numbers 22:28). According to the second school of thought, this "miracle" was incorporated ab initio (from the beginning) into the basic laws of the universe. In making this assertion, however, the rabbis encountered serious consequences for free will, for God, knowing the future need of each preprogrammed miracle, must therefore have also known of the human actions leading up to that need; if an action is known in advance, the possibility of choosing a different action is cut off. Therefore, the most fervent adherents of free will are forced, perhaps somewhat paradoxically, to admit in the possibility of miracles, in a sense allowing for God's free will too.

What does science have to say about all this? Very little. As religious philosophers for centuries have noted, science deals with reproducible phenomena of the world that multiple observers can independently and repeatedly examine. The very nature of miracles takes them outside the realm of scientific investigation. I hasten to point out that while remaining sensitive and alert to the possibility of fantastic miracles, we should also be humbly mindful that we do not know everything. Perhaps what seems to us a miracle is simply a still-undiscovered facet of normal nature. Arthur C. Clarke said that in the eyes of a primitive civilization, advanced technology was indistinguishable from magic. Recognizing that miracles can appear to be magical, we should not forget our own limited understanding of what is really, naturally possible.

9 BEFORE AND AFTER

The creation of the universe involved not only the creation of matter and space, but very possibly also the creation of time. The relativistic principle that space and time are wedded aspects of a four-dimensional space-time suggests that just as we cannot sensibly ask what lies outside the universe, so too we cannot ask what came before the universe: there was no "before." There are, nevertheless, at least two questions that can be asked: What happens as we trace the earliest events of the universe back even further than we have so far? And, are the rules that govern the universe — the existence of only four forces, that gravity is attractive, the symmetries and laws of conservation, and the other curious rules of nature that scientists have elucidated — all inevitable? If so, why, and if not, how did they come to be the laws of the universe in which we live?

An accurate understanding of the universe before inflation, when the size of the universe was less than about the Planck length of 10^{-35} meters across, depends on whether or not the Higgs boson (introduced in chapter 4) actually exists, the exact nature of the Higgs field, and whether or not alternative concepts such as the string theory of particles correctly describe reality. As physicists and astronomers work toward producing a unified theory that includes both gravity and quantum mechanics, they look toward a new generation of high-energy particle colliders and advanced technology space telescopes to probe these mysteries experimentally. Still, some general outlines of what might have occurred at the very earliest moments have been developed by theorists who extrapolate known principles as far back as they think sensible, given the intrinsic limits of the theories.

Stephen Hawking and James Hartle built on their calculations of black holes to model the nature of the very early universe, before the period of inflationary growth. They advanced what they call the "no boundary condition model," a precise analogy to the relativistic principle that space is finite but has no boundary: it is like the surface of a balloon to an ant that can walk around on it forever without encountering an edge while measuring, nevertheless, the balloon's size. So too the temporal domain of the earliest universe may have no "edge." Hawking and Hartle argue that when the universe was so tiny that quantum mechanical effects could not be ignored, the Heisenberg uncertainty principle, which as we have seen conjoins energy and time intervals together via the Planck constant, also wedded space and time, causing space-time to curve and close in on itself in four dimensions. The result, they suggest, was a smooth, unbounded "surface" with a very counterintuitive characteristic: it bent "before" into "there." The universe has no edges but is finite in size; it has no before, but originated in a beginning. According to Hawking, "The universe would be completely self-contained and not affected by anything outside itself." Although Hawking has continued to refine these ideas, which like other cosmological concepts may change, the notion of unbounded time has been given new respectability.

Whether or not Hawking and Hartle's hypothesis is accurate, an explanation needs to be found for the fact that certain rules were in place to govern the Creation. The rabbis of the Talmud make the following observation regarding these operational rules of nature: "Seven things were created before the world was created, and these are: the Torah [the first five books of the Bible], Repentance, the Garden of Eden, Gehenna, the Throne of Glory, the Temple, and the name of the Messiah." These seven supernatural things may symbolize seven more general fundamentals: the rule of physical law (Torah); the existence of intelligence and free will, i.e., human self-consciousness (Repentance); both reward and punishment, i.e., principles of causality (the Garden of Eden and Gehenna); the principles of matter, i.e., bosons, fermions, and their properties (the Throne of Glory, since early matter is metaphorically traced in the literature to the Throne of Glory); the governing rules of the beginning moments of the big bang (the Temple, because the Temple is the center of existence); and the later evolution of the universe and the rules determining its future (the Messiah). These seven in turn are grounded in the seven lower sefirot. Other rabbis cite eight preworldly things, or a variant on the set of seven, but most agree something was in place before the world as we know it began to take shape.

THE END

Our main inquiry has been into the beginning, but it is certainly not inappropriate to contemplate, where possible, the other extreme — the end, if there indeed is an end. Jewish religious mystics delved into the mysteries of the beginning in an attempt to understand humanity's source and thereby, perhaps, its purpose. A similar sort of spirit drives the modern scientific quest. Both public interest and scientific enterprises include as one motivation a search for origins and meaning in life: why were we created? Meaning is inextricably linked to the roles we play and how we live our lives as we move beyond the starting point and toward the future and a Messianic era. Insofar as the future hopes and speculations of religions converge on an Edenlike vision, they imagine an ending that evokes the beginning, the biblical Eden. Both science and religion, as they conjecture about the end, do so from perspectives rooted in their understandings of the beginning.

We live in the world of *Assiyah*, the kabbalistic World of Doing, embedded in the tenth and last sefirah, *Malkhut*. In *Malkhut* we live out the practicalities of daily existence, and at the most mystical level, we pay attention. If intelligent life is the purpose of the Creation, in any of the senses we have discussed, then can it be said that the Creation has now reached its successful conclusion? The Jewish mystics would not say so. Humanity's purposeful task, *tikkun olam*, is a partnership with God, a relationship the Kabbalah describes as helping complete the Creation by figuratively repairing the vessels broken in those early moments of the big bang. True, we have the gift of intelligence, but that does not imply the goal itself has been reached, or even that it will be reached soon. Human free will, which powers awareness, inherently allows for uncertainty and even failure. How and when we succeed, or for that matter if we ever can succeed, is usually tied to the ambiguous principles of the Messianic age. The many theological sources by no means agree on whether the arrival of the Messianic age is contingent on our success in performing *tikkun olam*, or perhaps contingent on our failure, or our trying, or whether it is independent of our efforts. The notion of the resurrection of the dead, a fundamental belief in both normative Judaism and also in the Kabbalah, and the principles of reincarnation that are more closely associated in Judaism with the Kabbalah, are also part of the rich and complex theology surrounding the stages in humanity's moral development beyond the Creation.

From an evolutionary perspective we should first consider whether we have deluded ourselves about our own (that is, humanity's) importance. Perhaps some more highly evolved creature in the remote future is the real "goal" of the Creation. My own opinion is that the advent of modern genetics and bioengineering have at least had the effect of giving us control over our future genetic development. It will not be left to random mutations or environmental selection. For better or for worse, future generations, even distant ones, will probably differ from us only in ways we permit or enable. Excepting some catastrophic event, human made or natural, that eliminates us as one such event did the dinosaurs, I believe we are the final result of evolution just because we now can control our evolution. Actually, I suspect that a self-adjusting capability should necessarily be part of any purposeful cosmic plan that has an evolved, aware creature as its goal. Likewise needed is our ability to control wisely our environment. The fact that we appear close to mastering these techniques surely means that we, and not some future being, *are* meant for the role. The primary questions are, then, are we up to the task, do we have the wisdom as well as the know-how, and how much time is there left?

Only a few decades ago modern astronomers were amazed to discover how close the expanding universe was to marginal "closure," the situation in which expansion is exactly balanced by gravitational restraining forces (described in chapter 4). Many astrophysicists philosophically preferred a plainly closed universe, in which gravity was strong enough to balance the expansion and then some, so that our universe would someday collapse in a time on the same order of length as the current age of the universe, about fourteen billion years, only to rebound in an infinite series of bounces over infinite time, thus reinstating the eternity and nonsingularity of the cosmos. The problem with this scenario for a closed universe is that it does not work: there is not enough mass-energy in the universe to produce a collapse, since cosmic mass is the source of cosmic gravity. The insights of the theory of inflation described earlier offered a solution to the problem of balance. The rapid period of cosmic inflation automatically stretched out space by a whopping amount, making the universe appear today exactly balanced between closure and open expansion. Inflation follows naturally, not accidentally, from the nature of particle physics and the big bang itself.

Perhaps some kind of new observations will discover that the universe is fully closed and ultimately destined to collapse after all. Astronomers today realize from analyzing the stately motions of galaxies that the universe contains a vast reservoir of unseen dark matter, whose existence came as a surprise. There could be others waiting. While some theorists expect a collapsing universe to bounce outward eventually, others have calculated that a collapsing universe could compress into a black hole singularity, where it will remain; this is known as the "big crunch" scenario. In either case, humanity still has many billions of years to live, since we have not even reached the turnaround point in the process.

In the next tens of billions of years, the universe will see its main sequence stars, those like the Sun, which are gradually burning their hydrogen into helium, consume all their fuel and alter drastically. Very massive stars will end their lives relatively quickly, as supernovas. Those that more closely resemble the Sun will evolve more slowly, fusing their helium, carbon, oxygen, nitrogen, and other products into still heavier elements until they can no longer sustain the high temperatures needed for these fusion reactions and they begin to cool off and shrink to dead ashes, called white dwarf stars. Were the universe to collapse, galaxies and their matter would eventually recollide and generate heat from the gravitational energy released. According to calculations that depend sensitively on uncertain details of how the universe might collapse in this situation, even in the absence of stars, these cosmic heat sources might sustain an advanced civilization in the far distant future. Frank Tipler has advanced the highly controversial but interesting conjecture that because of relativistic time-dilation effects, our descendants living inside this collapsing universe would, according to their subjective sense of time, find themselves approaching the final collapse point infinitely slowly. To them, the universe would be both eternal and life sustaining.

These and similar theoretical concepts have multiplied and diversified over the past few decades, but meanwhile the growing precision and quantity of astrophysical measurements make it clear that the universe is not closed. Particularly ruinous to the notion of closure are recent observations that indicate the opposite is the case: the universe apparently is accelerating outward rather than slowing down, propelled by a previously unsuspected repulsive aspect of gravity. Models of inflation can account for this acceleration, even though the physics responsible still relies on that hoped-for grand unified theory. The universe, it seems, will continue to expand, probably forever, and so will be eternal (in the sense of existing forever), even though it began at the big bang.

An ever-expanding universe will, of course, last infinitely longer than even a collapsing universe, and far longer than the brief interval it has enjoyed so far. Stars and galaxies will evolve in much the same way as described above, but with no chance of gravitational resurrection. Entropy, that property of heat which leads everything to a less ordered state, will gradually reduce everything in the universe to a uniform, cold ember, replete with black hole remnants of stars that slowly evaporate: a universe incapable of doing anything. Since life is essentially a nonequilibrium process that takes energy and does work, life too will be extinguished. How long might this take? There are still details to sort out, but it seems likely that it will take not tens of billions of years but thousands of billions of years. Freeman Dyson has suggested an interesting proviso analogous to the collapsing scenario: the processes that sustain life and thought as the universe cools can be slowed down even more gradually by a superadvanced civilization. As a result, the subjective sense of time could appear to our distant descendants to leave an eternity still to live. Dyson's calculations have been contradicted by others using different assumptions about the nature of life, and there are some disagreements about how the universe will in fact develop. In any case, if the universe is indeed accelerating its outward expansion, our neighboring galaxies will eventually all disappear from our view, and the future for these remote humans will be a lonely one.

DISTANT HORIZONS AND COUNTLESS UNIVERSES

There is no reason why the universe could not be much bigger than the portion whose light finally has reached us 13.7 billion light-years later. Light from regions more distant than that has not had time enough to reach us. Making the universe larger does not alter any of the discussions we have had so far in this admittedly speculative chapter. Readers familiar with variants of the inflation model will know that the universe may actually be very much bigger than the dimensions we can directly measure. The basic reason is that by the period of inflation — the epoch of spontaneous symmetry breaking shortly after the moment of Creation — light might have had time, in principle, to travel a distance in the universe that exceeds considerably the portion that forms our currently observable universe. Were the actual universe as big as allowed by this light-travel distance (we don't know that it is, but if it were), then in some scenarios the universe at the moment of inflation was about 10^{23} times larger than the portion of the universe we can measure, and it may continue to be that much larger today. The exact size does not make any key differences to our discussion — it is forever inaccessible to our direct measurements — except perhaps in one way. If we, as intelligent life, play a role in collapsing a universal wavefunction, our actions might affect more distant parts of this meta-universe. We do not know if such processes could occur, in part because we do not yet understand how quantum mechanical effects occur, but research into the notion of nonlocality effects that I introduced in chapter 7 is active.

Our universe may not only be bigger than what we can see, it may also be just one of many universes. In early cosmic history, when the strong force spontaneously separated (or, "froze out") from the three forces, the stupendous pressure latent in the vacuum was released and exponentially inflated the universe in size. Then it stopped. The reason why the inflation ceased is just as seemingly arbitrary as the reason why it began in the first place. Astrophysicists ascribe the conduct of inflation to the nature of the vacuum (what it can do) and chance (what it did do). The vacuum is pictured as being in a state something like that of a radioactive atom about to decay and emit a particle. It was a matter of chance, but the vacuum in the inflating universe suddenly "decayed" into a state of normalcy, ending inflation about 10^{-33} seconds after it began.

Cosmologists like Alan Guth and Andrei Linde have hypothesized that the vacuum need not have undergone this spontaneous decay into normalcy everywhere. It may have done so only in a few places, each spot unconnected to the other. Each of these select regions, then — including the one that became our own universe —

stopped inflating and continued on its own more gradual expansion: each formed its *own* universe, with its own individual big bang history, and perhaps even with its own peculiar set of physical laws. Guth and Linde further speculate that other portions of the remaining, still inflating, vacuum will at some later time also experience decay, generating still other universes, and so on. They suggest that an infinite number of these universes could have been created, each even more remote from our own universe than are the meta-distant edges of our universe. We can never have any direct evidence of such universes.

Variants on these ideas suggest that black holes in our own universe, formed perhaps from the explosive death of stars, might generate daughter universes from a pinched space-time bubble on the other side of the black hole's horizon. In some exotic cases, Guth and others have conjectured that a vacuum bubble might even be generated within our universe with the just right conditions, perhaps in futuristic particle accelerators. Since the nature of the fields permits creation ex nihilo when the conditions are right, no material is needed for creating such a new universe, just the right (extreme) conditions. All this heady imagination helps to push our understanding to the limit, probing for logical or experimental flaws, and emphasizes the need for a theory that includes both gravity and quantum mechanics. Inflation models are regularly being contrived, revised, or rescinded.

One appealing feature of the many-universes model, especially to many scientists, is that the anthropic principle can be satisfied automatically. Infinite numbers of universes are created by exotic processes, but intelligent life arises only in those few universes in which the physics and boundary conditions are perfectly harmonized to produce it. Our universe happens to be one of those fortunate places, perfect for life in some of its corners. The concept is attractive to some people because it enables the natural order of things to produce consciousness and life as a consequence of many attempts, and it relegates our own comfortable universe — indeed our own being — to our particular good fortune.

We do not know how difficult it really is to generate life, much less intelligent life, and in thinking about life elsewhere in the universe we have confronted the possibility that any forms of life might be rare. Are there enough of these other, independent universes out there to satisfy the statistical odds required by a purely random, mechanistic anthropic principle? The current answer seems to be, possibly. String theory alone concludes that there are many different "landscapes" of possibility, about 10^{500} of them, apparently enough for random chance to produce a few universes tuned perfectly for life.

Perhaps life and our fastidious universe did arise from situations like these, but chance need not be the determining factor, the "final cause." Jewish mystical tradition records that God created many worlds before this one. It does not seem to me necessarily more excessive for God to use many universes to develop conditions right for humanity than to require many billions of stars or galaxies to do so. Perhaps the long chain of events is a necessary consequence of the particular physics that God has designed, natural laws that enable us to exist and to be intelligent. The Jewish mystics also believed that our universe is just the most recent version of many attempts. Ours is the one that finally worked, because the physical and the moral laws — the rules of consequences and free will — are not arbitrary features, but enabling ones that provided the basis for a creation that is stable, balanced, resourceful, and capable of fulfilling its Creator's will.

10 BRINGING TRUTH TO LIGHT

Why should you, the reader, take seriously this amazing account of the nature of the universe and its origins? Why should you believe that the fantastic descriptions we have encountered are literally true — that is, that they correspond to reality? The imagery is so cosmologically vast or microscopically small, either way far outside our normal experience; is it worth the effort to understand it? Some features of the world (not to mention the ideas that attempt to explain them) certainly seem incredible. Many scientists, even Einstein, debated the philosophical meaning of quantum theory and considered some interpretations quite unbelievable.

My response is that scientists describe what they see of the natural universe as best as they can. The truth of the observed particulars can be tested and confirmed (or rejected) by anyone — that is one of the essential pillars of the scientific method. Perhaps our questions will change someday, and we will look at the world with different tools, but if we ask "What does the observable universe look like?" the response will surely be close to the one presented in these pages. All scientific observations should, of course, be carefully scrutinized. People can make mistakes, but among our most valuable attributes is an ability to recognize error and recover. Not only are such aptitudes entwined with aspects of free will, they are related to awareness, with important consequences for the universe. Scientific knowledge, verified by independent scholarship, makes the modern picture of the universe as true as anything we know today. It is fully worth our most serious attention.

As for the scientific theories, those ideas aspiring to *explain* the observed features of the world coherently, they are in active flux. Scientists are continuously expanding and testing their inquiries, and their descriptive language is steadily improving as well. It is a compliment to science, not a rebuke, to say that its quest for truth entails the process of honest searching. Nevertheless, an evolving truth by no means has to deny all of its past forms, and as more is learned, that which is already known need not be discarded. Relativity did not spurn Newtonian mechanics; it absorbed and expanded it. By the same token the medieval mystics did not repudiate all traditional religious ideas; they adapted and reinterpreted them. The incredible picture of the Creation that modern cosmology has observed and modeled is both accurate and certain to improve. We know, for example, that the universe is expanding, but we don't yet know with certainty if it will ultimately stop enlarging, or perhaps even contract. We have, for example, a partial theory that so far works tolerably well for particles and forces, but a grand unified theory, or a theory of everything, that also encompasses a quantum mechanical description of gravity, has not been completed. What surprises might such a theory hold?

Fundamentally, the nature of scientific "truth" is a philosophical question, one that has been hotly contested among scientists and nonscientists, philosophers, historians, theologians, and religious literalists. Is it presumptuous or sensible for us to believe that science, being objective and rational, is somehow close to the ideal state of knowing? Many scientists believe that the reductionist approach of science, which asserts that all physical explanations can be found in ever subtler details (perhaps down to some limit like the Higgs boson), is the philosophically sound path to truth. Some philosophers of science argue to the contrary, that science is more of a social construct: people asking questions from a perspective laden with history and other marginally irrelevant baggage, and then answering those questions with a language that is limited and limiting, so that models and even observations are affected by cultural biases that preclude philosophical truth. These are interesting and valid arguments. I myself do not believe that science is a social construct. I believe the world makes itself increasingly known to those who open their eyes to it in increasingly perceptive ways. At the same time, however, I also recognize that language, including mathematics, can be restrictive. The seeker's task is to look in new and sensitive ways; the development of new tools and languages is part of the process. Ultimately, the world that we sense directly, or indirectly through our machines, is the source of our information.

Exactly the same question — Is it true? — can be asked about the religious accounts I have summarized, and my response is very nearly the same as the one I have given for science: the mystics have described what they understand from their sources in the best way they can. Their world, the source of their information, is an authentic source of knowledge. Their mystical insights are part of the human process of interpreting the world. Even Divine revelations, however, are perforce revelations to *people*, and as the rabbis pointed out, God speaks to people in their own languages, with the realization that every language lives in its own circumscribed world. I have done my best to present these insights fairly. Although innovative mysticism is today a much less active discipline than science, its ideas will grow and become enriched as people continue their explorations. Those engaged in a spiritual quest must return again and again to the revealed texts or inspired narratives, and to the words of teachers who help explain them. Like the scientist, the mystic is constrained to describe his or her experiences and insights in human language, a medium that is both limited and limiting, and like the scientist the mystic's creative task is to remain open and sensitive. What insights or new understanding might be forthcoming as we, as a species, mature?

Unfortunately, the question of religious truth has often been raised by people who are not struggling with doubt, but rather are possessed by certainty. The history of humanity is sadly replete with horrific violence and hatred when principles of belief, religious truths, are perceived as being questioned or threatened. Today's postmodern scientific world is no less infected with religious intolerance and fear. In perspective, it seems to me that competing truths between religions, or even within religions, as well as truths challenged by history, or science, or just by human sentiment, all serve to underscore the point that, to put it mildly, the truth is not especially obvious. The seeker is better advised to be both humble and open-minded in his or her quest. Perhaps humility is itself an objective for the religious soul; perhaps a gracious God has designed the world with ambivalent signals and free will to keep us modest and open-minded. In kabbalistic language, humility or perfect beauty (*Tiferet*) is the balanced confluence of both: loving, open attentiveness (*Hesed*) and self-assurance (*Gevurah*).

Our models, theories, and religious explanations are valuable only insofar as they bring insights and meaning to a growing abundance of information about the world we perceive. Explanations, insights, and meanings can — and should — change as we add new discoveries to the larger picture. The scientific stories and the mystical perceptions, the discoveries, confirmations, consistencies, and anomalies, are all a part of an ongoing process of interpretation. Humanity is young; there remain as many questions unsolved as answered. The scientist and the mystic both share constraints imposed by language and experience. Both must perforce be open to new ideas. One of my goals for this book has been to show that, at least in the arena of cosmology, it is possible to think about the same things in surprisingly different ways using vastly different vocabularies, and that the shared discourse can reveal insights that might otherwise have gone unnoticed.

DRAWING LESSONS

We have covered an astonishing range of topics prompted by our consideration of the Creation and that very first light. As an intellectual exercise, I hope the information has been interesting. As a meditation, I trust it has been inspiring. I think there are also some lessons to be learned.

At the outset of this book I spoke about the perceived division between our physical and our spiritual selves, and the common perception that science and religion are irreconcilable, or at best incompatible. I hope our examination of the Creation has helped to put these impressions to rest. The philosopher and mathematician Blaise Pascal wrote that the God of Abraham, Isaac, and Jacob is not the God of the philosophers. But if God is One, then God most assuredly is the simultaneous God of the philosophers and the forefathers. The disagreement is not about God's unity; it is about whose *idea* of God is more accurate, the philosophers' or the prophets'. My reply is that since God is the God of both, insights from both are valid and valuable. Science and religion are complementary, each teaching us something of God's manifold ways. The layperson should not feel he or she must take sides. Even someone with a fundamentally scientific outlook, or a religious one, can show interest in and respect for the views originating from other perspectives. Scientists and religious thinkers can share a courteous discourse characterized by the unthreatening exchange of old wisdom and new ideas, recent discoveries and surprising insights.

I also asked whether science can resolve any of the perplexities raised by religion today, and I answered yes. I hope that I have succeeded in guiding you through enough aspects of the shared discourse between science and religion that now you may consider such a question for yourself. I also suggested that a more valuable question to ask might be, Can science answer any of the questions raised by spiritual seekers? The answer to this question is also affirmative. Science offers something important to the spiritual process, because virtually everyone takes science so seriously. Together, science and technology dominate nearly every aspect of our lives. They have successfully, incredibly, transformed our world and the way we think about it. In my experience, most deeply religious people, and even many who adopt a literal interpretation of scriptures, believe me (the scientist) when I tell them, for example, about Hubble's discoveries: We observe that galaxies are moving away from us, and light from the farthest ones appears to have been traveling for billions of years. People believe in science because it works so well. They believe it even when they don't understand it, and even if they do not accept the scientific models. Despite possible misgivings about the potential uses of technology, people believe that modern medicines will cure illness, that satellite photos show the weather, and that an automobile is best repaired by a mechanic and not by prayer. A religious person might be at ease trusting in science because such trust does not threaten his or her spiritual needs. A nonreligious person might not only trust in science, he or she might even be accused of turning science into a sort of religion.

Science, like religion, is very much a human activity. Its discoveries not only amplify theories, they can upstage old concepts and force popular theories to be revised in strange ways. Indeed, a great strength of science is just this process of unpredicted growth through careful observation, analysis, and insight. The theories of special and general relativity, for example, are painfully counterintuitive. Masses increase, time intervals dilate, matter equals energy, space bends...it's bizarre. Nonetheless, relativity provides an accurate description of the world as it actually is and beautifully explains the congruence of the universe — how each observer can employ the same fundamental laws. Somehow our simple, commonsense conceptions of the world have been replaced by ones that are difficult to understand and challenging to believe. Aristotle's depiction of the universe, despite its appealingly self-evident quality, was completely mistaken about the nature of the Earth, the structure of the cosmos, and much else. The lesson is obvious: commonsense ideas are often wrong. Michael Hoskin, a historian of science, puts it this way: "The history of cosmology is not the easy story of the rejection of absurd ideas in favour of what (perhaps after a little thought) is seen to be patently true, but the heroic saga of the hard-won rejection of the patently true in favour of the absurd."

The implications of the trust (or belief) in science are exhilarating for those on a spiritual quest because belief in science is as much a vote of confidence for the scientific process as it is for the scientific findings, and that process is a humbling one. It is humbling to discover a truth you never knew before about a world that is already quite amazing and mysterious. And it is humbling to realize by this discovery that there very likely are many other ones waiting — that you don't know it all. Everyone who believes in the efficacy of science realizes that its story is not over. Facts will improve, models will evolve, and our understanding will inevitably get better. Unfinished stories may keep us living in permanent uncertainty, but the fringes of inquiry are where changes are most likely to occur. For true believers in science, therefore, a productive attitude includes intellectual openness to new ideas, respect for other honest practitioners who might just be on to something, and the meek admission that, yes, the story is not over. Science teaches us not to be threatened by new, or even contradictory ideas, but to welcome them. Thoughtful innovations advance the search for truth; they expand our horizons. Scientists trust that reason will ultimately unveil the truth, for God gave the gift of reason to humanity for a purpose — to be used — and made the world itself with a comprehensible structure. The process of open inquiry allows reason unfettered license and is a blessing. For every one of us, even nonscientists, these are healthy attitudes.

I think, moreover, that uncertainty is part of the excitement that leads to awe-wonder. Both scientists and mystics share an appreciation and wonder of the world, which every revelation amplifies anew. Whether a person believes the world was created by God, by natural laws, or by accident, listening to the discoveries, accomplishments, and insights of others leads us toward richer awareness. As Rabbi Ben Zoma succinctly put it in the Talmud, "Who is wise? Someone who learns from everyone."

Cosmology is one area of inquiry in which people can listen to and learn from one another, perhaps even acquiring new language tools or metaphors from beyond their conventional framework, but there are others we have touched on as well, such as consciousness. I think one of the profound lessons to be gathered from our consideration of the exchange between science and religion is that openness, tolerance, and respect — even when confronting apparently conflicting beliefs — are essential attitudes for a person's progress along the spiritual or scientific path.

The same scientific attitudes of openness, tolerance, and respect can be adopted into our religious and spiritual lives. Science welcomes, even depends upon, openness to give and take, novel insights, or contradictory ideas. We should appreciate the value of similar attitudes when searching God's spiritual world. Furthermore, when we recognize that even science and religion — those two apparent opposites — can carry on a rewarding conversation, then surely different forms of authentic spiritual discourse have room to tolerate, and even welcome, divergent views. A sensitive religious believer should be open, respectful, and humble, evincing the same attitudes that characterize the objective scientific believer. Commonsense ideas are often wrong; spiritual seekers should strive to be as honest in their searches as the seeker in the laboratory precisely because they are engaged in the pursuit of truth. Sad to say, religious people often have not been so noble, but because of the faith most people (including religious people) place in science, I suggest that modern science can convey this important lesson of openness and tolerance to everyone, including the religious community. Science teaches us that there are many different but equally valid paths to understanding, many legitimate approaches to the oneness that characterizes God's world. Science also teaches us that we do not have the final answers. We must persevere on the path to understanding, recognizing that even our conception of truth may evolve as we gain insight. I am an astronomer, but I welcome and value the scientific contributions of the zoologist, and those of all the alphabetic disciplines in between, as complementing our infinitesimal comprehension of God's glorious works. In these matters the spiritual path is not different from the scientific one. We are all engaged in the same holy task.

In chapter 1, I mentioned the "god of the gaps," the nature of the deity sometimes invoked by scientists to explain those features of the world left incomprehensible by gaps in scientific theories.

When creation ex nihilo was a mystery to science, God was needed to provide an explanation; likewise God was invoked to explain the near perfection of living creatures when that was a mystery. Stephen Hawking advocated an interesting and more physical variant to this notion — the "god of the edges." In the context of his theory that the universe has no edges — no boundaries in time — he justifiably noted that modern physical theories, which strive for completeness, have been excellent at explaining, more or less, all aspects of a complete system like the universe. What they cannot easily do is explain the edges of that entity, because boundaries perforce lie between a system and something else. Were the universe to have a border (which it doesn't), then God would be needed because the existence of an edge would suggest the existence of something beyond it. "If there is an edge," Hawking explains, "somebody has to decide what should happen at the edge. You would really have to invoke God." This is what Hawking means by a god of the edges, although since the concept also hinges on that which science does not explain, it is a type of god of the gaps. For the Kabbalists, and I suspect for many other mystics as well, this variant, with its relegation of God to the edges, has it backward: it is the intimate, unbounded *wholeness* of the world that is the salient attribute that signifies God, not its bounded finitude.

We live in an extraordinary time, in which seemingly every mystery has become or is becoming intelligible. The god of the gaps — the god of mystery — is no longer the default explanation for even that archetypical riddle, the Creation. But science in our miraculous era, although it refashions the inscrutable into the comprehensible, simultaneously transmutes the mundane into the wonderful. God is a deity of wonder as much as a deity of mystery; such is the import of understanding: the fabulous, real Tree of Knowledge.

CLOSING MEDITATION

Modern science and kabbalistic mysticism have provided us with joint insights about our wondrous universe:

We on Earth live at the perceived center of the cosmos. All other places share this property, as we saw in the discussion of general relativity, but ours is, nevertheless, a special kind of condition. The Creation itself took place here, as everywhere, ex nihilo from the basic laws of physics. The event occurred 13.73 billion years ago, although, paradoxically, it is likely that there was never a time when the universe did not exist.

We seem to be the purpose of the Creation. Our universe is the way it is, perfect for life, perhaps for our sake. We may be but an infinitesimal speck in the vastness of the cosmos, but the laws of physics and nature that guide the universe established the extraordinary conditions necessary for our existence. We do not know for certain if this circumstance is due to necessity or luck, but we are surely blessed.

We are engaged in a quest for knowledge and meaning. There is humility in recognizing as we search that we are sophisticated yet ignorant, and that there is a unity derived from God's Oneness that permeates and interconnects everything in the world. Learning about the world is therefore an ongoing pursuit, simultaneously scientific and religious in nature, in which we benefit from the combined efforts of all other seekers. Our growing knowledge transforms mystery into wisdom, and wisdom into wonder.

We share responsibility for the universe. Not only are we peculiar, complex, and intelligent, we have the gift of awareness. Our free will and self-consciousness, according to the still mysterious quantum mechanical framework of the universe, affect reality. Life may or may not be common in the universe — we do not know — but intelligent life is not very common. Perhaps we are alone.

We have also been bestowed with an awesome dominion over the Earth. By our actions we contribute to perfecting the world — *tikkun olam* — and by our actions, as the universe expands, most likely forever, we partner with the Divine for a Messianic age. Our good deeds help to illuminate the world, while meanwhile we ourselves strive for enlightenment.

"By Your light," says the Psalmist, "will I be enlightened" (Psalm 36:10).

Let there be light.

SCHEMATIC OF THE EVOLUTION OF THE COSMOS

The approximate, schematic figure on pages 218–19 summarizes the key physical eras and kabbalistic categories in the lifetime of the universe. Names and event times (or times that mark the end of an epoch) are given on the left side; the corresponding primary products of creation and landmark events are given on the right side. Please see chapter 5 for a more detailed description. Circles represent particles characteristic of each era, starting with quarks, and then respectively electrons and positrons, protons/neutrons and their antiparticles, and finally atomic nuclei; galaxies and stars are indicated late in the Epoch of Matter. (This figure has been adapted and modified, with permission, from Bennett, Donahue, Schneider, and Voit; color figure 23.2 and its notes, page 704).

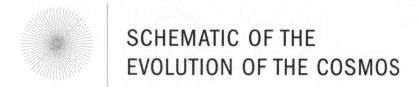

SCHEMATIC OF THE EVOLUTION OF THE COSMOS

WORLD	SEFIRAH	TIME SINCE BIG BANG (APPROX.)	EPOCH
Atzilut			
	Keter		
			Planck era
Briyah		10^{-43} second	
			GUT era; three unified forces
	Hokhmah	10^{-37} second	
	Binah		Inflation
Yetzirah		10^{-33} second	
			Epoch of Quarks
	Hesed	10^{-12} second	
	Gevurah		Epoch of Leptons
		10^{-4} second	
			Epoch of Radiation
	Tiferet	15 minutes	
			Epoch of Matter
		380,000 years	
Assiyah			
	Netzah	200 million years	
	Hod		
	Yesod	8 billion years	
	Malkhut	13.7 billion years	The present

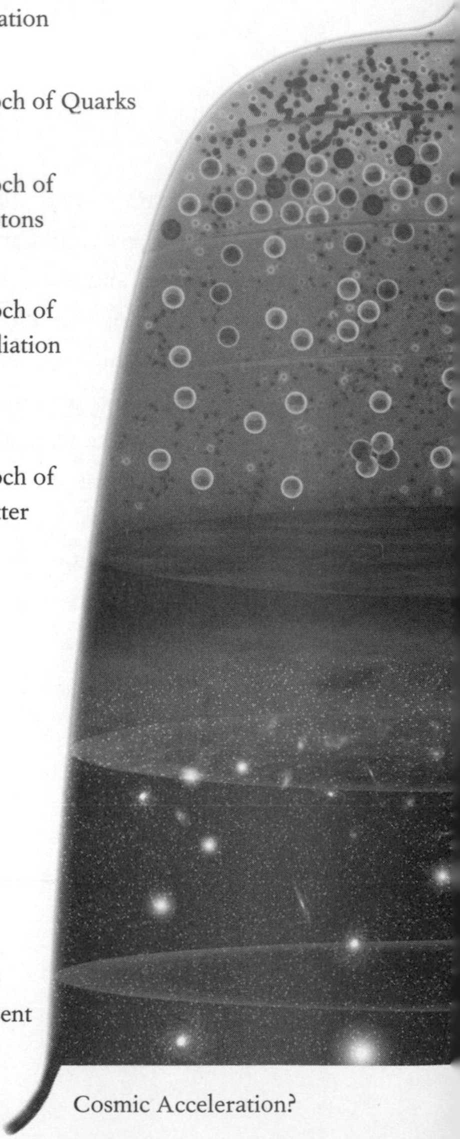

Cosmic Acceleration?

FROM THE BIG BANG TO LIFE, AND FROM KETER TO MALKHUT

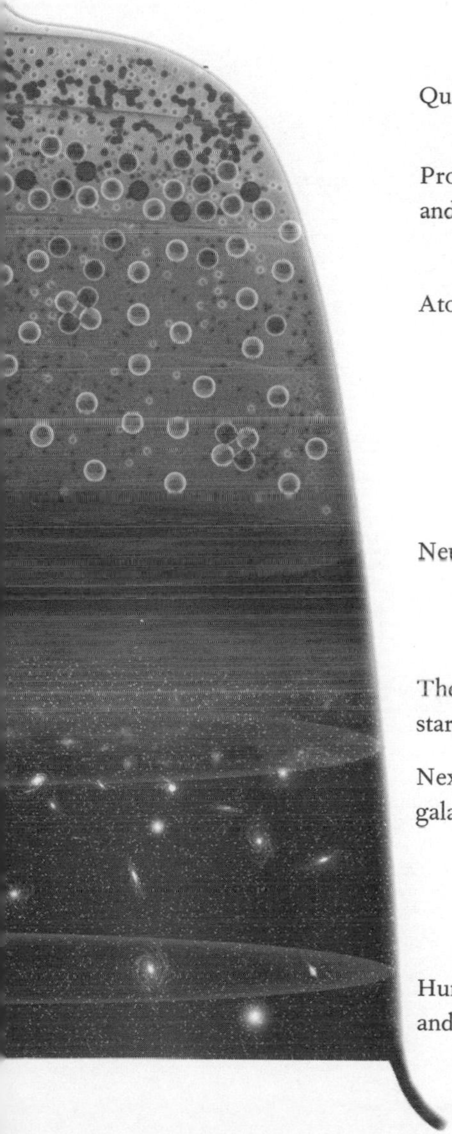

THE PRODUCTS OF CREATION	LANDMARK EVENTS
Light	*Gravity becomes a distinct force*
Higgs particles	*Strong force separates from the electromagnetic and weak forces*
Quarks, leptons	*Matter and antimatter annihilate each other*
Protons, neutrons, and electrons	*Electromagnetic and weak forces separate*
Atomic nuclei	
Neutral atoms	*The time of recombination: the cosmic microwave background radiation propagates freely*
The first galaxies and stars	
Next generations of galaxies and stars	
	Formation of the Sun and its solar system, including Earth
Humanity and consciousness	

TREE OF LIFE – LADDER OF SEFIROT

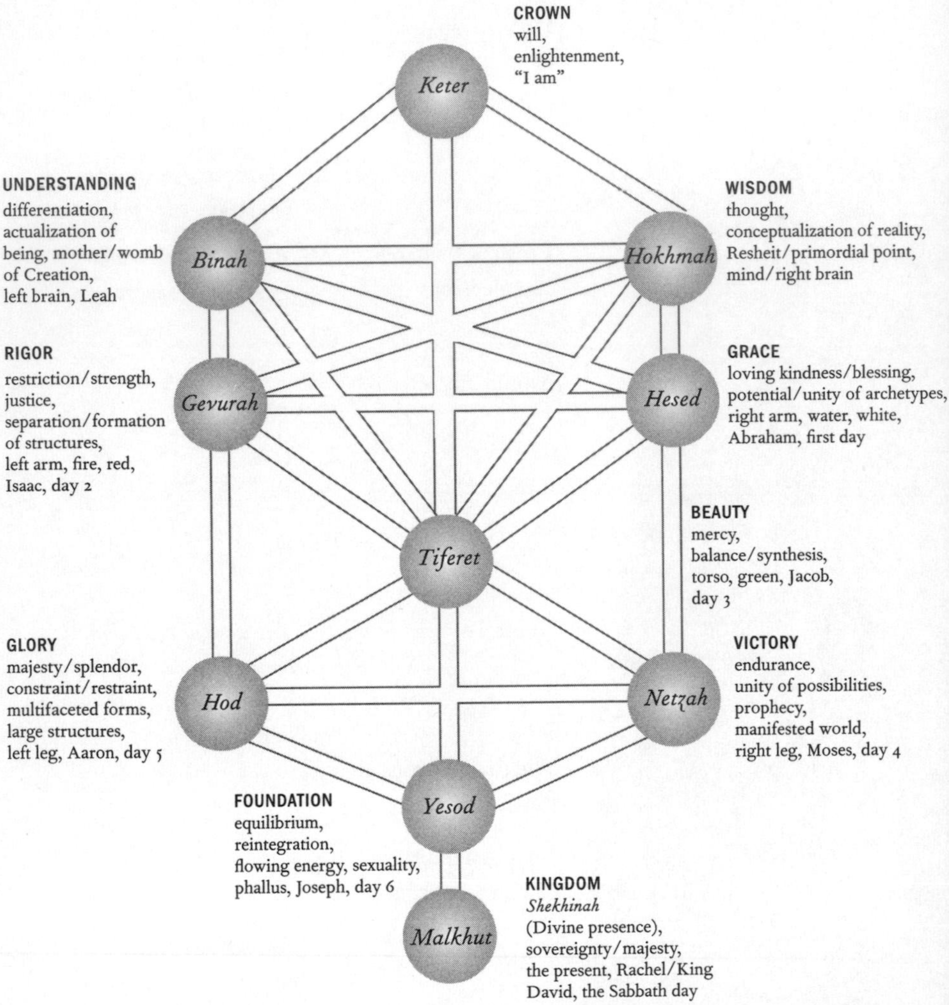

CROWN
will,
enlightenment,
"I am"
Keter
UNDERSTANDING
differentiation,
actualization of
being, mother/womb
of Creation,
left brain, Leah
Binah
WISDOM
thought,
conceptualization of reality,
Resheit/primordial point,
mind/right brain
Hokhmah
RIGOR
restriction/strength,
justice,
separation/formation
of structures,
left arm, fire, red,
Isaac, day 2
Gevurah
GRACE
loving kindness/blessing,
potential/unity of archetypes,
right arm, water, white,
Abraham, first day
Hesed
BEAUTY
mercy,
balance/synthesis,
torso, green, Jacob,
day 3
Tiferet
GLORY
majesty/splendor,
constraint/restraint,
multifaceted forms,
large structures,
left leg, Aaron, day 5
Hod
VICTORY
endurance,
unity of possibilities,
prophecy,
manifested world,
right leg, Moses, day 4
Netzah
FOUNDATION
equilibrium,
reintegration,
flowing energy, sexuality,
phallus, Joseph, day 6
Yesod
KINGDOM
Shekhinah
(Divine presence),
sovereignty/majesty,
the present, Rachel/King
David, the Sabbath day
Malkhut

NOTES AND COMMENTS

For each section, any comments and recommendations for further reading that apply to the entire section come first. Notations referring to specific quotations and topics, organized by page number, follow.

BOOK EPIGRAPHS

vii "From this verse...": *Zohar* I, 16b.

vii "It was the discovery...": Michael Rowan-Robinson, *Ripples in the Cosmos.*

vii "One of the great afflictions...": Rabbi Abraham Isaac Kook, from *The Lights of Holiness,* quoted in Ben Zion Bokser, *Abraham Isaac Kook: The Lights of Penitence, the Moral Principles, the Lights of Holiness, Essays, Letters, and Poems,* p. 195

PREFACE

xvi "If I am not for myself, who will be for me?": Babylonian Talmud, Avot, Chapter 1, Mishnah 14. All citations of the Talmud are from I. Epstein, ed., *The Babylonian Talmud: Translated into English.* The Tractate of Avot is also known as *The Ethics of the Fathers* and is readily available in many excellent translations in separate editions.

xvi "The abundant love with which God loves us": from the daily prayer book.

xviii "May my many errors be forgiven...": Isaac Luria, quoted in Hayyim Vital, *Sefer Etz Hayyim Hashalem,* 14.

CHAPTER 1. RELIGION AND SCIENCE IN HARMONY

This first section introduces the important and controversial issues that prompted me to write *Let There Be Light,* issues that, I imagine, have more passionate writing about them than do all the rest of the topics in this book combined. As a general remark about my supplemental reading recommendations, I should say that I strongly prefer books written by professionals in the given field over other, sometimes equally excellent (and occasionally superior) expositions on the topic by science or religion writers. I do so partly because these firsthand authors and their books are closer to the original material, and partly because readers who have finished *Let There Be Light* should be able to handle these more detailed descriptions. But please bear in mind that my recommended reading lists are by no means all-inclusive; I am a browser at bookstores, and I urge everyone to be the same.

For readers who are interested in some of the current thinking about ways to integrate science and religion, I can recommend a few of many books that are available, in particular ones by three scientists who became theologians. These books have strong Christian perspectives and generally bring in a much wider range of biblical material and theology than I try to do here. They are easy to read, although somewhat scholarly in affect. *Religion and Science: Historical and Contemporary Issues,* by Ian G. Barbour, is the place to begin. This book subsumes much of Barbour's earlier writing. It has an excellent, helpful historical overview of thinking about science and religion from the time of Galileo and Newton forward, a review of the philosophical considerations, and discussions on quantum physics and cosmology covering (in more detail, and from an explicitly Christian perspective) many of the topics I address in this book. Sir John Polkinghorne has written prolifically and produced a series of relatively short, focused books, including *Belief in God in an Age of Science, Science and Theology: An Introduction,* and *The Faith of a Physicist;* in the last he reviews different concepts of God, including theism, pantheism, panentheism (the belief that God is nature, but more than just nature), and the "god of the gaps." In *One World: The Interaction of Science and Theology* he succinctly describes ten qualities of the "scientific view of the world" — for example, elusiveness, intelligibility —

which I think most nonscientists would also agree with, and which capture neatly many of the areas of shared analysis. Arthur Peacocke's *Theology for a Scientific Age: Being and Becoming Natural, Divine, and Human* is a thoughtful and accessible presentation on the nature of the Divinity in the light of modern science. Peacocke's *Paths from Science towards God: The End of All Our Exploring* is also good.

I would like to recommend two books by a theologian (not an ex-scientist) who writes in a clear and interesting manner about modern science and theology: Philip Clayton's *God and Contemporary Science: Edinburgh Studies in Constructive Theology* and *The Problem of God in Modern Thought*. Adopting an explicitly Christian perspective, Clayton carefully analyzes many of the arguments and claims made by authors in the field of science and religion, including some presented in *Let There Be Light*. His chapter "Creation and Cosmology" in *God and Contemporary Science* sorts through the possible lessons theology can learn from cosmology.

One physicist who has broached many of the subjects I raise in this book, but from a quasi-religious perspective, is Paul Davies. He writes of himself that he belongs to "the group of scientists who do not subscribe to a conventional religion but nevertheless deny that the universe is a purposeless accident." Davies is a prolific science author, and all of his books are worth reading, but I recommend especially his book *The Mind of God: The Scientific Basis for a Rational World*, an excellent account of this unconventionally "religious" physicist's view of God. Davies reviews clearly some of the ways philosophers and scientists think about God and presents excellent discussions on many of the topics that I cover in this book, including the Creation, relativity, quantum mechanics, and the mind. Davies's first book on this subject matter, *God and the New Physics,* also discusses many of the subjects I raise here.

Charles Townes, a religious scientist and winner of a Nobel Prize in physics and of the Templeton Prize (a major annual award given by the John Templeton Foundation for "discoveries about spiritual realities"), has written an autobiographical book, *Making Waves,* about his discovery of the maser and laser. It contains an important chapter on basic research, fascinating personal recollections and observations on the process of discovery, and five insightful essays on science and religion. (Full disclosure: Townes was my Ph.D. thesis supervisor.)

I recommend a popular book written by the cosmologist Joel Primack and his wife, Nancy Abrams, *The View from the Center of the Universe,* about the importance of realizing the spiritual lessons inherent in the modern scientific view of the world. It approaches many of the same issues I address in *Let There Be Light,* especially in big bang cosmology.

Finally, I recommend two authors who are scientists, not theologians, but whose perspectives on science and religion are completely different from those of the authors I have mentioned thus far (and from my own): both are outspoken critics of religion. Their points are generally stimulating and well articulated; both have won awards for popular writing, and both adopt a more or less conventional atheistic view, supported by numerous examples. Steven Weinberg is a Nobel laureate in physics and one of the great scientists and thinkers of our time. A powerful advocate for the reductionist philosophy, he played a major role in many of the theoretical cosmological discoveries I discuss in this book. He has written two popular books that are, among other things, critical of religion: *Facing Up: Science and Its Cultural Adversaries* and *Dreams of a Final Theory,* which is largely about the grand unified theory of physics. Richard Dawkins, writing in *Unweaving the Rainbow: Science, Delusion, and the Appetite for Wonder* and *The Selfish Gene,* is an eloquent proponent of the wonder of the natural world but is unapologetically hostile toward religion. His field is evolutionary biology, from which he derives most of his thought-provoking examples. I will not address many of the negative observations that these authors have made about religion, but all serious spiritual seekers should read what these authors have to say and decide how they would respond. As the first-century sage Rabbi Elazar ben Arokh urged, "Know how to respond to a skeptic" (Babylonian Talmud, Avot, Chapter 2, Mishnah 14), or more literally "to an Epicurean," that is, a person who argues that the world is run by chance.

2 Galileo Galilei's famous comment is from his 1615 letter to the Grand Duchess Cristina of Tuscany. He writes, "I would say here something that was heard from an ecclesiastic of the most eminent degree [i.e., Cesare Cardinal Baronio]: 'That the intention of the Holy Ghost is to teach us how one goes to heaven, not how heaven goes.' " This translation of the quotation is from Fordham University's *Internet Modern History Sourcebook: Galileo Galilei, Letter to the Grand Duchess Cristina of*

Tuscany, 1615, www.fordham.edu/halsall/mod/galileo-tuscany.html. The attribution of the quote to Cesare Cardinal Baronio is from Dava Sobel, *Galileo's Daughter,* p. 65.

2 "The idea that because they were right...": George Lemaître, quoted in Helge Kragh, *Cosmology and Controversy,* p. 59.

3 "Many [believers] fear...": Hugh Ross, *A Matter of Days,* p. 19.

4 "We should not immediately refute...": Kook, from *Letters,* quoted in Bokser, *Abraham Isaac Kook,* p. 134.

Cosmology and Kabbalah

There are a few outstanding popular works on the Kabbalah, and if you have time to read only one or two, it should be one of the following. Arthur Green's short *Guide to the Zohar,* which he wrote as the introduction to Daniel Matt's masterful new translation of the *Zohar,* is brilliant, clear, and the best overall scholarly introduction I have seen. Daniel Matt's *The Essential Kabbalah* is a poetic compilation of original kabbalistic passages from a wide range of sources, which he has collected and beautifully translated. If you are looking for some original source material to read, this is the place to start. Matt's introduction and endnotes are excellent. Matt's book *Zohar: The Book of Enlightenment* is another good popular introduction. I am a huge fan of Louis Jacobs, and his book *Jewish Mystical Testimonies* is a superb collection of precisely that: Jewish mystical testimonies written by ancient Kabbalists, modern rationalists, and many types in between. Finally, I recommend *The Thirteen Petalled Rose,* an overview of Jewish mystical ideas, by the modern Talmudic giant Adin Steinsaltz; Yehuda Liebes's *Studies in the Zohar,* which also discusses at length possible Christian influences on the *Zohar;* Moshe Hallamish's *Introduction to the Kabbalah,* a very good general, but scholarly, introduction; Allen Afterman's *Kabbalah and Consciousness and the Poetry of Allen Afterman;* and last but by no means least, Lawrence Fine's superb *Physician of the Soul, Healer of the Cosmos: Isaac Luria and His Kabbalistic Fellowship.* Fine's book has two excellent chapters on the concept of *tikkun olam,* which I discuss in chapters 5 and 7.

Serious readers will want to sample more scholarly analyses, and the place to begin is with Gershom Scholem's 1941 classic, *Major Trends in Jewish Mysticism,* and his systematic *Kabbalah.* More recently, Moshe

Idel (one of Scholem's disciples) has published numerous innovative and well-received books exploring various aspects of the Kabbalah, in particular *Kabbalah: New Perspectives* and *Studies in Ecstatic Kabbalah*. The original sources of the Kabbalah are increasingly available in English, but be forewarned: the material is recondite, even in English. The best translations come with lots of commentary to help decode meanings, explain obscure references, and provide context; that's good, because you will certainly put most of your attention into the commentaries. Isaiah Tishby's anthology of *Zohar* texts translated into Hebrew has itself been translated into English by David Goldstein as *The Wisdom of the Zohar: An Anthology of Texts*. I particularly like it because it topically organizes the material, and also because of Tishby's long and excellent introductions to each section. Daniel Matt's translation of the *Zohar* in *The Zohar: Pritzker Edition* is in my opinion the best of several straightforward English translations available. Matt's work has meticulous footnotes to help, but even so the material is slow going.

Aryeh Kaplan, an orthodox rabbi and devout practitioner, has written a series of lucid translations and explanations of classic kabbalistic material, including *The Sefer Yetzirah: The Book of Creation in Theory and Practice*, and *The Bahir-Illumination* (these editions include the Hebrew text as well). Kaplan is also the author of numerous other books on Jewish mysticism, meditation, and religion. I recommend his books in part because they are reliably accurate and traditional in perspective. Leonard R. Glotzer's *Fundamentals of Jewish Mysticism: The Book of Creation and Its Commentaries* is a thorough and readable translation and exposition of the *Sefer Yetzirah* and its concepts. The best English book I have found on the original material in the *Etz Hayyim* is *The Tree of Life: Hayyim Vital's Introduction to the Kabbalah of Isaac Luria*, by Donald Wilder Menzi and Zwe Padeh. It is a translation of just the first part of that work, but that is the part that deals with the first steps in the Creation, so it overlaps nicely with what I cover here, and it is full of effective illustrations and tables.

There are some other fine translations of kabbalistic material. Lawrence Fine's *Safed Spirituality: Rules of Mystical Piety, the Beginning of Wisdom*, Aryeh Kaplan's *Meditation and Kabbalah*, and Daniel Matt's *Zohar: The Book of Enlightenment* and *Zohar: Annotated and Explained* are all good examples.

For readers seeking more of an immediate connection to personal spirituality, I highly recommend Arthur Green's *Ehyeh: A Kabbalah for Tomorrow,* which also has excellent introductory discussions, and Tamar Frankiel's *The Gift of Kabbalah: Discovering the Secrets of Heaven, Renewing Your Life on Earth.*

7 On the importance of cosmology to people, I wrote an article about popular opinion and astronomy, "Public Attitudes towards Space Science," in *Space Science Reviews* 105, no. 1–2 (2003), p. 493, published by Springer Netherlands.

9 "There is no such thing as mysticism in the abstract...": Gershom G. Scholem, *Major Trends in Jewish Mysticism,* pp. 6, 206.

10 "a mystical novel...": Daniel C. Matt, *The Essential Kabbalah: The Heart of Jewish Mysticism,* p. 6.

10 "Jewish theosophy...": Scholem, *Major Trends,* p. 206.

10 "The Kabbalah was indeed produced by mystics...": Louis Jacobs, *Jewish Mystical Testimonies,* p. 1.

12 "How? And how many? And when?": Hayyim Vital, *Sefer Etz Hayyim Hashalem,* First Palace, Gate 1, Branch 1. (For this and other citations from Vital's *Etz Hayyim,* see also the translation in Menzi and Padeh, *The Tree of Life.*)

12 "the true nature of reality": Kook, *The Lights of Holiness,* quoted in Bokser, *Abraham Isaac Kook,* p. 195.

Preconceptions and Prejudices

13 "Cosmic religious experience...": Albert Einstein, *Cosmic Religion with Other Opinions and Aphorisms,* 1931, quoted in Alice Calaprice, ed., *The Expanded Quotable Einstein,* p. 208.

14 "Those who desire to arrive at the palace...": Moses Maimonides, *The Guide for the Perplexed,* part 3, chapter 51.

Plato, in his *Phaedrus* and *Symposium,* presents the world of Ideals as the object of mystical contemplation. Isaac Newton, noting the apparent perfection of the world, wrote, "It is not to be conceived that mere mechanical causes could give birth to so many regular motions, since the comets range over all part of the heavens in very eccentric orbits. . . . This most beautiful system of the sun, planets, and comets could only proceed from the counsel and dominion of an intelligent and powerful Being" (quoted in Milton K. Munitz, *Theories of the Universe: From Babylonian Myth to Modern Science*, p. 208).

Motivations and Questions

15 Stephen Hawking is one of the great mathematical physicists of our time. He has in addition written some half-dozen books for the general public, including *A Brief History of Time* and *The Universe in a Nutshell*, the latter filled with many exuberant color images designed to explain complex ideas of relativity and cosmology, though with mixed success.

CHAPTER 2. TWO VIEWS OF COSMOLOGY

22 "Why does the Torah start with the letter *bet?*": *B'Resheit Rabbah* 1:10.

23 The *Zohar* introduces the term *Resheit* in its discussion of the first word of scripture (*Zohar* I, 15a); all of the various transposed readings of the word *B'Resheit* are from passages in the *Zohar*.

23 *B'Resheit Rabbah* (or, Genesis Rabbah) is a collection of midrashim on passages in the first book of the Bible. It is one of the earliest, classic midrashim, and several English translations are available. I highly recommend Rabbi Wilfred Shuchat's *The Creation According to the Midrash Rabbah*, a clear translation and insightful explication of the Creation story in Genesis Rabbah, to those encountering midrash for the first time, as well as to people already familiar with midrashic homiletics. While it presents the Hebrew text and proceeds at a sophisticated level, the presentation is very accessible.

Disparate Views of Creation

A beautiful, slightly alternative view of the science versus religion debate on cosmology from the point of view of a Buddhist physicist is Trinh Xuan Thuan's *The Secret Melody: And Man Created the Universe;* it also has good historical background material and technical explanations of modern physics. Alan Lightman's *Ancient Light: Our Changing View of the Universe* is a clear explication of popular cosmology by a scientist who specializes in poetic personal essays, books on science for a popular audience, and fiction.

24 [Newton] wondered why the universe did not collapse...: Newton's views on possible gravitational collapse of the universe were expressed in one of his letters to the theologian Richard Bentley, c. 1692. Newton explained his view that "if the matter was evenly distributed throughout an infinite space, it could never convene into one mass," although it would condense into many smaller masses, namely, the "Sun and fixed stars." Four of his letters to Bentley, as well as the Scholium (preface) to his "Fundamental Principles of Natural Philosophy," are reprinted in Munitz, *Theories of the Universe.*

24 "the Universe in its totality has never been different...": Maimonides, citing Aristotle and his own views on Creation ex nihilo and the Greek philosophy of time and creation, in *Guide for the Perplexed*, part 2, chapter 13.

25 "Those who follow the Law of Moses...": ibid.

25 "the open book of Heaven": Galileo Galilei, from his 1615 letter to the Grand Duchess Cristina of Tuscany, quoted in Sobel, *Galileo's Daughter*, p. 65.

26 "I believe that the intention of Holy Writ...": Galileo Galilei, from a long letter to the Benedictine monk (and one of his favorite students) Benedetto Castelli in 1613, portions of which also appear in his 1615 letter to Cristina of Tuscany. Galileo also wrote in this letter, "[Madama Cristina propounded that] Holy Scripture cannot err and the decrees therein contained are absolutely true and inviolable. I should only have added that, though Scripture cannot err, its expounders and interpreters are liable to err in many ways.... Holy Scripture and Nature are both emanations from the divine word: the former dictated by the Holy Spirit, the latter the observant executrix of God's commands." Sobel, *Galileo's Daughter*, p. 65, pp. 63–64.

The Modern Scientific Picture

Neil deGrasse Tyson and Donald Goldsmith have written a clear and beautifully illustrated volume on modern astronomy and astrophysics called *Origins: Fourteen Billion Years of Cosmic Evolution;* it is the companion volume to an episode of *Nova* on PBS. The story of the Cosmic Background Explorer (COBE) is well told from a personal point of view by John C. Mather, the originator of the project and its "project scientist," in *The Very First Light*. This book, which Mather wrote with John Boslough, also provides a good historical perspective on the ideas and early ballooning experiments that laid the groundwork for the COBE mission. A member of the COBE team and lead on one of the instruments, George Smoot, wrote *Wrinkles in Time* with Keay Davidson, describing COBE's remarkable discovery that the cosmic microwave background radiation is *not* absolutely uniform. Another good book on the cosmic background radiation is Marcus Chown's *Afterglow of Creation: From the Fireball to the Discovery of Cosmic Ripples.*

If I were challenged to demonstrate how science reveals the world as it is, not as we may preconceive it to be, I would use the example of the discovery of the acceleration of the universe. This jaw-dropping, unexpected, and completely counterintuitive result is well described by one of its discoverers, the supernova expert Robert Kirshner, in his book *The Extravagant Universe: Exploding Stars, Dark Energy, and the Accelerating Cosmos*.

35 Supernovas in very remote galaxies have enabled astronomers to estimate distances...: Here is a little more detail on measuring the distance of supernovas. As mentioned, the light from a star or supernova propagates in all directions, spreading and dimming with distance. The amount of light collected by a telescope here on Earth depends inversely on the supernova's distance squared. (There is also a slight correction needed for possible diminution of the light by any intervening haze.) For example, a candle ten feet away from a book shines one hundred times less light on it than a candle only one foot away, because while the amount of candlelight is constant is both cases, the area the candle illuminates gets bigger by the distance squared — and so the light of the more distant candle is spread over an area one hundred times larger. The same is true of stars and supernovas. Comparing the natural brightness of the candle or supernova with the measured amount of light results in a determination of its distance.

CHAPTER 3. THE PARADOX OF "WITHOUT-LIMIT"

The Age and Shape of the Universe

39 "At the very beginning of the King's authority...": *Zohar* I, 15a.

40 "like a very tiny point, having no substance": Rabbi Moshe ben Nachman (Nachmanides), *Commentary on the Torah,* commentary to Genesis 1:3.

40 "The universe began at time zero...": Joseph Silk, *A Short History of the Universe.* Silk's introduction to cosmology is very good for people looking for slightly more technical explanations than I provide here, and it is accompanied by some very helpful graphs and figures. *A Short History of the Universe,* published in 1994, has been updated and reissued as *On the Shores of the Unknown: A Short History of the Universe* (2005). Silk's earlier book, *The Big Bang,* recently revised, is also excellent and includes more math and more general astronomical material.

General Relativity: A Scientific Perspective on Unity

40 George Gamow's classic 1961 book, *One, Two, Three — Infinity* popularized the balloon model of the cosmos. The best popular discussion of general and special relativity that I have seen is in Brian Greene's *The Fabric of the Cosmos.* For people willing to consider some simple math, at the high-school level, Edward Harrison's book *Cosmology: The Science of the Universe,* 2nd ed., is outstanding. I recommend it not only for its discussion of relativity, but also for its unusually clear and very interesting presentation of all aspects of modern cosmology. Note: for this book — indeed for any of the cosmology or physics books — be certain to get the latest edition (2000, in the case of Harrison's *Cosmology*).

42 "When the Holy One, Blessed Be He, wished to create the world...": *Zohar* I, 156a, 16a, b.

42 Some other accessible discussions of general relativity are to be found in Richard Wolfson's excellent *Simply Einstein: Relativity Demystified,* which includes discussion of paradoxes, black holes, space-time, and more; Walter Scheider's *A Serious but Not Ponderous Book about Relativity,* whose emphasis is on pedagogy; Stan Gibilisco's *Understanding Einstein's Theories of Relativity: Man's New Perspective on the Cosmos;* Jim Al-Khalili's outstanding *Black Holes, Wormholes, and Time Machines;* Paul Davies's *Space and Time in the Modern Universe,* a good presentation by a very successful popular writer; and Stephen Hawking et al., *The Future of Spacetime,* a collection of easy-to-read popular essays by physicists and science writers.

43 Curvature of space: The curvature of a surface is a measure of how "bent" it is. A ball's surface, which bends inward to close, has a positive

value of curvature; a saddle's surface bends outward in a way that never closes and has a negative value of curvature. A flat surface has neither positive nor negative curvature — it is zero, and is not bent, this is the Euclidean case. General relativity describes space whether its curvature is positive (ball), negative (saddle), or zero (flat). Current measurements suggest that on the cosmological scale the curvature of space is close to zero. Flat space is *not* two-dimensional like a sheet — but its triangles sum to 180 degrees.

48 "Come see the secret of the affair!": *Zohar* III, 65a.

48 "God's unity is not an element superadded...": Maimonides, *Guide for the Perplexed*, part 3, chapter 57.

Special Relativity: The Coupling of Space and Time

All of the books mentioned in the preceding general relativity section treat special relativity as well, and are recommended. Richard Feynman has written several popular books about basic physics and elementary particles. For more sophisticated readers, *The Feynman Lectures on Physics* and *Six Not-So-Easy Pieces* explain relativity and space-time.

54 Stephen Hawking and James Hartle's ideas are briefly described in Hawking's *A Brief History of Time*, p. 136.

56 "each level is independent even though they are all one...": *Zohar* III, 65a.

CHAPTER 4. THE COSMIC CAST

All of the recommended physics books in this chapter address the full range of cosmological issues I cover, but I list them under the topics that they are best at explaining.

The Four Forces

Richard Feynman's *The Character of Physical Law* is a very accessible overview of the forces. Steven Weinberg, in *Dreams of a Final Theory: The Scientist's Search for the Ultimate Laws of Nature*, provides a clear and interesting account of the development of modern ideas of the forces and particles, a field in which he played a major role, and the importance of a grand unified theory of physics.

Alan H. Guth's book *The Inflationary Universe: The Quest for a New Theory of Cosmic Origins* is excellent in its description of the fundamental ideas about forces and particles that motivated his research.

57 The values for only thirty-one physical quantities...: The thirty-one fundamental constants are discussed, and their current values tabulated, in M. Tegmark, A. Aguirre, M. J. Rees, and F. Wilczek, "Dimensionless Constants, Cosmology, and Other Dark Matters," *Physical Review D* 73, no. 2, id. 023505 (2006).

The Particles and Their Forms

Brian Greene's first book, *The Elegant Universe*, is primarily about string theory, but part of his story involves the physics of the elementary particles, which he explains extremely well. In his book *Quintessence*, Lawrence Krauss writes about the main alternative explanation to the cosmological constant as an explanation for an accelerating universe. Along the way he describes dark matter and the evidence for it with considerable skill and specificity. Barry Parker's *Search for a Supertheory: From Atoms to Superstrings* is also a good discussion that emphasizes particle physics. Timothy Ferris is a popular writer, rather than a researcher like the previous authors; in *The Whole Shebang, a State of the Universe(s) Report*, he provides a clear description of dark matter and many of the other cosmological topics I address. Tom Siegfried's *Strange Matters: Undiscovered Ideas at the Frontiers of Space and Time*, and Barry Parker's *Invisible Matter and the Fate of the Universe* have good discussions on dark matter in the context of cosmology.

A Unified Description of Forces and Particles

74 "Action at a distance" refers to a rather peculiar property of nature: Newton was criticized by the German mathematician Gottfried Wilhelm Leibnitz and other continental scientists for his theory of gravity precisely *because* it did not offer an explanation for action at a distance. Leibniz wrote, "'Tis also a supernatural thing, that bodies should attract one another at a distance, without any intermediate means" (H. G. Alexander, *The Leibniz-Clarke Correspondence*, quoted in David Park, *The Grand Contraption*, p. 220). Newton's answer: "Hitherto I have not been able to discover the cause of these properties of gravity

from phenomena, and I frame no hypotheses; for whatever is not deduced from the phenomena is to be called a hypothesis, and hypotheses, whether metaphysical or physical, whether of occult qualities, or mechanical, have no place in experimental philosophy" (quoted in Munitz, *Theories of the Universe*, p. 210; the original quotation appeared in the General Scholium [preface] Newton wrote for his work "Fundamental Principles of Natural Philosophy").

76 The field is called the Higgs field, and the particle associated with it is called the *Higgs boson*. . . : The Higgs particle and the Higgs field are well described in Alan Guth's *The Inflationary Universe*, pp. 138–45, and Brian Greene's *The Fabric of the Cosmos*, pp. 256–63. Gordon Kane's *Supersymmetry: Squarks, Photinos, and the Unveiling of the Ultimate Laws of Nature* is a particularly good and explicit description of the Higgs field and its boson and the idea of supersymmetry. See also Barry Parker's *Einstein's Dream: The Search for a Unified Theory of the Universe.*

Strings

77 The best popular book about string theory is certainly Brian Greene's *The Elegant Universe*. Greene goes into considerable detail describing the history of string theory, how it fits into our current understanding of particles, why it might be able to offer answers to the outstanding puzzles, and (not least) what it means to think about matter as being composed of vibrating strings and not of tiny points.

The Inflationary Universe

It is not really possible to sort out the topic of inflation from that of cosmology in general in any good book written since 1988. Here are some especially enjoyable popular cosmology books that include good descriptions of inflation: Kirshner, *The Extravagant Universe*, an excellent introduction to these ideas; Charles Seife, *Alpha and Omega: The Search for the Beginning and the End of the Universe;* Michael Rowan-Robinson, *The Nine Numbers of the Cosmos;* Ralph Alpher and Robert Herman, *Genesis of the Big Bang* (this introduction is largely a history by two of the founders of modern cosmology); and James Trefil's inclusive *The Moment of Creation: Big Bang Physics from Before the First Millisecond to the Present Universe.*

For more technically inclined readers I also recommend Harrison, *Cosmology*, 2nd ed.

81 The theory of inflation was proposed by the physicist Alan Guth...: Guth's book *The Inflationary Universe* is one of the best popular explanations of the theory of inflation and is also terrific in describing the fundamental ideas in physics that motivate it. This is definitely the book to begin with when looking deeper into inflation. Other books I recommend include Greene, *The Fabric of the Cosmos* (especially chapter 10), and Ferris, *The Whole Shebang*. They also describe the concepts of isotropy and flatness.

The Sefirot: Force and Substance in the Kabbalah

87 "The Holy One said, 'Let there be light.'": Nachmanides, *Commentary on the Torah*, commentary to Genesis 1:3.

88 "Come see! When the Holy One...": *Zohar* I, 14a.

88 "Why are they called the sefirot?": *The Bahir*, 125. All citations of *The Bahir* are from Aryeh Kaplan, *The Bahir-Illumination*.

88 "The God who reveals Himself...": Tishby, *The Wisdom of the Zohar*, vol. 1, pp. 269–71.

88 ...the ten sefirot constitute the thirty-two paths by which the world was made...: The *Sefer Yetzirah* (1:1) begins, "With thirty-two mystical paths of wisdom [*hokhmah*]...[God] engraved and created His world." All citations of the *Sefer Yetzirah* are from Aryeh Kaplan, *The Sefer Yetzirah: The Book of Creation in Theory and Practice.*

88 Good discussions of the sefirot are to be found in the books I recommended in the notes to chapter 1. See also Green, *Ehyeh;* Hallamish, *An Introduction to the Kabbalah;* and Fine, *Safed Spirituality.*

88 I pointed out to my colleague and friend, the cosmologist Max Tegmark, that the thirty-one fundamental physical constants he calculates in his paper "Dimensionless Constants, Cosmology, and Other Dark Matters" are strikingly similar in quantity to the thirty-one fundamental particles (the twenty-nine known particles plus the presumed Higgs boson and graviton). He told me he thought the coincidence was cute, but remarked that actually the latest results of the WMAP satellite on the cosmic microwave background radiation suggest there are really thirty-two fundamental physical constants.

89 "The ten sefirot are the secret of existence...": Moses de Leon, quoted in Matt, *The Essential Kabbalah*, p. 69. Moses de Leon is the rabbinical personality who first began to circulate written fragments of the *Zohar* in Spain around 1300. Gershom Scholem and many other scholars attribute the composition of the text of the *Zohar* to him. *Shekel haKodesh* (the Holy Shekel), from which this quote was taken, is one of his accredited works.

89 "What is 'His hidden force?' ": *The Bahir*, 148.

90 "There are ten sefirot.": Kaplan, *Sefer Yetzirah* 1:9–11, 3–4.

90 "The world was created by means of ten sefirot.": Nachmanides, *Commentary on the Torah*, commentary to Genesis 1:1.

90 "There are ten sefirot without concreteness...": Kaplan, *Sefer Yetzirah* 1:5.

91 "At the beginning of everything...": Vital, *Sefer Etz Hayyim Hashalem*, First Palace, Gate 1, Branch 3.

One from Many: The Revelations of Symmetry

For readers interested in understanding symmetry in physical laws of nature, Richard Feynman's short book *The Character of Physical Law* is an excellent place to start. Feynman discusses in his typically lucid but precise way not only symmetry, but also the great conservation principles and the relationship between mathematics and physics. His book *The Meaning of It All*, although a bit overstated in its title, is a clear and concise exposition of his philosophy. *The Equation That Couldn't Be Solved: How Mathematical Genius Discovered the Language of Symmetry*, by Mario Livio, is an excellent popular exposition-cum-history of the ideas of symmetry. Weinberg, *Dreams of a Final Theory*, has a good discussion of symmetry, as does Ferris, *The Whole Shebang*. Kane's *Supersymmetry* is excellent.

For slightly more technically minded people, Feynman's other books are all highly recommended, including *Six Not-So-Easy Pieces*. Vincent Icke's book *The Force of Symmetry* is a very readable, detailed, but nonmathematical description of all aspects of symmetry, covering everything from waves and quantum mechanics to the nature of the forces and particles. Hermann Weyl himself wrote a book called *Symmetry*, which is good but too complicated for most lay readers.

The *Sefer Yetzirah,* as noted in the main text, contains an intricate, abstruse, quasi-mathematical explication of the sefirot, the Hebrew letters, and the vowel and musical marks. It heavily relies on symmetrical permutations and combinations. Rabbi Aryeh Kaplan, in his book *Sefer Yetzirah,* offers an excellent guide through this complex material with many charts and diagrams. His book on meditation and the Kabbalah, *Inner Space: Introduction to Kabbalah, Meditation, and Prophecy,* edited from his lectures by Abraham Sutton, has an excellent chapter on the *partzufim* and the *olamot.*

93 "A thing is symmetrical...": Feynman, *The Character of Physical Law,* p. 84.

98 God "renews every day the workings of the Creation": Babylonian Talmud, Chagiga 12b.

CHAPTER 5. MOMENTS OF CREATION

Most of the astronomy and cosmology books I cite in this chapter address in one way or another the gamut of remarkable events that transpired in the first few hundred thousand years of the universe. I list particular volumes under the sections they cover best, but by all means take advantage of their complete presentations.

100 "[The Kabbalist] is not an introspective mystic...": Tishby, *The Wisdom of the Zohar,* vol. 2, p. 655. Please note that in this introduction, Tishby also emphasizes that the *Zohar* has a complex and even paradoxical view of nature, some aspects of which are at variance with the sentiments of this quotation.

100 "One of the great afflictions of man's spiritual world...": Kook, *The Lights of Holiness,* quoted in Bokser, *Abraham Isaac Kook,* p. 195.

The Sefirot in Creation

Gershom Scholem's thorough and scholarly introduction to mysticism in his book *Kabbalah* contains a lengthy review of all the sefirot and their characteristics. Isaiah Tishby also has an excellent overview of the nature of the sefirot in his introduction to the *Zohar*'s passages on *Atzilut* in *The Wisdom of the Zohar,* vol. 1, p. 229. Leonard Glotzer's *The Fundamentals of Jewish Mysticism* is also very good, especially the introduction and the chapter 1 translation of the *Sefer Yetzirah* with commentary. All the books on Kabbalah that I mention in the notes to chapter 1 also contain sections describing the sefirot.

100 "the secret of existence": Moses de Leon, quoted in Matt, *The Essential Kabbalah*, p. 69.

101 "Here the six great supernal extremities...": *Zohar* I, 3b.

101 "Next came substance from spirit...": Kaplan, *Sefer Yetzirah* 1:11.

102 "*Keter Elyon* is called...": Moses de Leon, *Shekel haKodesh*, quoted in Matt, *The Essential Kabbalah*, p. 69.

102 "constitut[ing] the most primal and recondite level...": Green, *A Guide to the Zohar*, p. 41.

Before the Big Bang: The World of Atzilut

103 As noted earlier, Aryeh Kaplan's book *Inner Space* has a good discussion of the four worlds (*olamot*). Tishby's essay "The Account of Creation," in *The Wisdom of the Zohar*, vol. 2, reviews the origins of the concept of the worlds and their various levels of significance. He agrees with Scholem's conclusion that the theory of the four worlds was the result of a long process of development, concluded only in the fourteenth century. The main body of the *Zohar* itself does not explicitly invoke this arrangement, although it is hinted at, for example, in one section of the *Zohar Hadash* 17b.

106 "According to kabbalistic theology...": Fine, *Physician of the Soul*, pp. 55–56.

107 "Know that before the emanations emanated...": Vital, *Etz Hayyim*, First Palace, Gate 1, Branch 2.

107 The idea of *tzimtzum* (contraction) is important to later Kabbalah and some of the notions discussed in this section. Gershom Scholem traces the basic ideas of *tzimtzum* to pre-Zoharic literature, including the writing of Nachmanides, but emphasizes the centrality of the concept to Isaac Luria and the Tzefat Kabbalists. See Scholem, *Kabbalah*, pp. 129–35.

The Big Bang through the Great Inflation: The World of Briyah

Alan Guth's *The Inflationary Universe* has the best exposition of this esoteric early period of time, heavily influenced of course by his own theories of inflation. Excellent discussions are also in Brian Greene's *The Fabric of the Cosmos*. Sir Martin Rees, Great Britain's astronomer royal and a prolific theorist, is also a wonderful popular writer. His book *Before the Beginning: Our Universe and Others* has two chapters devoted to explaining the pre- and postinflation periods of the big bang; the book also addresses in easy language numerous other topics that I cover in this book. I recommend Rees's other books too: *Just Six Numbers: The Deep Forces That Shape the Universe* and *Our Cosmic Habitat*.

For readers willing to tackle a bit more complicated material, Joseph Silk has written several superb books on cosmology that are very well organized and clearly written; they do not shy away from an occasional graph or equation. *A Short History of the Universe* (1994) is terrific and has been updated and reissued as *On the Shores of the Unknown: A Short History of the Universe* (2005). The third edition of his first book, *The Big Bang*, is also excellent. I again recommend Edward Harrison's *Cosmology;* chapter 20 skillfully takes the reader from the Planck time to the first galaxies.

108 The size of the early universe: It is a little bit tricky to talk about cosmic distances accurately without getting technical, but a few words of clarification are in order. At the time of inflation, about 10^{-35} seconds, the size of the universe as set by the maximum distance light could travel was about 10^{-26} meters, but the actual dimension of the early universe is not known and might have been much larger than the light-travel distance. The minimum value is commonly used in inflation scenarios because all regions in this size universe could communicate with one another to ensure that our universe then, and so today, would be uniform (isotropic) as observed. Inflation then swelled the size of the universe by at least a factor of about 10^{25}, growing this minimum region to centimeter-size before it began its more steady, normal expansion into the universe we can see today. As noted in the main text, most of these fantastic numbers, especially those associated with inflationary models, are highly uncertain. I have not attempted to explain all the provisos and variations that come with the calculations, and the values in this book should therefore be taken as illustrative and not literally accurate.

From Inflation to Atoms: The World of Yetzirah

118 Everyone should read the short, groundbreaking volume about the epoch of radiation first published in 1977 by Steven Weinberg, *The First*

Three Minutes: A Modern View of the Origin of the Universe (the most recent edition is from 1993). Although we have learned a tremendous amount about inflation and the cosmic microwave background radiation since 1977, Weinberg's portrayal of the creation of the first atoms remains essentially unchanged. Chapter 6 in Lawrence Krauss's *Quintessence* provides a clear discussion of this early period. A good general discussion of elementary particles is provided by Alan Guth in *The Inflationary Universe,* which also has a skillful elucidation of the origin of the asymmetry between matter and antimatter. Bruce Schumm's book *Deep Down Things* presents an insider's accessible, detailed discussion of modern elementary-particle physics.

122 "The sixth [of the sefirot] is the adorned, glorious, delightful throne...": *The Bahir,* 146.

123 "The struggle to integrate love and judgment...": Green, *A Guide to the Zohar,* p. 47.

The Parting Radiation and Matter to the Formation of Galaxies, Stars, Planets, and Life: The World of Assiyah

124 ...matter gradually became more important than radiation...: As the universe expanded and stretched space, it also stretched out light waves — that is, the wavelengths of all the light waves became longer. This is also the reason why the cosmic background radiation, which was predominantly visible when it was produced, is now invisible microwave radiation — it has been stretched to longer wavelengths. The energy of light depends on its wavelength; an ultraviolet photon packs more punch than a photon at radio wavelengths, for example. As the universe expanded, each cubic centimeter of space found itself left with less and less energy from radiation, for two reasons: this stretching of wavelength, and the fact that the radiation contained progressively fewer photons, because they were spreading out to fill a larger volume. The number of particles in a given volume also decreased with time, but only for the second reason — particles were not "stretched." As a result of this difference in the dilution of matter and radiation during expansion, eventually every cubic centimeter of space had more matter-energy in it than radiation-energy. The epoch of radiation eventually gave way to

the epoch of matter. It happened that this transition from radiation domination to matter domination occurred at about the same time that the temperature cooled enough for electrons to recombine with nuclei and form atoms. John Mather and John Boslough, in *The Very First Light*, provide a very good overview of the importance of the cosmic microwave background radiation and the history of its detection.

132 "'By understanding He continually established the heavens': *Zohar* I, 207a.

CHAPTER 6. COSMIC WISDOM

The Awesome Universe

There is a wonderful quotation from Maimonides' view on love that I want to share: "What is the correct form of love of God? It is in the person who loves God with a love so great, abundant, and mighty that his soul is bound to the love of God, and he devotes himself to it continuously.... One can love the Holy One, blessed be He, only through the knowledge that one has of Him. According to the extent of knowledge is the extent of love. If the former is small, so is the latter; if the former is great, the latter is too. Therefore a person should concentrate on studying and acquiring sciences and skills that will reveal to him his Master, as far as it is in his power to know and understand" (from Maimonides, *Hilkhot Teshuvah: The Ways of Repentance*). Here is another quotation from Maimonides: "And which is the path that leads us to love and fear God? When a person contemplates His great and wondrous works and His creatures and recognizes therefrom His wisdom which is beyond assessing and endless, he at once loves, praises, and extols, and is filled with a great longing to know the great Name, as David said [Psalm 42:3], 'My soul is thirsty of God, for the living God.' And when he contemplates these very matters he at once recoils and becomes afraid realizing that he is but a lowly and dull creature, of little knowledge, standing before the Perfect One, as David said [Psalms 8:4–5], 'When I see the heavens, the work of Your fingers, what is man that You are mindful of him?'" (Maimonides, *Hilkhot Yesodei haTorah*). Both of these translations are from Ben Zion Bokser, *The Jewish Mystical Tradition*, pp. 80–81.

139 "Rabbi Elazar and Rabbi Abba were staying together one night": *Zohar* II, 171a–172a.

140 "*Yirah* [awe or fear] is of three types": *Zohar* I, 11b.

138 The momentous principles of awe-fear (*yirah*) and love (*ahavah*), and the closely related spiritual pursuit of self-effacement and oneness, are widely explored in the kabbalistic literature in their multiple forms. Isaiah Tishby has a lengthy essay on love and fear in the context of prayer and devotion in volume 3, part 5, section 2 of *The Wisdom of the Zohar*. The eleventh-century rabbi Bahya ibn Pakuda, in his *Duties of the Heart*, explains in a more systematic way his philosophy of love of God. The founder of the "Chabad" movement of Hassidic thought, Rabbi Schneur Zalman of Liadi (1745–1813) presents his intricate kabbalistic philosophy in *Tanya*, which has a particularly elaborate exposition of the concepts of love and awe-fear in chapters 41 and following. (Very good, copiously annotated English translations of the *Tanya* are available, such as the 1984 Kehot Publication Society edition.) Still and all, the homiletical associations of awe-*yirah* and love-*ahavah* to science and the scientific quest are much less considered. Daniel Matt addresses these ideas from a theological perspective in his book *God and the Big Bang*. The material in *Let There Be Light*, however, is primarily my own speculation.

*Wisdom (*Hokhmah*) and the Universe*

141 "Rabbi Yudai said...": *Zohar* I, 3b.

142 "In the beginning [*B'Resheit*] — At the very beginning...": *Zohar* I, 15a.

The Anthropic Principle

John Barrow and Frank Tipler's book *The Anthropic Cosmological Principle* is a wonderfully thorough and accessible investigation of this complicated notion, and it is a classic. The book provides a long historical and philosophical background (about 250 pages) to an idea with ancient roots and surprising modern twists, one that rather directly draws our perceptions of the physical world into religious concepts, thereby (potentially) endowing them with meaning. The book also contains six detailed chapters on physics and other branches of science. The arguments are made with easy mathematics, and although they can be intricate I think the conclusions are all readily understandable. Many of the examples in *Let There Be Light* are also in *The Anthropic Cosmological Principle*, but the latter has many more and considers a wider range of natural sciences.

In 1692 Richard Bentley initiated a correspondence with Isaac Newton probing Newton's ideas about nature, and in particular the cosmological implications of his new theory of gravity. Newton's "Four Letters to Richard Bentley" are reproduced in Munitz, *Theories of the Universe*, and provide a clear and fascinating insight into his views of God, nature, and gravity.

Leonard Susskind's book *The Cosmic Landscape* provides a technical and historical presentation of the string theory's "landscape" (which idea Susskind helped to pioneer). Brian Greene's *The Elegant Universe* is an excellent explanation of string theory.

Paul Davies, in chapter 8 of *The Mind of God*, explores one physicist's take on a "designer universe." For more background on intelligent design, see the sources I mention in the notes to chapter 1. Also see William Dembski's *Intelligent Design: The Bridge between Science and Theology*, a thoughtful, nonscholarly argument in support of ideas of intelligent design and the relationship between science and religion. *God and the New Biology*, by the theologian Arthur Peacocke, critically examines the reductionist assumptions of modern biology.

150 "This most beautiful system..." and "Hitherto I have not been able to discover...": Isaac Newton, in the General Scholium (preface) to his work "Fundamental Principles of Natural Philosophy," as quoted in Munitz, *Theories of the Universe*, pp. 208, 210.

152 "Everything in the world came into being...": *Zohar* III, 48a.

152 "The whole world...": Babylonian Talmud, Berachot 6b.

152 String theory...can actually predict so many different, physically possible kinds of universes — about 10^{500} of them in the 'landscape'...: The number 10^{500} is fabulously large, vastly bigger than any meaningful, physical number. For example, the shortest length physics can intelligently discuss is the Planck length, about 10^{-35} meters; an atom is gigantic in contrast, at about 10^{-10} meters. If we used this smallest of

physical lengths, the Planck length, to measure the largest length in the universe, its measurable size, we find the entire measurable universe is only a paltry 10^{61} Planck lengths in size. No other physically meaningful number is much bigger, and none are close to the landscape figure, which is so far a purely mathematical construct.

CHAPTER 7. A QUANTUM OF SENSE

The best place to start for a better understanding of quantum theory is still Feynman's classic undergraduate text *Lectures on Physics* vol. 3, chapters 1 and 2. Chapter 4 is a particularly enlightening discussion of bosons, fermions, how they behave, and what is meant by "identical particles." One of the best popular summaries of the controversial issues of quantum mechanics is *Einstein, Bohr, and the Quantum Dilemma*, by Andrew Whitaker. I find the discussion of quantum reality in chapter 7 of the popular book *Paradigms Lost: Images of Man in the Mirror of Science* by John Casti very clear.

Most of the popular cosmology books cited earlier perforce include some discussion of quantum theory. For readers desiring a comprehensive discussion, Roger Penrose is a brilliant mathematician, innovative scientist, and popularizer of his particular take on mind and matter. All of his books are extremely interesting but require some serious concentration and patience. His first book, *The Emperor's New Mind: Concerning Computers, Minds, and the Laws of Physics*, has an excellent section (chapter 6) on the meaning of quantum mechanics. The book also covers several other topics I discuss in *Let There Be Light*.

The theologian and physicist John Polkinghorne has an extremely good introduction to quantum ideas in the small volume *Quantum Theory: A Very Short Introduction*. Chapter 6, "Lessons and Meanings," is particularly interesting. Philip Clayton addresses theological implications of quantum mechanics in *Mind and Emergence: From Quantum to Consciousness.*

153 "Understanding the *order* in the universe...": Townes, *Making Waves,* p. 161.

154 "We find that nature... In every elementary quantum process...": John Wheeler, *At Home in the Universe,* pp. 120, 272.

160 "In the experiments...": Werner Heisenberg, from the Gifford Lectures on Physics and Philosophy (1955–56), published as *Physics and Beyond: Encounters and Conversation*, trans. Arnold J. Pomerans, p. 160.

*Quantum Mechanics and Awareness (*Yirah*)*

For more insight into the meaning of quantum mechanics, I recommend that you first familiarize yourself with some of the books on quantum mechanics I recommended in the previous section. The controversies over interpretation — the "Copenhagen interpretation" of Niels Bohr; "hidden variable" suggestions; Einstein's reservations and the Einstein-Podolsky-Rosen paradox; variants suggested by Wigner, Schrödinger, Heisenberg, David Bohm, and John Bell; and (not least) Zurek's decoherence theory — are what the rabbis call "disputes for the sake of Heaven," that is, legitimate arguments advanced in the search for truth. Richard Feynman's *The Character of Physical Law* is excellent. Physics professor Andrew Whitaker's *Einstein, Bohr, and the Quantum Dilemma* is a detailed and complete popular discussion focused on just these issues; it has the best popular description I have seen of the difficult-to-understand decoherence theory (pp. 289–97) and presents analogous ideas such as quantum diffusion, stochastic behavior, and spontaneous collapse. *The Meaning of Quantum Theory* by the science writer Jim Baggott is also very good. Tony Hey and Patrick Walters's *The Quantum Universe* is easy reading, Kenneth Ford's *The Quantum World: Quantum Physics for Everyone* likewise (with an emphasis on particle physics). Jim Al-Khalili's *Quantum: A Guide for the Perplexed* has chapters by different authorities on Schrodinger's cat, decoherence, the meaning of quantum mechanics, and GUT.

Sam Trieman's *The Odd Quantum* is a bit harder to follow and more sophisticated but very good. Nonlocality and its philosophical implications are the principle foci of Menas Kafatos and Robert Nadeau's *The Conscious Universe*, but the book has good general chapters about quantum ideas as well. Henry P. Stapp's *Mind, Matter, and Quantum Mechanics* is a detailed exposition and analysis of choice, meaning, nonlocality, and other topics.

163 "The result of an observation...": Eugene Wigner quoted in John Wheeler and Wojciech Zurek, eds., *Quantum Theory and Measurement*, pp. 172–73.

164 "Decoherence is a process..." "settles these questions...": Wojciech Zurek, "Decoherence, Einselection, and the Existential Interpretation (The Rough Guide)," in *Philosophical Transactions of the Royal Society of London, A,* vol. 356 (1998), pp. 1793–1821.

166 "These considerations lead us at the end...": Wheeler, *At Home in the Universe,* p. 292.

166 "What this means, in short...": Menas Kafatos and Robert Nadeau, *The Conscious Universe: Part and Whole in Modern Physical Theory,* p. 9.

168 "I think it is safe to say...": Feynman, *The Character of Physical Law,* p. 129.

168 "What I am going to tell you about...": Richard Feynman, *QED—The Strange Theory of Light and Matter,* p. 9.

Purpose and the Kabbalah

169 "When the most secret of secrets sought to be revealed...": *Zohar* I, 2a.

169 The concept of *tikkun olam,* repairing the world, is fundamental to the Kabbalah and mainstream Jewish theology. Most of the books on the Kabbalah that I recommended earlier will address *tikkun olam* and the notion of "raising the holy sparks." Chapter 8 in Daniel Matt's *God and the Big Bang* discusses how to bring these ideas into everyday life. Lawrence Fine, in *Physician of the Soul,* devotes chapters 6 and 7 to *tikkun.*

170 "One must direct one's heart..." "The end of all...": *Zohar* II, 56b–57a, 25a.

170 "Beloved is humanity who were created...": Babylonian Talmud, Avot, Chapter 3, Mishnah 14.

From Nothing, Everything: Creation ex Nihilo

171 "the heavens have been formed out of absolutely nothing..." "even time itself...": Maimonides, *Guide for the Perplexed,* part 2, chapter 13.

172 "When the Holy One, Blessed Be He, created His worlds...": *Zohar; Zohar Hadash,* 17b; see for example Tishby, *The Wisdom of the Zohar,* vol. 2, p. 572.

172 "absolute, certain nothingness": Nachmanides, *Commentary on the Torah,* commentary to Genesis 1:1.

173 "...the energy stored in a gravitational field is described by *negative* energy...": A point of clarification about negative energy in the gravitational field might be helpful. The energy is "negative" in the following sense: as positive energy is subtracted from the field, for example to give to matter in motion, its total becomes less by a bigger amount. This is analogous to increasing the debt on a credit card, whose negative balance becomes larger and larger even as more and more money is spent.

173 "Inflation is the ultimate free lunch": Guth, *The Inflationary Universe,* p. 1. This book has the best overall discussion of the material in this section, including more recent variations on Guth's ideas of inflation. Discussions can also be found in most of the cosmology texts I have mentioned.

CHAPTER 8. MIRACULOUS WILL

Intelligence and Self-Awareness

Mind: A Brief Introduction, by John R. Searle, a noted philosopher of the mind-body dilemma, is a wonderfully interesting, cogent historical and philosophical review. It is a must-read for people interested in consciousness. Roger Penrose, in *The Emperor's New Mind,* discusses all of the topics touched on in this chapter: mind, physics (quantum mechanics especially), astrophysics, cosmology, Turing tests, and the mathematical underpinnings of them all. His subsequent book, *Shadows of the Mind: A Search for the Missing Science of Consciousness,* is a sequel and in some ways a recapitulation of the first, but it is a little more polished. In it he advances his own hypothetical, and controversial, solution to a science of consciousness. These books are slow reading, but they are well worth the effort, particularly for his discussions of Godel's theorem on the fundamental limits of what can be proven. Penrose's small volume *The Large, the Small, and the Human Mind* is also good. Hubert L. Dreyfus's *What Computers Can't Do: The Limits of Artificial Intelligence* and *What Computers Still Can't Do: A Critique of Artificial Reason* provide articulate reasons *against* thinking that computers can someday be "intelligent."

Free Will

This section is obviously an extraordinarily condensed personal perspective on what I might argue is *the* fundamental perplexity of religion and philosophy. Nearly all of the other topics in this book have convincing answers — or at least partial answers with progress under way toward more complete ones. But this topic is so interesting, exciting, and meaningful in part because it does not yet have any convincing answers. Roger Penrose's books have excellent presentations on chaos, complexity, and noncomputability. Chaos theory is very clearly discussed in the historical review of its invention by James Gleick, *Chaos: Making a New Science*. Searle's *Mind* is terrific.

More detailed arguments about free will, backed up by the results of the latest neurological experiments, are set forth in *The Illusion of Conscious Will*, by Daniel Wegner; *How the Mind Works*, by Steven Pinker; and *Bright Air, Brilliant Fire: On the Matter of the Mind*, by Gerald M. Edelman.

178 "Everything is foreseen...": Babylonian Talmud, Avot, Chapter 3, Mishnah 15.

178 "Everything is in the hands of Heaven...": Babylonian Talmud, Megilah 25a.

179 "Everything is in the hands of Heaven.... So it seems...": Rabbi Mordekhai Yosef of Izbitz (the "Mai-Hashiloah"), part 1, p. 27 in parasha *Vayerah*.

Intelligent Life in the Universe

An excellent place to begin further reading on life in the universe is Donald Goldsmith and Tobias Owen's *The Search for Life in the Universe*. Carl Sagan was the most visible and most public astronomer in SETI, the Search for Extraterrestrial Intelligence. He may be best known for his science fiction novel *Contact* (and the movie of the same name). His book *The Dragons of Eden: Speculations on the Evolution of Human Intelligence* is good, as is his classic TV series and book on astronomy, *Cosmos*. The SETI Institute has published several volumes, including *How Might Life Evolve on Other Worlds? SETI Academy Planet Project*.

A convincing case that life is not common is made in *Rare Earth: Why Complex Life Is Uncommon in the Universe*, by Donald Brownlee and

Peter Ward. For a more biological perspective, try *The Thread of Life: The Story of Genes and Genetic Engineering,* by Susan Aldridge, or *Life Evolving: Molecules, Mind, and Meaning,* by Christian de Duve. Edward O. Wilson, a distinguished professor of evolutionary biology, is biology's premier spokesperson for reductionist science, and his books are readable and interesting. I recommend in particular *Consilience: The Unity of Knowledge* and *The Diversity of Life.* For a moving, poetic counterview to Wilson's, I recommend the tiny volume *Life Is a Miracle: An Essay against Modern Superstition,* by Wendell Berry.

189 "The chance that this alternative set will contain...": Stephen Jay Gould, *Full House,* pp. 214–16.

Miracles

The Talmud is impressive in part because it thoughtfully incorporates many divergent views, and rabbinic opinions of miracles provide no exception. Nevertheless there is a preponderant perspective. In the tractate Pesachim 54a, a lengthy discussion on miracles can be found. Perhaps this is also the place to recommend Stephen Jay Gould's last book, *The Hedgehog, the Fox, and the Magister's Pox: Mending the Gap between Science and the Humanities.* Loren Eiseley's classic, *The Immense Journey,* remains as apt as ever.

191 "The most amazing thing about the universe...": Albert Einstein, quoted in Calaprice, *The Expanded Quotable Einstein,* p. 278.

CHAPTER 9. BEFORE AND AFTER

The rabbinic discussion about miracles closely tracks the rabbis' thoughts on the Creation and pre-Creation because of the opinion that miracles were events preplanned into the universe. (The spin I put on their concepts is my own, however.) Stephen Hawking briefly presents his and Hartle's ideas in his popular books, including *A Brief History of Time* and *The Universe in a Nutshell. Before the Beginning: Our Universe and Others,* by Martin Rees, is an excellent scientific review of this topic. I recommend all of Rees's popular books.

194 "The universe would be completely self-contained...": Hawking, *A Brief History of Time,* p. 136.

195 "Seven things were created before the world...": Babylonian Talmud, Pesachim 54a; see also Nedarim 39b.

The End

Most introductory astronomy books will have sections on the life and death of stars and other topics related to beginnings and endings, which, although I treat them in separate sections here, are intimately related. A few excellent books that concentrate specifically on such matters include Paul Davies, *The Last Three Minutes: Conjectures about the Ultimate Fate of the Universe,* and Lee Smolin, *The Life of the Cosmos,* a book that advances his own interesting variation on cosmological evolution.

199 Frank Tipler's *The Physics of Immortality* is an unusual speculation about the science of immortality. Carrying the idea of infinite lifetimes in a closed universe even further, he conjectures that the contracting universe would contain within its closed boundaries all information about its history, including information about people, in a form that might even be recoverable and useful. He has speculated that an incredibly advanced civilization could have the knowledge, time, energy, and maybe even technology to gather, interpret, and manipulate this information to reconstruct all previous life in what would effectively be a resurrection of the dead. One of the strengths of his ideas is that he proposes observational tests; one of its weaknesses is that it now seems to fail these tests. See also Freeman Dyson, "Time without End: Physics and Biology in an Open Universe," *Reviews of Modern Physics* 51, no. 3 (July 1979).

Distant Horizons and Countless Universes

This topic is a particularly important one for scientists attempting to address anthropic ideas, because it offers a natural basis for the random occurrence of statistically unusual events (life, for instance). Nearly all of the books on the anthropic principle that I recommended above have a discussion of multiworld theories. Alan Guth's book *The Inflationary Universe,* Lee Smolin's book *The Life of the Cosmos,* and Leonard Susskind's book *The Cosmic Landscape* present three variations on this theme. See also Brian Greene's *The Elegant Universe,* chapter 14.

200 The estimated possible size of the universe I cite here, a fantastic 10^{23} times larger than the size of the universe *we can see*, comes from Guth's calculations. Over the past decade, numerous variants to the "standard inflation model" have been proposed and have calculated other sizes for the possible universe. One version, by Andrei Linde, is larger by ten to the power 10^{12} (ten to the power one trillion).

CHAPTER 10. BRINGING TRUTH TO LIGHT

On the social construction of science, I recommend *Who Rules in Science? An Opinionated Guide to the Wars*, by James Robert Brown. Another leading book on this topic is *Science, Truth, and Democracy*, by the Columbia University philosopher Philip Kitcher. Strong and cogent critics of social construction theories include Steven Weinberg, in *Facing Up: Science and Its Cultural Adversaries*, and (more antagonistically) Richard Dawkins, in *The Ancestor's Tale: A Pilgrimage to the Dawn of Evolution*.

Paul Davies's *God and the New Physics* is a physicist's sensitive efforts to think about the topics raised in this chapter. Chapter 5, on "holism vs. reductionism," is particularly interesting, and in it he calls attention to what he sees as the "abandonment" of pure reductionism by physicists in favor of a holistic worldview captured, for example, in Gary Zukav's *The Dancing Wu Li Masters: An Overview of the New Physics* and Fritjof Capra's *The Tao of Physics*. Although I agree with Davies's perspective, he overstates the case; the "bootstrap" models of particle physics featured in these two books have since yielded to the quark vision I present here. Davies also thoughtfully addresses, at considerably greater length than I do here, the issues of free will, miracles, and the soul.

Ellen Bernstein's *Splendor of Creation: A Biblical Ecology* is a persuasive, poetic vision of our biblically mandated responsibilities to nature. The theologian Arthur Peacocke, in *God and the New Biology*, has excellent chapters on "nature as creation" and the biblical imperatives to steward the Earth and its environment.

Drawing Lessons

I recommend a book by the prolific popular astronomy writer Chet Raymo, *Skeptics and True Believers: The Exhilarating Connections between*

Science and Religion. In it, Raymo writes, "I am one of those people, trained in science, who cannot quite accept the idea of God nor quite leave it alone.... It seems to me that science is part of the traditional religious quest for the God of creation" (p. 1). He pointedly adds, "I am today a thoroughgoing Skeptic who believes that words like *God, soul, sacred, spirituality, sacrament,* and *grace* can retain their currency in an age of science.... I hunger for a faith that is open to the new cosmology" (p. 8). His book, the sensitive inquiry of a lyrical skeptic, touches on many of our other topics.

211 "The history of cosmology is not the easy story...": Michael Hoskin, *The Cambridge Illustrated History of Astronomy*, p. 32. I particularly like Hoskin's piercing quotation. Here is a more complete excerpt: "It is important to recognize that this Aristotelian cosmology drew strength from being an intellectual formulation that reinforced common sense, in contrast to modern science which contradicts what seems self-evident. Aristotle tells us that the Earth is at rest beneath our feet, that we are on terra firma, whereas today's astronomers would have us believe that we are hurtling through space at an almost unimaginable speed.... The history of cosmology is not the easy story of the rejection of absurd ideas in favour of what (perhaps after a little thought) is seen to be patently true, but the heroic saga of the hard-won rejection of the patently true in favour of the absurd."

212 "Who is wise?": Babylonian Talmud, Avot, Chapter 4, Mishnah 1.

214 "If there is an edge...": Stephen Hawking, quoted in Renée Weber, *Dialogues with Scientists and Sages: The Search for Unity*, p. 201.

References

Afterman, Allen. *Kabbalah and Consciousness and the Poetry of Allen Afterman*. Riverdale-on-Hudson, NY: Sheep Meadow Press, 1992.

Albert, David Z. *Quantum Mechanics and Experience*. Cambridge, MA: Harvard University Press, 1992.

Aldridge, Susan. *The Thread of Life: The Story of Genes and Genetic Engineering*. Cambridge: Cambridge University Press, 1996.

Alpher, Ralph, and Robert Herman. *Genesis of the Big Bang*. Oxford: Oxford University Press, 2001.

Ashlag, Yehuda. *An Entrance to the Tree of Life: A Key to the Portals of Jewish Mysticism*. Compiled and edited by Philip S. Berg. Jerusalem, Israel; New York: Press of the Research Centre of Kabbalah, 1977.

Baggott, Jim. *The Meaning of Quantum Theory*. Oxford: Oxford University Press, 1992.

Barbour, Ian G. *Religion and Science: Historical and Contemporary Issues*. San Francisco: HarperSanFrancisco, 1997.

Barrow, John D., and Frank J. Tipler. *The Anthropic Cosmological Principle*. Oxford: Oxford University Press, 1986.

Bennett, Jeffrey, Megan Donahue, Nicholas Schneider, and Mark Voit. *The Cosmic Perspective*. 3rd edition. San Francisco: Pearson Addison-Wesley, 2004.

Bernstein, Ellen. *Splendor of Creation: A Biblical Ecology*. Cleveland, OH: Pilgrim Press, 2005.

Berry, Wendell. *Life Is a Miracle: An Essay against Modern Superstition*. Washington, DC: Counterpoint, 2000.

Bohm, David. *The Special Theory of Relativity*. New York: W. A. Benjamin Inc., 1965.

Bokser, Ben Zion. *Abraham Isaac Kook: The Lights of Penitence, the Moral Principles, the Lights of Holiness, Essays, Letters, and Poems*. Classics of Western Spirituality. New York: Paulist Press, 1978.

———. *The Jewish Mystical Tradition*. New York: Pilgrim Press, 1981.

Brewster, Sir David. *Memoirs of the Life, Writings, and Discoveries of Sir Isaac Newton*. Edinburgh: Thomas Constable and Co., 1955.

Brown, James Robert. *Who Rules in Science? An Opinionated Guide to the Wars*. Cambridge, MA: Harvard University Press, 2001.

Brownlee, Donald, and Peter D. Ward. *Rare Earth: Why Complex Life Is Uncommon in the Universe*. New York: Copernicus, 2000.

Calaprice, Alice, ed. *The Expanded Quotable Einstein*. Princeton, NJ: Princeton University Press, 2000.

Capra, Fritjof. *The Tao of Physics*. Berkeley, CA: Shambhala Publications, 1975.

Casti, John L. *Paradigms Lost: Images of Man in the Mirror of Science*. New York: William Morrow, 1989.

———. *Would-Be Worlds*. New York: John Wiley and Sons, 1997.

Chown, Marcus. *Afterglow of Creation: From the Fireball to the Discovery of Cosmic Ripples*. Sausalito, CA: University Science Books, 1996.

Clayton, Philip. *God and Contemporary Science: Edinburgh Studies in Constructive Theology*. Grand Rapids, MI: W. B. Eerdmans, 1997.

———. *Mind and Emergence: From Quantum to Consciousness*. Oxford: Oxford University Press, 2004.

———. *The Problem of God in Modern Thought*. Grand Rapids, MI: W. B. Eerdmans, 2000.

———, and Arthur Peacocke. *In Whom We Live and Move and Have Our Being: Panentheistic Reflections on God's Presence in a Scientific World*. Grand Rapids, MI: W. B. Eerdmans, 2004.

Coles, Peter, and Francesco Lucchin. *Cosmology*. New York: John Wiley and Sons, 1995.

Crowe, Michael J. *Modern Theories of the Universe from Heschel to Hubble*. New York: Dover Publications, 1994.

———. *Theories of the World from Antiquity to the Copernican Revolution*. New York: Dover Publications, 1990.

Davies, Paul. *About Time*. New York: Touchstone, 1995.
———. *Are We Alone?* London: Penguin Books, 1995.
———. *The Cosmic Blueprint*. London: Penguin Books, 1987.
———. *God and the New Physics*. New York: Simon and Schuster, 1983.
———. *The Last Three Minutes: Conjectures about the Ultimate Fate of the Universe*. New York: Basic Books, 1994.
———. *The Mind of God: The Scientific Basis for a Rational World*. New York: Simon and Schuster, 1992.
———. *The New Physics*. Cambridge: Cambridge University Press, 1989.
———. *The Physics of Time Asymmetry*. Berkeley and Los Angeles: University of California Press, 1974.
———. *Space and Time in the Modern Universe*. New York: Cambridge University Press, 1977.
Dawkins, Richard. *The Ancestor's Tale: A Pilgrimage to the Dawn of Evolution*. Boston: Houghton Mifflin, 2004.
———. *The Selfish Gene*. New York: Oxford University Press, 1990.
———. *Unweaving the Rainbow: Science, Delusion, and the Appetite for Wonder*. Boston: Houghton Mifflin, 1998.
de Duve, Christian. *Life Evolving: Molecules, Mind, and Meaning*. Oxford: Oxford University Press, 2002.
Delsemme, Armand. *Our Cosmic Origins*. Cambridge: Cambridge University Press, 1998.
Dembski, William. *Intelligent Design: The Bridge between Science and Theology*. Dovers Grove, IL: InterVarsity Press, 1999.
Dreyfus, Hubert L. *What Computers Can't Do: The Limits of Artificial Intelligence*. New York: Harper and Row, 1979.
———. *What Computers Still Can't Do: A Critique of Artificial Reason*. Cambridge, MA: MIT Press, 1992.
Dyson, Freeman, "Time without End: Physics and Biology in an Open Universe." *Reviews of Modern Physics* 51, no. 3 (July 1979).
Edelman, Gerald M. *Bright Air, Brilliant Fire: On the Matter of the Mind*. New York: Basic Books, 1992.
Einstein, Albert. *The Meaning of Relativity*. Princeton, NJ: Princeton University Press, 1956.
Eiseley, Loren. *The Immense Journey*. New York: Vintage Books, 1946.
Epstein, Isadore, ed. *The Babylonian Talmud: Translated into English*. London: Soncino Press, 1961.

Ferris, Timothy. *The Whole Shebang, a State of the Universe(s) Report*. New York: Simon and Schuster, 1997.

Feynman, Richard P. *The Character of Physical Law*. Cambridge, MA: MIT Press, 1965.

———. *The Meaning of It All*. Reading, MA: Perseus Books, 1998.

———. *QED—The Strange Theory of Light and Matter*. Princeton, NJ: Princeton University Press, 1985.

———. *Six Not-So-Easy Pieces*. New York: Helix Books, 1963.

———, Robert B. Leighton, and Matthew Sands. *The Feynman Lectures on Physics*. 3 volumes. New York: Addison-Wesley Publishing Co., 1965.

Fine, Lawrence. *Physician of the Soul, Healer of the Cosmos: Isaac Luria and His Kabbalistic Fellowship*. Studies in Jewish History. Palo Alto, CA: Stanford University Press, 2003.

———. *Safed Spirituality: Rules of Mystical Piety, the Beginning of Wisdom*. New York: Paulist Press, 1984.

Ford, Kenneth. *The Quantum World: Quantum Physics for Everyone*. Cambridge, MA: Harvard University Press, 2004.

Frankiel, Tamar. *The Gift of Kabbalah: Discovering the Secrets of Heaven, Renewing Your Life on Earth*. Woodstock, VT: Jewish Lights, 2001.

Gamow, George. *One, Two, Three — Infinity: Facts and Speculations of Science*. New York: Dover Publications, 1988.

Gibilisco, Stan. *Understanding Einstein's Theories of Relativity: Man's New Perspective on the Cosmos*. Blue Ridge Summit, PA: Tab Books, 1983.

Gingerich, Owen. *The Eye of Heaven*. New York: American Institute of Physics, 1993.

———. *The Great Copernicus Chase*. Cambridge: Cambridge University Press, 1992.

Gleick, James. *Chaos: Making a New Science*. New York: Penguin, 1988.

Glotzer, Leonard R. *The Fundamentals of Jewish Mysticism: The Book of Creation and Its Commentaries*. Northvale, NJ: J. Aronson, 1992.

Goldsmith, Donald, and Tobias Owen. *The Search for Life in the Universe*. New York: Addison-Wesley Publishing Co., 1992.

Gorner, G., and S. Gottlober. *The Evolution of the Universe*. New York: John Wiley and Sons, 1997.

Gould, Stephen Jay. *Full House*. New York: Three Rivers Press, 1996.

———. *The Hedgehog, the Fox, and the Magister's Pox: Mending the Gap between Science and the Humanities*. New York: Harmony Books, 2003.

Green, Arthur. *Ehyeh: A Kabbalah for Tomorrow*. Woodstock, VT: Jewish Lights, 2003.

———. *A Guide to the Zohar*. Palo Alto, CA: Stanford University Press, 2004.

Greene, Brian. *The Elegant Universe*. New York: Vintage Books, 1999.

———. *The Fabric of the Cosmos*. New York: Vintage Books, 2004.

Guth, Alan H. *The Inflationary Universe: The Quest for a New Theory of Cosmic Origins*. New York: Helix Books, 1997.

Hallamish, Mosheh. *An Introduction to the Kabbalah*. Translated by Ruth Bar-Ilan and Ora Wiskind-Elper. Albany, NY: State University of New York Press, 1999.

Harrison, Edward. *Cosmology: The Science of the Universe*. 2nd ed. Cambridge: Cambridge University Press, 2000.

Hawking, Stephen W. *A Brief History of Time*. New York: Bantam Books, 1988.

———. *The Universe in a Nutshell*. New York: Bantam Books, 2001.

———, and Roger Penrose. *The Nature of Space and Time*. Princeton, NJ: Princeton University Press, 1996.

———, Kip Thorne, Igor Novikov, Timothy Ferris, and Alan Lightman. *The Future of Spacetime*. New York: W. W. Norton, 2002.

Hawkins, Michael, with Celia Fitzgerald. *Hunting Down the Universe*. Reading, MA: Perseus Books, 1997.

Heisenberg, Werner. *Physics and Beyond: Encounters and Conversation*. Translated by Arnold J. Pomerans. Originally presented as the Gifford Lectures on Physics and Philosophy (1955–56). London: G. Allen and Unwin, 1971.

Hey, Tony, and Patrick Walters. *The Quantum Universe*. Cambridge: Cambridge University Press, 1987.

Hoffman, Edward. *The Way of Splendor*. Boulder, Colo.; London: Shambhala, 1981.

Hoskin, Michael, ed. *The Cambridge Illustrated History of Astronomy*. Cambridge: Cambridge University Press, 1997.

ibn Pakuda, Bahya ben Joseph. *The Duties of the Heart*. Translated with commentary by Yaakov Feldman. Northvale, NJ: J. Aronson, 1996.

Icke, Vincent. *The Force of Symmetry*. Cambridge: Cambridge University Press, 1995.

Idel, Moshe. *Kabbalah: New Perspectives*. New Haven, CT: Yale University Press, 1988.

———. *Studies in Ecstatic Kabbalah*. Albany, NY: State University of New York Press, 1988.

Jacobs, Louis. *Jewish Ethics, Philosophy, and Mysticism*. New York: Behrman House, 1969.

———. *Jewish Mystical Testimonies*. New York: Schocken, 1977.

Kafatos, Menas, and Robert Nadeau. *The Conscious Universe: Part and Whole in Modern Physical Theory*. New York: Springer-Verlag, 1990.

Kane, Gordon. *Supersymmetry: Squarks, Photinos, and the Unveiling of the Ultimate Laws of Nature*. Cambridge, MA: Perseus Publishing, 2000.

Kaplan, Aryeh. *The Bahir-Illumination*. York Beach, Maine: Samuel Weiser, 1979.

———. *Inner Space: Introduction to Kabbalah, Meditation, and Prophecy*. Edited by Abraham Sutton. Jerusalem: Israel Moznaim Publishing Co., 1990.

———. *Meditation and Kabbalah*. York Beach, Maine: Samuel Weiser, 1982.

———. *The Sefer Yetzirah: The Book of Creation in Theory and Practice*. York Beach, Maine: Samuel Weiser, 1997.

Al-Khalili, Jim. *Black Holes, Wormholes, and Time Machines*. Bristol, England; Philadelphia: Institute of Physics Publishing, 1999.

———. *Quantum: A Guide for the Perplexed*. London: Weidenfeld and Nicolson, 2003.

Kirshner, Robert P. *The Extravagant Universe: Exploding Stars, Dark Energy, and the Accelerating Cosmos*. With a new epilogue by the author. Princeton, NJ, and Oxford: Princeton University Press, 2004.

Kitcher, Philip. *Science, Truth, and Democracy*. New York: Oxford University Press, 2001.

Kragh, Helge. *Cosmology and Controversy: The Historical Development of Two Theories of the Universe*. Princeton, NJ: Princeton University Press, 1996.

Krauss, Lawrence M. *The Physics of Star Trek*. New York: Harper Perennial, 1995.

———. *Quintessence*. New York: Basic Books, 2000.

Liebes, Yehuda. *Studies in the Zohar*. Translated by Arnold Schwartz, Stephanie Nakache, and Penina Peli. Albany, NY: State University of New York Press, 1993.

Lightman, Alan. *Ancient Light: Our Changing View of the Universe*. Cambridge, MA: Harvard University Press, 1991.

Livio, Mario. *The Equation That Couldn't Be Solved: How Mathematical Genius Discovered the Language of Symmetry*. New York: Simon and Schuster, 2005.

Maimonides, Moses. *The Guide for the Perplexed*. Translated by M. Friedländer. London: Dover Publications, 1956.

Mather, John C., and John Boslough. *The Very First Light*. New York: Basic Books, 1996.

Matt, Daniel C. *The Essential Kabbalah: The Heart of Jewish Mysticism*. San Francisco: HarperSanFrancisco, 1995.

———. *God and the Big Bang*. Woodstock, VT: Jewish Lights, 1996.

———. *Zohar: Annotated and Explained*. Woodstock, VT: SkyLight Path Publishing, 2002.

———. *Zohar: The Book of Enlightenment*. Classics of Western Spirituality. New York: Paulist Press, 1983.

———. *The Zohar: Pritzker Edition*. Palo Alto, CA: Stanford University Press, 2004.

Menzi, Donald Wilder, and Zwe Padeh. *The Tree of Life: Hayyim Vital's Introduction to the Kabbalah of Isaac Luria*. Northvale, NJ: J. Aronson, 1999.

Mordekhai Yosef of Izbitz. *Mai Hashiloah*. Reprint, B'nai Brak, Israel: Mishor, 1990.

Moss, Ian. *Quantum Theory, Black Holes, and Inflation*. New York: John Wiley and Sons, 1996.

Munitz, Milton K. *Theories of the Universe: From Babylonian Myth to Modern Science*. New York: The Free Press, 1957.

Nachmanides (Rabbi Moshe ben Nachman). *Commentary on the Torah.* Translated and annotated with an index by Charles B. Chavel. New York: Shilo, 1999.

North, John. *Astronomy and Cosmology*. New York: W. W. Norton, 1995.

Park, David. *The Grand Contraption*. Princeton, NJ: Princeton University Press, 2005.

Parker, Barry. *Einstein's Dream: The Search for a Unified Theory of the Universe*. New York: Plenum Press, 1987.

———. *Invisible Matter and the Fate of the Universe*. New York: Plenum Press, 1989.

———. *Search for a Supertheory: From Atoms to Superstrings*. New York: Plenum Press, 1987.

Peacock, John A. *Cosmological Physics*. Cambridge: Cambridge University Press, 1999.

Peacocke, Arthur. *God and the New Biology*. London: Dent, 1986.

———. *Paths from Science towards God: The End of All Our Exploring*. Oxford: Oneworld Publications, 2001.

———. *Theology for a Scientific Age: Being and Becoming Natural, Divine, and Human*. Minneapolis, MN: Fortress Press, 1993.

Peebles, P. J. E. *Principles of Physical Cosmology*. Princeton, NJ: Princeton University Press, 1993.

Penrose, Roger. *The Emperor's New Mind: Concerning Computers, Minds, and the Laws of Physics*. Oxford: Oxford University Press, 1989.

———. *The Large, the Small, and the Human Mind*. Edited by Malcolm Longair. Cambridge: Cambridge University Press, 1997.

———. *Shadows of the Mind: A Search for the Missing Science of Consciousness*. Oxford: Oxford University Press, 1994.

Perkins, Donald. *Particle Astrophysics*. Oxford: Oxford University Press, 2003.

Pinker, Steven. *How the Mind Works*. New York: W. W. Norton, 1997.

Polkinghorne, John. *Belief in God in an Age of Science*. New Haven, CT: Yale University Press, 1998.

———. *The Faith of a Physicist*. Princeton, NJ: Princeton University Press, 1994.

———. *One World: The Interaction of Science and Theology*. London: SPCK, 1986.

———. *Quantum Theory: A Very Short Introduction*. Oxford: Oxford University Press, 2002.

———. *Science and Providence: God's Interaction with the World*. London: SPCK, 1989.

———. *Science and Theology: An Introduction*. London: SPCK; Minneapolis: Fortress Press, 1998.

Primack, Joel, and Nancy Abrams. *The View from the Center of the Universe*. New York: Riverhead Books, 2006.

Raymo, Chet. *Skeptics and True Believers: The Exhilarating Connections between Science and Religion*. New York: Walker and Co., 1998.

Rees, Martin. *Before the Beginning: Our Universe and Others*. Reading, MA: Helix Books, 1998.

———. *Just Six Numbers: The Deep Forces That Shape the Universe*. New York: Basic Books, 2000.

———. *Our Cosmic Habitat*. Princeton, NJ: Princeton University Press, 2001.

Roos, Matts. *Introduction to Cosmology*. New York: John Wiley and Sons, 1997.

Ross, Hugh. *A Matter of Days: Resolving a Creation Controversy*. Colorado Springs, CO: NavPress, 2004.

Rowan-Robinson, Michael. *The Nine Numbers of the Cosmos*. New York: Oxford University Press, 1999.

———. *Ripples in the Cosmos: A View behind the Scenes of the New Cosmology*. Oxford; New York: W. H. Freeman Spektrum, 1993.

Runes, Dagobert D. *The Wisdom of the Kabbalah*. New York: The Citadel Press, 1967.

Sagan, Carl. *The Dragons of Eden: Speculations on the Evolution of Human Intelligence*. New York: Random House, 1977.

Scheider, Walter. *A Serious but Not Ponderous Book about Relativity*. Manchester, England: Cavendish Press, 2000.

Schneur Zalman of Liadi. *Likutie Amarim: Tanya*. Toronto: Kehot Publication Society, 1984.

Scholem, Gershom G. *Kabbalah*. New York: Quadrangle, 1974.

———. *Major Trends in Jewish Mysticism*. New York: Schocken, 1941.

———. *On the Kabbalah and Its Symbolism*. New York: Schocken, 1969.

———. *Zohar, The Book of Splendor*. New York: Schocken, 1949.

Schumm, Bruce A. *Deep Down Things*. Baltimore, MD: Johns Hopkins University Press, 2004.

Searle, John R. *Mind: A Brief Introduction*. Oxford: Oxford University Press, 2004.

Seife, Charles. *Alpha and Omega: The Search for the Beginning and the End of the Universe*. New York: Viking, 2003.

SETI Academy Planet Project. *How Might Life Evolve on Other Worlds?* N.p.: Teacher Ideas Press, 1995.

Shuchat, Wilfred. *The Creation According to the Midrash Rabbah*. Jerusalem, Israel; New York: Devora Publishing, 2002.

Siegfried, Tom. *Strange Matters: Undiscovered Ideas at the Frontiers of Space and Time*. Washington, D.C.: Joseph Henry Press, 2002.

Silk, Joseph. *The Big Bang*. 3rd edition. New York: W. H. Freeman and Co., 2001.

———. *On the Shores of the Unknown: A Short History of the Universe*. Cambridge and New York: Cambridge University Press, 2005.

———. *A Short History of the Universe*. New York: Scientific American Library, 1994.

Smith, Howard A. "Public Attitudes towards Space Science," *Space Science Reviews* 105, no. 1-2 (2003). Published by Springer Netherlands.

Smolin, Lee. *The Life of the Cosmos*. Oxford: Oxford University Press, 1997.

Smoot, George, and Keay Davidson. *Wrinkles in Time*. New York: William Morrow, 1993.

Sobel, Dava. *Galileo's Daughter*. New York: Penguin Books, 2000.

Stapp, Henry P. *Mind, Matter, and Quantum Mechanics*. Berlin: Springer-Verlag, 2004.

Steinsaltz, Adin. *The Thirteen Petalled Rose*. New York: Basic Books, 1980.

Sullivan, J. W. N. *Isaac Newton*. New York: The Macmillan Co., 1938.

Susskind, Leonard. *The Cosmic Landscape*. New York: Little, Brown and Co., 2006.

Taylor, John C. *Hidden Unity in Nature's Laws*. Cambridge: Cambridge University Press, 2001.

Tegmark, M., A. Aguirre, M. J. Rees, and F. Wilczek. "Dimensionless Constants, Cosmology, and Other Dark Matters," *Physical Review D*. Vol. 73, no. 2, id. 023505 (2006).

Thuan, Trinh Xuan. *The Secret Melody: And Man Created the Universe.* Oxford: Oxford University Press, 1995.

Tipler, Frank J. *The Physics of Immortality*. New York: Doubleday, 1994.

Tishby, Isaiah. *The Wisdom of the Zohar: An Anthology of Texts*. 3 vols. Translated by David Goldstein. London: Littman Library of Jewish Civilization, 1961.

Townes, Charles H. *Making Waves*. Woodbury, NY: A. I. P. Press, 1995.

Trefil, James. *The Moment of Creation: Big Bang Physics from Before the First Millisecond to the Present Universe*. New York: Collier, 1984.

Trieman, Sam. *The Odd Quantum*. Princeton, NJ: Princeton University Press, 1999.

Tyson, Neil deGrasse, and Donald Goldsmith. *Origins: Fourteen Billion Years of Cosmic Evolution*. New York: W. W. Norton, 2004.

Vital, Hayyim. *Sefer Etz Hayyim Hashalem*. Tel Aviv, Israel: Barznai, 2004.

Watts, Alan W. *The Joyous Cosmology*. New York: Vintage Books, 1962.

Weber, Renée. *Dialogues with Scientists and Sages: The Search for Unity*. London: Routledge and Kegan Paul, 1986.

Wegner, Daniel M. *The Illusion of Conscious Will*. Cambridge, MA: MIT Press, 2002.

Weinberg, Steven. *Dreams of a Final Theory: The Scientist's Search for the Ultimate Laws of Nature*. New York: Pantheon, 1992.

———. *Facing Up: Science and Its Cultural Adversaries*. Cambridge, MA: Harvard University Press, 2001.

———. *The First Three Minutes: A Modern View of the Origin of the Universe*. Updated ed. New York: Basic Books, 1993.

Weyl, Hermann. *Symmetry*. Princeton, NJ: Princeton University Press, 1952.

Wheeler, John A. *At Home in the Universe*. Woodbury, NY: A. I. P. Press, 1994.

———. and Wojciech Hubert Zurek, eds. *Quantum Theory and Measurement*. Princeton, NJ: Princeton University Press, 1983.

Whitaker, Andrew. *Einstein, Bohr, and the Quantum Dilemma*. Cambridge: Cambridge University Press, 1996.

Wilson, Edward O. *Consilience: The Unity of Knowledge*. New York: Knopf, 1998.

———. *The Diversity of Life*. Cambridge, MA: Harvard University Press, Belknap Press, 1992.

Wolfson, Richard. *Simply Einstein: Relativity Demystified.* New York: W. W. Norton, 2003.

Zukav, Gary. *The Dancing Wu Li Masters: An Overview of the New Physics.* New York: Bantam Books, 1979.

Zurek, Wojciech H. "Decoherence, Einselection, and the Existential Interpretation (The Rough Guide)." Pp. 1793–1821 in *Philosophical Transactions of the Royal Society of London, A.* Volume 356 (1998).

INDEX

Note: Following the usage in the text, "Creation" is capitalized in the index, even though it does not always refer to biblical Creation. Page numbers in italics refer to illustrations.

C

H

M

N

O

P

Q

R

T

Y

Z

ABOUT THE AUTHOR

Howard A. Smith, PhD, is a senior astrophysicist at the Harvard-Smithsonian Center for Astrophysics in Cambridge, Massachusetts, with over two hundred published articles in astronomy and astrophysics. His research emphasizes the origins of stars and galaxies, in particular using techniques of infrared astronomy and spectroscopy. He has been the principal investigator on numerous national and international research grants and programs. A co-investigator on the European Space Agency's Infrared Space Observatory satellite, he led the Extragalactic Science program for its Long Wavelength Spectrometer team. He is currently a senior member of several teams with NASA's Spitzer Space Telescope. In addition to his research activities, he is involved in public education and outreach activities. He has been recognized by Harvard for excellence in teaching undergraduates.

Prior to moving to Cambridge, Dr. Smith was the chair of the Laboratory for Astrophysics, the astronomy department of the Smithsonian Institution's National Air and Space Museum in Washington, DC, where he supervised a staff of scientists and educators. He also played a key role in developing museum galleries, education programs, videos, and IMAX movies, including the Academy Award nominee *Cosmic Voyage*. For three years he served as a rotating discipline scientist at NASA headquarters, where he was responsible for grants in theory, data analysis, long-term research, and some proposed NASA missions. Before joining the Smithsonian, he led a research program at the Naval Research Laboratory.

Dr. Smith holds two undergraduate degrees from MIT, in physics and in humanities and science, and a PhD in physics from the University of California, Berkeley. He is a member of the American Physical Society, the American Astronomical Society, the Royal Astronomical Society, the International Astronomical Union, and the American Association for the Advancement of Science. A traditional and observant Jew, he has lectured on cosmology and Kabbalah for over twenty years. He is married with three children.

NEW WORLD LIBRARY is dedicated to publishing books and other media that inspire and challenge us to improve the quality of our lives and the world.

We are a socially and environmentally aware company, and we make every attempt to embody the ideals presented in our publications. We recognize that we have an ethical responsibility to our customers, our employees, and our planet.

We serve our customers by creating the finest publications possible on personal growth, creativity, spirituality, wellness, and other areas of emerging importance. We serve our employees with generous benefits, significant profit sharing, and constant encouragement to pursue our most expansive dreams. As members of the Green Press Initiative, we print an increasing number of books with soy-based ink on 100 percent postconsumer waste recycled paper. Also, we power our offices with solar energy and contribute to nonprofit organizations working to make the world a better place for us all.

Our products are available
in bookstores everywhere.
For our catalog, please contact:

New World Library
14 Pamaron Way
Novato, California 94949

Phone: 415-884-2100 or 800-972-6657
Catalog requests: Ext. 50
Orders: Ext. 52
Fax: 415-884-2199

Email: escort@newworldlibrary.com
Website: www.newworldlibrary.com